Places to Go with Children
IN
SOUTHERN CALIFORNIA

Places to Go with Children
IN
SOUTHERN CALIFORNIA

Stephanie Kegan

Chronicle Books • San Francisco

Copyright © 1989 by Stephanie Kegan. All rights reserved. No part of this book may be reproduced in any form without written permission from the publisher.

Printed in the United States of America.

Library of Congress Cataloging-in-Publication Data
Kegan, Stephanie.
    Places to go with children in Southern California/Stephanie Kegan.—Completely rev. and expanded.
    p. cm.
    Includes index.
    ISBN 0-87701-578-3
    1. California, Southern—Description and travel—Guide-books. 2. Family recreation—California, Southern—Guide-books. I. Title
F867.K3   1989
917.94'90453—dc19   88-39400
                                                                                                  CIP

Editing: Carolyn Miller
Book and cover design: Seventeenth Street Studios
Cover photo: San Diego Convention and Visitors Bureau
Composition: Another Point, Inc.

10 9 8 7 6 5 4 3 2 1

Chronicle Books
275 Fifth Street
San Francisco, California
94103

For Nora

With special appreciation to Ruth Ann Laws

Contents

Introduction, vii

Los Angeles County, 1
Downtown Los Angeles, 2
East Los Angeles, 15
South Central Los Angeles, 16
North Central Los Angeles, 22
Los Feliz and Hollywood, 25
Mid-Wilshire, 34
Beverly Hills and West Los Angeles, 37
Santa Monica, Pacific Palisades, and Malibu, 40
South Bay and Beach Cities, 47
Los Angeles Harbor Area, Catalina, and Long Beach, 49
The San Fernando Valley, 59
Saugus/Newhall and Valencia Area, 66
Burbank, Glendale, Pasadena, and the San Gabriel Mountains, 69
Claremont, Pomona, and Vicinity, 81

Orange County, 85
Buena Park/Anaheim, 86
Garden Grove, Santa Ana, and Orange, 91
Fullerton/La Habra, 95
Huntington Beach, Fountain Valley, and the Newport Beach Area, 97
Irvine and South Orange County, 100

Riverside and San Bernardino Counties, 107
In and Around Riverside and San Bernardino, 108
In and Around Palm Springs, 114
Barstow, Victorville, and Vicinity, 123

San Diego County, 129
San Diego, 130
Up the Coast, 148
Inland, 151

Inyo, Kern, and Tulare Counties, 161
In and Around Bakersfield, 162
The Bishop Area, 167
Death Valley, 170

Santa Barbara, Ventura, and San Luis Obispo Counties, 175
In and Around Santa Barbara, 176
Ventura, Thousand Oaks Area, and the Santa Clara Valley, 184
The Santa Ynez Valley, 190
San Luis Obispo and Morro Bay, 194

Special Annual Events, 201

Index, 217

Introduction

All too frequently, Southern California is depicted as a maze of freeways connecting a coastline of beach-partying young adults to an interior roughly divided into Hollywood in the north and Disneyland in the south. What usually gets lost in the hyperbole is the fact that Southern California offers families a greater variety of places to have fun together than just about anywhere else in the world.

The geography of Southern California includes hundreds of miles of beaches, mountain regions, and vast deserts—offering a nearly endless variety of out-of-doors enjoyments. Here, too, are city, regional, and historical parks, some practically large enough to be cities themselves, world-famous zoos, exciting new museums—some just for kids—and all sorts of other scientific and cultural attractions, not to mention the country's greatest concentration of amusement parks.

Because Southern California offers so much to see and do in such a large area, learning about and selecting from all that is available can be a bit overwhelming for visitors and residents alike. Moreover, families have special needs. Not all attractions are suitable for children—even some that purport to be.

I hope this book makes finding and selecting enjoyable places to go with children—from very young ones on up—a little easier. The book you are holding is the fourth edition of *Places to Go with Children in Southern California*. Over the years, since the first edition was published in 1977, an informal network of parents and others has emerged to offer me suggestions of places they have discovered. And, once again, I have driven over Southern California—looking, checking, exploring, following up on tips. This time I had a child of my own to accompany me.

As in the previous editions, I tried to look at each site through the eyes of a child: Just how tall do you have to be to see over the gate in front of the exhibit? Are the docents or proprietors friendly to children? Can you make noise? Can anything be touched? Are there places nearby to run and be active? Most important, what did the kids themselves have to say? No matter how nice a destination seemed in theory, if the place did not measure up to a visit by actual children, the listing did not go in the book.

Revisiting places, I was saddened to see that some had fallen into disrepair and could no longer be recommended. I was sorry to see that some outstanding attractions for families, such as Marineland, had closed. On the other hand, it has been wonderful to witness the growth in the number of new museums and other attractions either designed specifically for children or offering them special programs.

The emphasis of this book is on places that the whole family can enjoy. Naturally, a few attractions will appeal just to young children, and some will be appreciated only by older children. I have tried to keep in mind also that every child (and every family) is different. A botanical garden, for example, may bore some kids to tears, while others will be completely happy looking at flowers. I have tried to give enough information in each listing so that parents and children can decide which places are just right for them.

The places described in the book have been arranged by location and proximity to one another to make planning for outings easier and to give parents a backup choice in case something doesn't work out. And, as much as possible, I have tried to emphasize places that do not cost much or are free.

A few pointers:

- Always call ahead. This is the most important advice I can give you. (I have gone to a place that I just knew would be open, only to find it closed for repairs. I have also driven up and down the street looking for a place that I knew was there, only to learn that it had been replaced by something else the week before. And I am supposed to know better.)
- The prices given are accurate at the time of writing, but as we all know, prices are always going up.
- Local chambers of commerce and tourist offices are great sources for free maps, brochures describing local activities, and hotel and restaurant guides.
- Although this may seem like terribly obvious advice, be sure to have a good map handy and to study it before starting out.
- A blanket and a picnic kit of plastic knives and forks, paper plates, small cups, napkins, and a bottle opener will give you the option of being prepared for an impromptu picnic. A simple first-aid kit kept in the car can save an outing. Car snacks can be a good idea, too.
- Finally, dress in layers. In Southern California, it is frequently cool in the morning, hot in the afternoon, and quite cool in the evening.

Most important of all: Have fun!

Los Angeles County

Stretching from the ocean across a huge metropolis, north into snow-capped mountains, and beyond into the desert, Los Angeles County is a place where kids can experience just about every kind of outdoor activity imaginable, from surfboarding to tobogganing. Children can see places in this county that served as ranches for cowboys, hideouts for bandits, sets for movie stars, and gooey traps for prehistoric beasts. And, despite what some outsiders might think, Los Angeles is an area rich in cultural attractions—a growing number of them designed for children.

Perhaps one of the most exciting things about Los Angeles is its ethnic diversity. Within a few downtown blocks, kids can get a taste of Japan in Little Tokyo, China on North Spring Street, and Mexico on Olvera Street. All in all, there may be a greater variety of things to do in Los Angeles County and better weather to enjoy them than anywhere else in the country. What's more—despite budget cuts and the spiraling cost of just about everything—there are still plenty of places here for families to have fun without spending a lot of money.

Los Angeles, however, is not a very manageable area. No one place provides a representative sample of what the area has to offer. It is difficult, although not impossible, to get around without a car. The Southern California Rapid Transit District's customer relations department (phone: 213-626-4455) can help you plan your trips by public transportation. The Los Angeles Visitors Information Centers, located downtown at 696 South Figueroa Street in the Hilton Tower (phone: 213-689-8822), and in Hollywood at 6541 Hollywood Boulevard (phone: 213-461-4213), are excellent resources for tourists.

You can climb aboard a locomotive at the Griffith Park Travel Town.

Downtown Los Angeles

El Pueblo de Los Angeles Historic Monument
Between Main Street, Sunset Boulevard, Macy Street, Alameda Street, and Arcadia Street. (213) 628-1274. Open daily. Free. Visitors Center located in the Sepulveda House, 622 North Main Street (front entrance) and W-12 Olvera Street (rear entrance). Monday–Friday, 10 A.M.–3 P.M.; Saturday, 10 A.M.–4:30 P.M.

In 1781, forty-four bedraggled men, women, and children arrived from northern Mexico after a difficult seven-month journey, to found the Pueblo of Los Angeles. The settlers—eleven families of predominantly black, Indian, and mixed heritages—built earth huts around a central plaza, changing forever the lives of the native Indians living nearby. The city grew up around the plaza, and today the area and its original buildings are preserved as El Pueblo de Los Angeles Historic Monument. It's a lively, fun place—as well as a historic one—that includes the city's first firehouse and its oldest street, recreated as a Mexican marketplace.

A good place to begin your tour is at the Visitors Center, located in the 1887 Sepulveda House. (You can enter from either Main or Olvera street; the Victorian facade faces Main Street.) Constructed in the Eastlake Victorian style, the Sepulveda House was a commercial building with an upstairs rooming house. The Visitors Center, housed in a restored Victorian shop (it once sold fireplace mantles), shows a free eighteen-minute film on the history of the pueblo. The film plays at 11 A.M. and 2 P.M., and by appointment. As you leave Sepulveda House toward Olvera Street, you can peer behind glass to see the restored bedroom of Señora Sepulveda, the building's original owner.

You can also take a free guided walking tour of El Pueblo Tuesday through Saturday from 10 A.M. to 1 P.M. on the hour. The tours begin at the Docent Center, 130 Paseo de la Plaza, located next to the firehouse on the south side of the Plaza. The tour docents are well informed, friendly, and accustomed to children. The tours last an hour and include the basements of the Garnier buildings, which you cannot see on your own. The Garnier buildings, built in 1890 for Chinese tenants, are connected by underground tunnels. The basements, which have a colorful past, now house historical exhibits.

Olvera Street
North of the Plaza between North Main and Alameda streets. (213) 625-5045. Daily, from about 10 A.M. to around 8 P.M.

One of the oldest streets in Los Angeles, Olvera Street was transformed from a rundown dirt road into a brick-paved Mexican marketplace lined with shops and *puestos* (stalls) in 1930. Bustling, full of tourists, and very commercial, Olvera Street still manages to convey a colorful sense of the past. Children can see candles being dipped, a glassblower shaping glass, and an authentic blacksmith at work. At the north end of the street they can see a water trough carved by mission Indians in 1820.

Marvelous piñatas and Mexican handicrafts ranging from inexpensive to expensive are sold in the marketplace. There are a number of places to eat, including La Luz del Dia (southwest corner of Olvera Street), where, if you climb the stairs leading to the restrooms, you can get a good view of women making tortillas by hand. Usually musicians stroll around Olvera Street, too.

The Plaza, south of Olvera Street, is a good place to stop and rest. Once the center of pueblo life, the Plaza now hosts a number of celebrations including the Blessing of the Animals, Mardi Gras, and Cinco de Mayo. The iron-grilled kiosk in the middle of the plaza serves as a center for concerts.

Avila Adobe
10 Olvera Street, El Pueblo de Los Angeles Historic Monument. (213) 628-1274. Tuesday–Friday, 10 A.M.–3 P.M.; Saturday and Sunday, 10 A.M.–4:25 P.M. Free.

The Avila Adobe is the oldest existing residence in the city of Los Angeles. Built in 1818 by Francisco Avila, one-time mayor of the pueblo, the seven-room adobe was the pueblo's most elegant dwelling. Saved from demolition in the 1920s by some civic-minded citizens, the adobe was completely restored—using original building materials—after being damaged in the 1971 earthquake.

The adobe has been furnished in the style of a typical well-to-do California family of the early 1840s. You'll see the father's office, where he kept his ledgers and the cowhides used for barter, the indoor kitchen (most cooking was done outdoors) with its wooden bathtub, and the elegant parents' bedroom. Kids, of course, will be most interested in the children's bedroom with its cowhide bed, wooden cradle, chamber pot, clothes, and

4 LOS ANGELES COUNTY

The Plaza offers a break from the bustle of Olvera Street.

dolls. Outside is a packed-earth patio with an outdoor kitchen and an old wagon.

Old Plaza Firehouse
134 Paseo de la Plaza (southeast corner of the Plaza). (213) 625-3741. Tuesday–Friday, 10 A.M.–3 P.M.; Saturday and Sunday, 10 A.M.–4:30 P.M.

Built in 1884, this two-story red brick building was Los Angeles's first official fire station. It has been authentically restored to the era of the 1880s and is now a museum of early fire-fighting memorabilia. One of the first fire engines used in the city is on display, along with an original pumper and a chemical wagon. There are a large number of photographs, a collection of fire hats, and some old fire alarms, which the fire fighter on duty will ring for you.

One-Day Train Rides
Union Passenger Station, 800 North Alameda Street. For reservations and information, phone (213) 624-0171.

Is there a kid (big or small) who doesn't love trains? The grand Union Station, with its marble floors, big leather chairs, and flower-filled patios, is a fitting starting point for a train adventure. You can travel to San Diego or Santa Barbara and back easily in a day.

The Amtrak to Santa Barbara leaves every day at 9:55 A.M. and arrives at 12:05 P.M.; it leaves Santa Barbara at 4:40 P.M. and arrives in Los Angeles at 7:30 P.M. After the train passes through the San Fernando Valley, it goes through two tunnels under the Santa Susana Pass to the Simi Valley. The train stops at Oxnard and then travels right along the Pacific. There is a full dining car for the treat of a moving lunch.

One-way fare to Santa Barbara is $17 for adults, $8.50 for ages 12–21, $4.25 for ages 2–11; ages 2 and under ride free.

Heading south, trains leave every day for San Diego at 6:15 A.M., 8 A.M., 10:45 A.M., 12:45 P.M., 2:45 P.M., 4 P.M., 5 P.M., and 8 P.M. The trip takes two hours and forty-five minutes. The last train from San Diego leaves for Los Angeles at 7:45 P.M. With younger children you might want to ride only as far as San Juan Capistrano or San Clemente. One-way fare to San Diego is $21.50 for adults, $11 for ages 12–21, $5.50 for ages 2–11; ages 2 and under ride free. A second adult fare is $11. If you travel Monday through

Thursday, however, the fare is considerably less: $28.50 round trip for adults and teenagers; $14.25 round trip for children.

Amtrak also offers special package tours to the San Diego Zoo, Sea World, Tijuana, and the San Diego Harbor. For more information on the tours, call Amtrak and ask for Amtrak tours.

Reservations are required for the Santa Barbara train and are a good idea for San Diego.

Chinatown

Bounded by Sunset Boulevard, North Hill and North Spring streets, and the Pasadena Freeway. The main gate is located at 900 North Broadway near College Street. Open daily. Free.

Chinatown is the cultural center of Los Angeles's large Chinese-American community. The present Chinatown dates from the 1930s, when the original Chinese settlement, located southeast of Olvera Street, had to relocate to make way for Union Station.

North Broadway is the main street of Chinatown. Here are Chinese restaurants and groceries, fresh fish and live poultry markets, as well as new shopping plazas. Central Chinatown in the 900 block of North Broadway is the section geared to tourists. As you enter the plaza through the pagoda gates, point out the carved animals and fish along the rooflines to your children. The animals provide the buildings with good luck. Your children will probably also enjoy seeing the mural of the fiery dragon painted on the bank building on the corner to your right. The shops along Gin Ling Way, although catering to tourists, are fun for browsing—you'll find lots of kites and inexpensive toys. At night, lantern-covered lights brighten the plaza.

The area along North Spring Street serves the community rather than tourists. The herb shop at 701 North Spring Street is particularly interesting.

Chinatown contains many good, moderately priced Chinese restaurants. Since Chinese families take their children out to eat with them, nearly every restaurant here is accustomed to children. If you would like some other kind of food, you can take your children to Little Joe's at 900 North Broadway—an old-fashioned, moderately priced spaghetti and meatball kind of place—or to Philippe the Original at 1001 North Alameda Street (one block east of North Spring Street at Ord). Known for its French dip sandwiches, Philippe's offers counter service, old booths, sawdust on the floor, and tradition.

San Antonio Winery
737 Lamar Street. (213) 223-1401. Monday–Thursday, 8 A.M.–7 P.M.; Friday, 8 A.M.-8 P.M.; Saturday, 9 A.M.–7 P.M.; Sunday, 10 A.M.–6 P.M. Free.

Commercial winemaking in California started on the site of what is now Union Station in downtown Los Angeles. Louis Vignes planted a vineyard there and established a wine-making business in the 1830s. The San Antonio Winery, founded in 1917 and still run by the original family, is the oldest winery in Los Angeles still in operation. On a self-conducted tour you'll see the original winery buildings, built from boxcar sidings, and some of the wine-making equipment, including the enormous aging vats. In addition to wine tasting for adults, there is a delicatessen and sandwich shop on the premises that serves wonderful food. You can eat inside among the barrels of aging wine or outside on a lovely patio. (The patio is not open on Sunday, though.) A jazz band plays for lunch Thursday through Sunday.

Los Angeles Children's Museum
310 North Main Street (in the Los Angeles Mall at street level). (213) 687-8800. Summer: Monday–Friday, 11:30 A.M.–5 P.M.; Saturday and Sunday, 10 A.M.–5 P.M. School year: Wednesday and Thursday, 2:30–5 P.M.; Saturday and Sunday, 10 A.M.–5 P.M. Phone for school holiday hours. Admission: $4 per person; under 2, free.

The Children's Museum aptly describes itself as a place "where kids can touch the world." Children are encouraged to touch, handle, feel, wear, ride, probe, construct, design, and otherwise discover the museum's many exhibits. In the "Ethnic L.A." exhibit, children use dress-up, craft-making, game-playing, and walk-in exhibits to experience the various ethnic cultures that make up Los Angeles. (A different culture is featured each year.) In the "Workshop Place," children use egg cartons, paper tubes, Styrofoam bits, colored paper, crayons, scissors, glue—you name it—to make, well, whatever. In the "City Streets" exhibit, children can crawl through a drainage pipe, see what is beneath the sidewalks, walk on a catwalk, wear a fire fighter's uniform, and sit on police motorcycle.

Children can create their own cartoon characters in Zoetrope, an animators' workshop designed by Walt Disney Productions. In the Health Education Learning Project, or "H.E.L.P." exhibit, children learn about health by playing in equipped doctor's and dentist's offices and a hospital emergency room. One of the most popular exhibits is the "Sticky City," where giant

Pretending to be a firefighter is part of the fun at the Los Angeles Children's Museum.

foam shapes with Velcro tapes offer all sorts of wild construction possibilities. "Softspace" is a softly sculptured play space for children under three and their parents. There is also a spectacular Lego construction area, a working television newsroom, a mini-recording studio, a computerized pianocorder, a children's theater, and much more. The Children's Museum is a place where kids can be themselves and where they learn by having fun.

The museum offers special workshops and events year around, and summer children's tours. Birthday parties are also available. A museum shop sells children's books, educational games, and toys. Membership in the museum is also available for individual children and adults, families, and organizations.

Little Tokyo
Centered around First Street from Main to Alameda streets.

Little Tokyo is the heart of Los Angeles's large Japanese-American community. It is an active and cohesive district with scores of businesses and restaurants. If you come here in the morning, you'll see the shopkeepers starting their day by washing their windows just as their counterparts in Japan do. As in Japan, the moderately priced restaurants here (including Shakey's Pizza) have plastic displays of their food dishes in the windows.

A great deal of recent development is evident in the area. The Japanese Village Plaza Mall (between First and Second streets, near Central Avenue) is a lovely shopping mall with stone paths and fountains. A shop children will enjoy is Mitsuru Toys (107 Japanese Village Plaza Mall), which sells all sorts of battery-powered toys. In addition to some first-class Japanese restaurants, the mall contains a number of Japanese-accented fast-food places where kids can try a teriyaki burger or a bowl of *ramen gyoza*. The Japanese Village Plaza Mall can be easily recognized by the traditional fireman's lookout towering over the First Street entrance.

Weller Court (between Los Angeles and San Pedro streets at the corner of Weller and Second streets) is another attractive shopping mall that is fun to explore. The three-level court, overlooking a central fountain, includes a number of shops and eating places, as well as a glass-walled elevator to ride.

At the corner of First and Los Angeles streets is the impressive New Otani Hotel. Take the elevator to the fifth level and stroll in a lovely, genuine Japanese rooftop garden with waterfalls. While adults will be soothed

Just like in Japan, restaurants in Little Tokyo have food displays in their windows.

by the garden's serenity, children will be fascinated by the odd perspective that comes from being high above the city streets while seeming to be at ground level.

The Japanese American Cultural and Community Center at 244 South San Pedro Street (phone: 231-628-2725) has displays and information on cultural events, such as Children's Day, which is held in May in Little Tokyo. The plaza in front of the center contains a huge, fascinating rock sculpture dedicated to the first generation of Japanese immigrants.

The Temporary Contemporary
152 North Central Avenue. (213) 626-6222. *Tuesday and Wednesday, 11 A.M.–6 P.M.; Thursday and Friday, 11 A.M.-8 P.M.; Saturday and Sunday, 11 A.M.–6 P.M.. Adults, $4; students and seniors, $2; under 12, free. Admission fee includes the Museum of Contemporary Art at California Plaza. Free to all, Thursday 5–8 P.M.*

In 1983, the Temporary Contemporary opened in Little Tokyo as an exhibit space for the Museum of Contemporary Art while the new museum building on Grand Avenue was being constructed. The temporary museum, located in a pair of converted warehouses, proved so popular that it became a more-or-less permanent auxiliary of the Museum of Contemporary Art.

Older children will enjoy the colorful warehouse space and many of the changing exhibits. (Younger children may find some of the artwork frightening.) The museum is easily accessed by wheelchairs and strollers. It makes a very nice outing for parents with babies.

Los Angeles Times Tours
202 West First Street (between Broadway and Spring Street). *Parking at 221 South Spring Street. (213) 237-5000. Monday–Friday (except holidays), at 11:15 A.M. and 3 P.M. Minimum age is 10. Free.*

No reservations are needed for this one-hour tour of the *Los Angeles Times*, which takes you through the editorial area, wire room, composing room (where the news stories are assembled into page form), and distribution area. You'll also see the high-speed presses, which are usually running. You can arrange for group tours by calling (213) 237-5757.

Grand Central Market
Broadway and Hill streets between Third and Fourth streets. (213) 624-2378. Monday–Saturday, 9 A.M.–6 P.M.; Sunday, 10 A.M.–5 P.M.

The block-deep Grand Central Market is a far cry from the local supermarkets or shopping malls that most kids know. More than fifty independently operated stalls sell everything from rare spices to octopus to pigs' heads. It's exciting to see all the produce piled high and the eggs spread out, seemingly by the acre, instead of in Styrofoam containers. Plastic wrap is practically unheard of; butchers put your meat in waxed paper, and vendors place your produce in paper bags. The majority of customers are Spanish speaking and most stalls have bilingual signs and staff. A big health-food stand in the center of the market sells carrot shakes to tired shoppers.

Los Angeles Philharmonic Symphonies for Youth/ Open House at the Bowl
Los Angeles Philharmonic Association, Education Department, The Music Center, 135 North Grand Avenue, No. 405; Los Angeles, CA 90012. (213) 972-0703. June–August: (213) 850-2077.

Each year the Los Angeles Philharmonic performs concerts especially for children ages six through twelve. The hour-long concerts have special children's themes and are geared for their attention spans. Each piece of music is introduced with informative remarks by the conductor, and there are appearances by outstanding guest artists. Storytellers, narrators, puppets, and young soloists are also featured parts of the programs, which are designed to instill an appreciation of music in children. The concerts are held in the elegant Dorothy Chandler Pavilion at 10 A.M. on five Saturdays during the school year. Seats are $5.

The Philharmonic Association also offers children an outstanding summer arts festival at the Hollywood Bowl. Called Open House at the Bowl, the festival offers six weeks of performances and workshops for children on weekday mornings. The lively programs include performances by dance, instrumental, theatrical, and puppet ensembles. A different program is featured each week. Performances are held Monday through Friday at 9:30 and 10:30 A.M. on the Open House Stage, located in the Box Office Circle area.

Workshops for children aged three and older follow the performances at 10:30 and 11:30 A.M. The workshops, which are divided into age groups, relate to the performances and might include making puppets or instruments, learning magic, or participating in music or drama. The festival also exposes children to the Los Angeles Philharmonic Orchestra, which rehearses at the Bowl most weekday mornings.

Open House at the Hollywood Bowl is very popular and space in the workshops is limited, so make your reservations early. Also, it can get very hot at the Bowl, so dress children accordingly. You might want to apply sunscreen to fair children—everything happens outside. Many of the performances are signed, and children in wheelchairs are easily accommodated with advance notice. Performances are $2.50 for adults and children aged three and older. There is a separate $1 fee for workshops for children only. For more information phone: (213) 850-2000.

Museum of Contemporary Art
250 South Grand Avenue. (213) 626-6222. Tuesday and Wednesday, 11 A.M.–6 P.M.; Thursday and Friday, 11 A.M.–8 P.M.; Saturday and Sunday, 11 A.M.–6 P.M.. Adults, $4; students and seniors, $2; under 12, free. Admission fee also covers the Temporary Contemporary. Free to all, Thursday, 5–8 P.M.

The artwork at the Museum of Contemporary Art begins with the museum building, a stunning red sandstone structure with pyramid-shaped skylights designed by the Japanese architect Arata Isozaki. Inside the bright galleries are displays from the museum's permanent collection—international paintings, sculpture, photography, and environmental works from the 1940s on—and changing exhibitions.

Although almost everyone will appreciate seeing the outside of the museum building and the lovely courtyard fountains, a visit inside is probably best made with older children. The museum acoustics are such that one small child can make a great deal of noise. More important, young children may find some of the artwork frightening.

Holographic Visions
Lower level, 300 South Grand Avenue (adjacent to the Museum of Contemporary Art. (213) 687-7171. Tuesday–Sunday, 11 A.M.–6 P.M. Open on Thursday and Friday until 8 P.M. Free.

Holographic art is displayed in this museum next door to the Museum of Contemporary Art. Kids and adults alike are fascinated by the magical-seeming visions. Placards in the gallery explain how holograms work.

Wells Fargo History Museum
333 South Grand Avenue (on the northwest corner of the Wells Fargo Bank Center; entrance is on the corner of Third and Hope streets, up the stairway). (213) 253-7166. Monday–Friday, 9 A.M.–5 P.M. Free.

Stagecoaches are the highlight of this shiny public-relations museum devoted to Wells Fargo history. Children can see (but not touch) a restored nineteenth-century Concord stagecoach resting on a replica of a "corduroy road": logs placed crosswise over muddy trails so that vehicles could pass. A partially built coach, along with original coachmaker's tools, gives children an idea of how stagecoaches were built. There is also a stagecoach cabin that children can climb into; inside they will hear a tape that describes an 1859 stage journey from Saint Louis to San Francisco.

Other displays that would interest children include Winchester rifles, gold nuggets, nineteenth-century reward posters, a turn-of-the-century safe, Pony Express saddles, and a replica of an 1850s Wells Fargo office complete with gold scales and a telegraph machine. There is also a small theater that plays free movies relating to Wells Fargo history and the era of the West.

Los Angeles Bonaventure Hotel
404 South Figueroa. (213) 624-1000.

Children interested in what the buildings of the future may look like will enjoy a trip to the Bonaventure Hotel. (In fact, the hotel has been used as a set in science-fiction space films.) You cannot miss the hotel, with its five skyscraping mirrored cylinders and its glass elevators gliding outside. Designed by architect John Portman, the hotel is quite something on the inside, too. You can enter the hotel lobby, located in the square base of the building, from either Flower or Figueroa streets. The space-age lobby, circled by reflecting pools, is several stories high, with overhead balconies. Don't miss taking a ride on the glass-walled elevators; it's quite a thrill for kids to see the view outside as they zoom thirty-five floors up on the exterior of the building.

There are several inexpensive places to eat or snack in the hotel's shopping gallery, including Carl's Jr., the Bagel Nosh, and McConnell's Ice Cream. Or, you might want to explore Bunker Hill a bit and head over to the rather elegant McDonald's in the Court at Wells Fargo Center. To get to the Court, take the skywalk from the fifth floor of the Bonaventure, which leads east over Flower Street. On the other side of the skywalk, you'll find the new Stuart M. Ketchum downtown YMCA. (Take a peek inside to watch the swimmers through the glass in the lobby.) Then continue along Fourth Street to the Court at Wells Fargo Center (350 South Hope Street) with its lovely skylit atrium and indoor garden. The McDonald's inside the court is decorated in mauve and gray, with a terrace that offers a great view of downtown.

Clifton's Cafeterias
Clifton's Silver Spoon, 515 West Seventh Street at Olive. (213) 485-1726. Monday–Friday, 7 A.M.–3:30 P.M. Clifton's Brookdale, 648 South Broadway at Seventh Street. (213) 627-1673. Monday–Thursday, 6 A.M.–8 P.M.; until 8:30 on Friday, Saturday, and Sunday. Other Clifton's cafeterias are located in West Covina (818-960-4741), Lakewood (213-636-8747), Whittier (213-698-9479), and Laguna Hills (714-855-6661).

Clifton's is not your ordinary cafeteria chain. The original cafeteria, established in 1931, let its customers pay whatever they wanted for a meal and no one was turned away hungry. Of course those days are long gone, but the Brookdale cafeteria still retains the flavor of the original, with the same redwood-forest atmosphere complete with waterfall and brook. The Silver Spoon cafeteria has three dining rooms with different menus. There is a buffet upstairs in a Victorian setting, a conventional cafeteria, and a basement soup kitchen.

The food at these cafeterias is inexpensive and reasonably good. Children under twelve get a special Treasure Tray for $1.49. After eating they can choose a free gift from the Treasure Chest. Decorated cakes are available for birthday parties if you call three days in advance.

Pacific Coast Stock Exchange
233 South Beaudry. (213) 977-4700. Weekdays, 7:30 A.M.–1:30 P.M. Free.

The trading floor of the Pacific Coast Stock Exchange is second in size only to New York's. You can get a firsthand look at the action from a viewing gallery on the twelfth floor.

East Los Angeles

Lincoln Park/Plaza de la Raza
3501 Valley Boulevard (park entrance is a block east of the intersection of Valley Boulevard and Mission Road). Plaza de la Raza, phone: (213) 223-2475. Free.

This park is the home of the Plaza de la Raza (Place of the People), a community-supported Mexican-American cultural center. Cultural instruction with a Hispanic emphasis is given in classes that include dance, music, arts and crafts, piano, guitar, drama, and other subjects. There is a small fee for the classes, which are open to all. Plaza de la Raza also sponsors presentations of Mexican-American music, dance, drama, and other cultural events.

Scattered among the park's forty-six acres are picnic tables, barbecues, a gymnasium, ball fields, and a swimming pool. The park has a lake with ducks to feed, and there is a fishing program for youngsters. There is also a children's playground with an Aztec motif.

El Mercado
3425 East First Street. (213) 268-3451. Daily, 10 A.M.–8 P.M.

You can give your children a taste of Mexico without going farther than East First Street on a visit to El Mercado, a bustling three-floor indoor Mexican market. On the main floor is a large supermarket surrounded on the outside by stalls selling everything from piñatas to fresh shrimp. Most interesting of all is the *tortillería,* where you can watch conveyor belts carrying fresh hot tortillas. Upstairs is a series of restaurants and snack bars where you can sit at a table and watch the action on the mezzanine below while you eat. Mariachi bands are usually strolling around, too.

South Central Los Angeles

Children's Film and Television Center of America
University of Southern California School of Cinema/TV, University Park, Los Angeles. (213) 743-8632. Screenings are held at the Rialto Theater in South Pasadena on the second Saturday of the month; the Samuel Goldwyn Pavilion on the third Saturday of the month; and U.S.C. Norris Cinema Theater on the fourth Saturday. Adults, $3; children, $2. Free to members.

Affiliated with the School of Cinema/TV at the University of Southern California, the Children's Film and Television Center of America is dedicated to offering an entertaining, positive alternative to commercial children's programming. The organization sponsors the annual International Children's Film Festival in Los Angeles and conducts monthly programs of quality films for children. The films play at the Rialto Theater (1023 Fair Oaks, South Pasadena) on the second Saturday of each month; the Samuel Goldwyn Pavilion (Westside Pavilion, Pico between Westwood Boulevard and Overland, West Los Angeles) on the third Saturday; and the USC Norris Cinema Theater (USC Campus, Exposition Boulevard between Figueroa and Vermont) on the fourth Saturday.

All programs begin at 11 A.M., last approximately ninety minutes, and are suitable for children aged three to eleven. The films are open to everyone, as is membership in the center's nonprofit organization.

California Museum of Science and Industry
700 State Drive, Exposition Park. (213) 744-7400. Daily, 10 A.M.–5 P.M. Free.

Always a fascinating museum for children, the California Museum of Science and Industry recently underwent a $43 million renovation. Tripled in size, the museum complex is now the country's second-largest science museum, ranking after the Smithsonian Institute in Washington, D.C.

Children can not only touch the exhibits in this museum, they can activate them, manipulate them, go inside them, and even converse with them. In "The Energy Experience" exhibit, children learn about energy through question-and-answer video games; in the "Bicycle Company" exhibit, children can design their own bicycles on a computer and then become man-

The Museum of Science and Industry is full of fascinating exhibits.

agers of a bicycle factory; in "The Creative Computer" exhibit, children can create their own computer art.

Mathematical principles are demonstrated in ten exciting displays, complete with ringing bells and flashing lights. The transportation exhibit features computerized model electric trains. An agriculture exhibit features live chicks hatching in an incubator (chicken farmers bring the eggs to the museum every other day and take the newly hatched chicks back to the farm), honey-producing bees, and genetically cloned plants.

Some of the most fascinating exhibits are housed in the new seven-story Aerospace Building. Included among the displays are the Gemini 11 space capsule, the Apollo 12 lunar descent engine, the Intelstat III communications satellite, a T-38 Air Force trainer, and a replica of the Space Shuttle. On the ground floor, children can design their own airplanes, tap into a weather satellite, or call up a satellite image of another part of the world.

Also outstanding is the octagonal Mitsubishi IMAX Theater, which offers viewers a five-story motion-picture screen and six-channel stereo sound. One of the films shown in the theater is *The Dream Is Alive,* which was shot by the astronauts on the Space Shuttle. The theater is open daily. Phone (213) 744-2015 for show information. Admission is $4.75 for adults and $3 for students and children. Outside the theater is the outdoor Air and Space Garden, which includes a United Airlines DC-8.

In the renovated Hall of Health, the focus is on choices people can make to enhance their own health. At the "Health for Life" exhibit visitors insert personalized "credit" cards to check their breathing, pulse, heartrate, balance, stress level, and other vital signs.

Another exciting part of the museum complex is the California Museum of Afro-American History and Culture. This 44,000-square-foot structure highlights the contributions of Black Americans to science, education, politics, religion, and sports.

The Mark Taper Hall of Economics and Finance is still another new structure in the museum complex. The nation's only separate museum facility devoted to the United States economy, the Hall of Economics and Finance uses dozens of one-of-a-kind exhibits to make economics interesting and entertaining.

In addition to its regular exhibits, the Museum of Science and Industry has a number of temporary exhibits that change frequently. The museum also offers a superb program of Saturday Science Workshops for children aged 4¾ through eighth graders. Each workshop is geared to a specific grade level. Kindergartners and first-graders can learn how animals adapt to their environments or about ocean surprises. Older children can build their own rockets, design their own planes, or take a trip aboard a marine research boat. Summer workshops are also held. Phone the museum for a schedule and an application.

Natural History Museum of Los Angeles County
900 Exposition Boulevard (on the west side of the Rose Garden in Exposition Park). (213) 744-3414 or 744-3466 (tape). Tuesday–Sunday, 10 A.M.–5 P.M. Adults, $3; senior citizens and students, $1.50; ages 5–12, 75¢; under 5, free. Free second Tuesday of every month.

One of the largest and most prominent museums of its kind in the country, the always popular Natural History Museum has recently undergone a major expansion. The highlight for kids is the new Discovery Center (open 11 A.M.–3 P.M., Tuesday–Sunday), a hands-on exploratory center designed for children of all ages. Located on the main level, near the original rotunda area, the Discovery Center gives kids the opportunity to handle all sorts of artifacts and scientific specimens. They can walk through a North American forest habitat, take fossil rubbings from a realistic-looking rock wall, study water drops under a microscope, try on costumes from around the world, and check out discovery boxes filled with special activities and things to examine.

PLACES TO GO WITH CHILDREN IN SOUTHERN CALIFORNIA 19

The Gem Hall is just one of the many exhibits at the Natural History Museum of Los Angeles County.

The Natural History Museum is too big to see it all in a single visit. Among the other highlights for children are the habitat halls showing North American, African, and exotic mammals in their natural environments, the new hall of birds featuring electronically animated bird habitats, the megamouth shark display, and of course the dinosaurs. Kids will also enjoy the multimedia chaparral exhibit, which surrounds visitors in the sights, sounds, and even the smells of a chaparral ecology.

Children will also be interested in the American and California history exhibits, which include a replica of a colonial kitchen and an 1889 streetcar, and the antique cars collection on the lower level.

The museum offers Saturday workshops for parents and children, summer natural science workshops for kindergartners through eighth graders, and twice-monthly special family events in the Discovery Center. For more information about classes phone (213) 744-3342; for information about summer workshops or Discovery Center events phone (213) 744-3335.

Visitors at the Natural History Museum of Los Angeles County ponder an ancient Aztec stone.

Exposition Park Rose Garden
900 Exposition Boulevard. Daily, 7 A.M.–5 P.M. Free.

Adjacent to the Natural History Museum is one of the largest rose gardens in the nation. The sunken garden contains more than sixteen thousand rosebushes and is a lovely spot for a stroll.

Watts Towers/Watts Towers Art Center
1765 East 107th Street, Watts. (213) 569-8181. Art Center hours: Tuesday–Saturday, 9 A.M.-5 P.M.

Sabatino (Simon) Rodia, an Italian tile setter, devoted thirty-three years of his life to the construction of these soaring towers. Singlehandedly, he wired steel reinforcing rods together into a lacy structure, stuccoed them with cement, pebbles, cup handles, old dishes, and other cast-off items. The neighbors made fun of him, calling his towers junk, but Rodia worked on anyway. By the time he died in 1965, his towers were recognized as remarkable works of art. Tours within the tower grounds are available to groups of fifteen or more, and reservations are necessary. (You can phone the art center to inquire about joining a tour group.) The Watts Towers Art Center (up the block at 1727 East 107th Street) displays the work of local artists and has special exhibitions.

Dominguez Adobe/Rancho San Pedro
18127 South Alameda Street, Compton. (213) 631-5981. Tuesday and Wednesday, 1–4 P.M.; second and third Sunday of the month, 1–4 P.M. Free.

Juan José Dominguez was a soldier with Father Serra's original expedition from Mexico to found the California missions. He was rewarded for his long service with a seventy-five-thousand-acre Spanish land grant that covered the area south of the Pueblo de Los Angeles to the water. The land grant passed to Juan José's nephew Manuel, who built a ranch house on it in 1826. The land is now covered by more than a half-dozen different cities, but you can still see the ranch house, which has been restored as a museum containing original furniture and artifacts of the era.

North Central Los Angeles

Elysian Park
Near the intersection of Pasadena and Golden State freeways. The main street through the park is Stadium Way. (From Pasadena Freeway, take the Stadium Way off ramp.) Park entrances are on Sunset Boulevard, Stadium Way, Scott Avenue, Academy Road, Morton Place, Riverside Drive-Golden State Freeway, and North Broadway. (211) 225-2044. Daily, 5:30 A.M.– 10 P.M. Free.

Just north of downtown Los Angeles is a 585-acre park, much of which is in a wilderness state. The park includes picnic areas, miles of hiking trails, a ten-acre rare-tree grove (in which the trees are labeled), a small lake, tennis courts, and baseball diamonds. A play area for small children is located in the arboretum in the area bounded by Eysian Park Road, Stadium Way, and Academy Road. The center of the park, along Stadium Way, is landscaped and is a good place for family picnics. The park is most enjoyable on weekdays when it is quiet. On weekends the park is extremely crowded.

Lawry's California Center
Avenue 26 at San Fernando Road. (Take the Figueroa Street off ramp from the Pasadena Freeway [110] northbound. Turn right on Figueroa, staying in the left lane to the corner of Avenue 26. Turn left on Avenue 26 and go 1½ blocks to the main entrance.) (213) 225-2491. Tours Monday–Friday, at 11:30 A.M., 12:30, 1:30, and 2:30 P.M. Free.

On a forty-five minute tour, visitors see how Lawry's products (seasonings, sauce mixes, and salad dressings) are made. The tour includes the production facilities, laboratories, and test kitchens. Small children have to be lifted to see parts of the tour, and there is a lot of walking. A garden surrounds the center, with exotic trees from Asia and South America and a collection of rare plants. You can have an informal lunch of Mexican food or barbecued meat dishes in the garden daily from 11 A.M. to 3 P.M. Dinner is available from May until November.

Heritage Square

Exit Pasadena Freeway on Avenue 43, go east to Homer Street (just on the other side of the freeway), then south to the end of the street. (818) 449-0193. Saturday, Sunday, and most holidays, 12–4 P.M. (Self-guided tours on Saturday. Guided tours on Sunday at 12:15, 1:15, 2:15, and 3:15 P.M.) Adults, $3; senior citizens and ages 13–17, $2; 12 and under, free.

Heritage Square is a haven for some of the city's endangered Victorian buildings. Eight significant structures, which would have otherwise been demolished, have been brought together in this ten-acre park. The buildings, including an 1897 church and the Palms Railroad station, have been arranged in a village setting of lawns, shade trees, and period lamp posts. The restoration work, supported by public contribution and carried out largely by volunteer craftsmen, is going slowly. So far the ground floor of the 1887 Hale House, originally at Avenue 45 and Figueroa, has been completely restored and furnished with period furniture. The Palms Depot has also been restored and furnished with railroad memorabilia. Some of the buildings that are in the process of restoration are also open. You are also welcome to picnic on the green.

Saturday, when you can look around on your own, is probably the best day to come with children. Better still, come during one of the park's special events, which include old-fashioned Fourth of July and Labor Day picnics, Christmas-season festivities, vintage car displays, brass band concerts, and more.

Southwest Museum

234 Museum Drive, Highland Park. (From central Los Angeles, take the Pasadena Freeway north to Avenue 43, go left on Avenue 43 to Figueroa, right on Figueroa, left on Avenue 45, right on Marmion Way, and left on Museum Drive.) (213) 221-2163. Tuesday–Saturday, 11 A.M.–5 P.M.; Sunday, 1–5 P.M. Adults, $3; seniors and students, $1.50; ages 7–18, $1; under 7, free.

Perched on a hill overlooking Highland Park, the Southwest Museum looks like a monastery. The museum is devoted to the history and culture of American Indians, particularly the Indians of California and the Southwest. The best way to enter the museum is through the long tunnel on Museum Drive, which is lined with dioramas depicting southwestern Indian life. (Children have to be about four feet tall to see the dioramas without being lifted. Preschool children might find the somewhat dark tunnel frighten-

Children watch an artist at work at the Southwest Museum.

ing, and children should probably be at least eight to enjoy the museum in general.) At the end of the tunnel is an elevator that takes you up 108 feet to the museum.

Inside the museum, some of the high points for children are a large totem pole, Indian headdresses and clothing, a replica of a Chumash Indian rock art site, some fascinating Indian masks, a collection of Hopi kachina dolls, and a full-size Southern Cheyenne tipi.

The museum also sponsors film series, some of which may be of interest to children; workshops for children; and family programs that include stories and songs.

Lummis Home
200 East Avenue 43, Highland Park. (From the Pasadena Freeway, take the Avenue 43 exit.) (213) 222-0546. Wednesday–Sunday, 1–4 P.M. Free.

Near the Southwest Museum is the home of its founder, Charles Lummis. A noted writer, editor, archaeologist, historian, and western enthusiast, Lummis built his home by hand using local stones, hand-hewn timber, and telegraph poles from the Santa Fe Railroad. A curator from the Historical

Society of Southern California will be pleased to give a personal tour of this remarkable home, point out Lummis's Early California memorabilia and his photos of southwestern Indians. Children should be at least eight or nine to appreciate the home. Outside is a lovely garden of native California plants.

Casa de Adobe
4603 North Figueroa Street, Highland Park. (213) 221-2163. Tuesday–Sunday, 11 A.M.–5 P.M. Free.

Located directly below the Southwest Museum, Casa de Adobe is a replica of an early-nineteenth-century Spanish-California ranch house, or hacienda. Furnished with antiques and reproductions of period furniture and family items, the hacienda rooms can be viewed through half-doors. Small children, however, will have to be lifted to see the rooms. (If a room is dark, feel free to switch on the light, then turn it off when you finish looking.)

Across the street is **Sycamore Grove Park**. A children's playground is located near the north end of the park.

Los Feliz and Hollywood

Griffith Park
Main entrances on Los Feliz Boulevard at Vermont Avenue, Western Avenue, and Riverside Drive. (Griffith Park lies just west of the Golden State Freeway [I-5], roughly between Los Feliz Boulevard on the south and the Ventura Freeway [134] on the north. Freeway off ramps leading to the park from I-5 are Los Feliz Boulevard, Griffith Park [direct entry], and Zoo Drive. Approaching the park on Freeway 134 eastbound, take either the Forest Lawn Drive or Victory Boulevard off ramp. From Freeway 134 westbound, take Zoo Drive or Forest Lawn Drive. After leaving the freeways, follow signs into the park.) (213) 665-5188. Daily, 5 A.M.–10:30 P.M. Bridle and hiking trails and mountain roads close at sunset. Free.

Children in Los Angeles have the largest city park in the United States for a playground. Covering more than four thousand acres, Griffith Park offers

26 LOS ANGELES COUNTY

Find a pony just your speed at the Griffith Park Pony Rides.

picnic areas, children's playgrounds, hiking and bridle trails, a famous zoo, a fascinating new museum, a miniature railroad, pony and stagecoach rides, an observatory and planetarium, an old-fashioned merry-go-round, and plenty of other kids to play with. A free map of the park, including hiking trails, is available at the Ranger Headquarters and Visitors Center, 4730 Crystal Springs Drive.

Griffith Observatory and Planetarium

2800 East Observatory Road (located at the north end of Vermont Avenue, on the south side of the park). (213) 664-1191. The Hall of Science is open daily in summer from 12:30–10 P.M. (Saturdays, 11:30 A.M.–10 P.M.) Winter hours: Tuesday–Friday, 2–10 P.M.; Saturday, 11:30 A.M.–10 P.M.; Sunday, 12:30-10 P.M. Free. Planetarium shows in summer: Monday–Friday, 1:30, 3, and 8 P.M.; Saturday and Sunday, 1:30, 3, 4:30, and 8 P.M. Winter: Tuesday–Friday, 3 and 8 P.M.; Saturday and Sunday, 1:30, 3, 4:30, and 8 P.M. Age 16 and older, $2.75; seniors, $1.50; ages 5–15, $1.50.

The Griffith Observatory houses one of the largest public telescopes in California. It is open for free viewing every clear evening, except Monday, from 7 to 10 P.M. (In the summer it is open daily from dark until 10 P.M.) For a recorded message on the current planet positions and sky events, phone (213) 663-8171.

The Hall of Science in the Observatory has exhibits in astronomy and the physical sciences. Highlights include a pendulum showing the rotation of the earth, a six-foot-three-inch-diameter globe of the earth, a seismograph that reacts to the vibrations of feet stomped on the floor, and a submarine periscope.

A huge projector fills the seventy-five-foot dome of the adjacent planetarium with realistic views of the skies as they appear at any time from any point on earth. The hour-long presentations change regularly. Shows are selected for their dramatic appeal as well as their astronomical interest. Children under five are not admitted to the planetarium shows—they might find them frightening—except for the special children's presentations at 1:30 P.M. on Saturday and Sunday (daily during the summer).

Older children and teenagers will enjoy the Laserium show at the Observatory. It's a laser-beam concert with high-fidelity rock or other music and impressive special effects. Shows are generally scheduled Tuesday through Thursday at 6:30 and 9:15 P.M.; Friday and Saturday at 6:30, 9:15, and 10:30 P.M.; and Sunday at 6:30 P.M. Summers add Monday shows and later shows on Sunday and weekdays. Tickets are $5.50 for adults and

$4.50 for ages five through twelve. Children under five are not permitted. Tickets are available through Ticketron or at the Observatory. If you plan to get your tickets at the Observatory, arrive forty-five minutes to one hour before the show time. (Attending both the planetarium show and laserium gives you preferred seating without waiting in line.) For laserium information phone (818) 997-3624.

Travel Town
On Zoo Drive near Griffith Park Drive, Griffith Park. (212) 662-5874. Monday–Friday, 10 A.M.–4 P.M.; Saturday and Sunday, 10 A.M.–5 P.M. Closes one hour later during the summer. Free.

The largest collection of steam locomotives west of the Mississippi River is located in this delightful outdoor museum. In addition to the locomotives are boxcars, cabooses, dining cars, and even yellow streetcars from the old days in Los Angeles. Children can climb aboard most of the trains, including the locomotive cabs, and let their imaginations go.

Travel Town is undergoing a major restoration. Volunteer groups are working to restore the railroad cars, and a new acquisition, an operating diesel switch locomotive, is helping to move cars. An indoor area of the museum houses a newly reorganized exhibit of fire-fighting equipment to tell the story of the Los Angeles Fire Department from 1869 to 1940.

There are plenty of benches for adults to sit on while the kids are climbing on trains, and you can picnic on the lawn. A miniature train leaving from Travel Town's restored Southern Pacific depot offers children rides for $1.25 (adults, $1.50). You can also arrange to have your child's birthday party in the Travel Town Birthday Car, which is decorated just for kids. (The car comes equipped with air-conditioning and a refrigerator/freezer).

On Sundays from 10:30 A.M. to 3:30 P.M., the Los Angeles Live Steamers Club members operate their own miniature steam engines on a layout of track east of Travel Town. The tiny trains are authentic in every detail, and children are welcome to ride them for free.

Pony, Stagecoach, and Miniature Train Rides
Crystal Springs Drive near Los Feliz Boulevard, Griffith Park. Pony/Stagecoach: (213) 664-3266. Monday–Friday, 10 A.M.–5 P.M.; Saturday and Sunday, 10 A.M.–5:30 P.M. Train: (213) 664-6788. Winter: Tuesday–Friday, 10 A.M.–4:30 P.M.; weekends, 10 A.M.–5 P.M. Summer: Monday–Friday, 10 A.M.–5 P.M.; weekends, 10 A.M.–6 P.M.

Children as young as a year old can ride the ponies here. A track of slowly walking ponies lets kids take their first rides with Mom or Dad walking next to them. A separate oval course has a medium track for children three and up and a fast track for children seven and older. Stagecoach rides are also offered. Stagecoach and pony rides are $1.

Nearby is another miniature train that provides rides for children and adults. The fare for people fourteen years and up is $1.50; those younger ride for $1.25.

Merry-Go-Round

Located just off Griffith Park Drive near the main concession stand in Griffith Park. Winter hours: Weekends and holidays, 11 A.M.–6 P.M. Summer hours: Daily, 11 A.M.–6 P.M.

Crafted in 1926, this lovely old (but well-preserved) four-abreast carousel offers rides for children and adults for 75¢.

Los Angeles Zoo

533 Zoo Drive (in Griffith Park near the intersection of the Ventura and Golden State freeways). (213) 666-4090. Open every day except Christmas, 10 A.M.–5 P.M. Open until 6 P.M. during summer. Adults, $4.50; senior citizens, $3.50; ages 2–12, $2; under 2, free.

More than two thousand animals from all over the world live here on some eighty acres of landscaped hilly terrain. The animals are grouped by area of origin—Africa, Eurasia, North America, South America, and Australia—residing in moat-enclosed environments designed to simulate their native habitats. In addition to all the regular kinds of zoo animals, the Los Angeles Zoo also has mountain tapirs, emperor tamarins, red-flanked duikers, and several other species available for viewing nowhere else in the United States. The zoo also contains a delightful koala bear exhibit, an aquatics section, an aviary, a reptile house, and a new children's zoo called Adventure Island. Animal shows are scheduled daily, and animal rides are available across from the Wildlife Theater.

The zoo has an attractive new entry with shops and snack bars. There are also snack bars inside the zoo, picnic areas, and playgrounds. Strollers and wheelchairs are available for rent. A family zoo membership, which includes unlimited free admission for all household members and free admission to more than eighty reciprocal zoos nationwide, is available for $35 a

Koalas are among the most popular attractions at the Los Angeles Zoo.

year. Week-long summer zoo camps running from 9 A.M. to 3 P.M. are also offered for children eight to eleven.

Gene Autry Western Heritage Museum
4700 Zoo Drive (in Griffith Park, across from the zoo parking lot). (213) 667-2000. Tuesday–Sunday, 10 A.M.–5 P.M. Adults, $4.75; students and seniors, $3.50; ages 2–12, $2.

The Gene Autry Western Heritage Museum is an exciting and major new museum devoted to the history of the American West. Seven permanent galleries designed by Walt Disney Imagineering depict the history of the West from the early explorations of the Spanish conquistadors to the present day. Exhibits range from traditional displays of artifacts to elaborate and creative multimedia presentations.

The focus of much of the museum is on the real everyday lives and occupations of the people who helped settle the West. For example, the tools and personal belongings carried on a journey west are featured in an exhibit with sounds and voices from the past. As counterpoint to this "real" West, the museum also depicts the West of romance created in films, television, novels, advertising, and art. Some of the exhibits, including a western "screen test," offer children an opportunity to participate.

The museum is housed in an attractive tri-level building that looks like a modern southwestern mission. The building includes a 250-seat theater, an education center, a research library, a cafe, and a museum store.

Happily Ever After
2640 Griffith Park Boulevard (near Hyperion Avenue), Los Angeles. (213) 668-1996. Monday–Saturday, 10 A.M.–7 P.M.; Sunday, noon–5 P.M.

This children's bookstore is located in a cozy yellow house. Babies and toddlers have their own book area, which includes an inviting basket of toys in the center of the floor. Another room contains a blue couch and a fine selection of books for preschool children through young adults. Picture books are arranged by subject—such as school concerns, siblings, and sleep problems—as well conventionally by author. Books for parents are shelved in a separate room that includes a large chair. The store also sells some educational toys, wooden stamps, and book-related cassettes and videotapes.

A story hour for toddlers is held on the first and third Wednesday of each month from 10:30 to 11 A.M. With their parents, children hear stories, learn hand games, and sing songs. (No pre-registration is necessary, although you should call before coming.) The store also holds author signings, concerts, and other special events, such as a Halloween party featuring ghost stories told around a campfire behind the store. Happily Ever After will also special order books for you and provide free gift wrapping.

Barnsdall Park
4800 Hollywood Boulevard. (213) 485-2116. Daily, 9 A.M.–10 P.M. Free.

Located on a hilltop surrounded by olive trees above the bustle of East Hollywood, Barnsdall Park has become a major cultural center in the city of Los Angeles. The park land once belonged to oil heiress Aline Barnsdall, who commissioned architect Frank Lloyd Wright to design her home, called Hollyhock House, on the crown of a hill. In addition to picnic facilities and children's play areas, the 13.5-acre park includes a municipal art gallery; an arts and crafts center; a junior arts center; and the Hollyhock House, which is open for tours to the public.

Los Angeles Municipal Art Gallery
Barnsdall Park. (213) 662-8139. Tuesday–Sunday, 12:30–5 P.M. Adults, $1; 13 and under, free.

The Los Angeles Municipal Art Gallery displays the works of contemporary Southern California artists in regularly changing exhibitions. The gallery is a good place for kids to get acquainted with the art work of others. Exhibitions frequently deal with some aspect of the creative process—for example, how artists perceive ordinary objects such as a telephone. Folk art, conceptual art, and works that children and others can participate in are included in the exhibitions. Most displays include statements by the artists, which help explain what their work is all about.

Visitors are allowed on days when exhibitions are being installed, which can be very interesting for children. The docents at the gallery are understanding with children and enjoy answering their questions. The annual Magical Mystery Tour, held at Christmas, is an exhibition of fantasy and fun artwork designed for children.

Junior Arts Center
Barnsdall park. (213) 485-4474. Gallery hours: Tuesday–Sunday, 12:30–5 P.M.

The Junior Arts Center offers an excellent program of arts workshops for children and young people aged three through eighteen. The classes—which include painting, drawing, clay, photography, movement, theater, film and video workshops, as well as other arts and crafts workshops—are taught by experienced artists and craftspersons. Workshop sessions are generally divided into seven-to-eight-week fall, winter, spring, and summer quarters and a shorter December arts program. Classes meet once a week and contain about twelve students. The fees average about $18 per session.

The gallery in the art center has changing shows designed for children. Other programs include Sunday Open Sunday, a series of free art workshops for the whole family on Sundays from 2–4 P.M., and special events such as story telling and art festivals. A visual arts program for children with handicaps is offered, and accommodations for handicapped children in other programs are readily made.

Hollyhock House
Barnsdall Park. (213) 662-7272. Tours: Tuesday, Wednesday, and Thursday, 10 A.M., 11 A.M., 12 P.M., and 1 P.M.; Saturday and the first, second, and third Sunday of each month, 12, 1, 2, and 3 P.M. Adults, $1.50; seniors, $1; 12 and under, free with an adult. Tickets are sold at the Municipal Art Gallery next to the house.

Aline Barnsdall's home was the first residence in Los Angeles designed by Frank Lloyd Wright, and it is the only Wright house open to the public on a regular basis. Wright decorated the main house with stylized designs of Barnsdall's favorite flower, the hollyhock. This remarkable house was restored in 1970 and refurbished with many of the original fixtures and furniture. The tour is best appreciated by older children and teenagers.

The Hollywood Studio Museum
2100 North Highland Avenue, Hollywood. (On the opposite side of the street and slightly south of the Hollywood Bowl.) (213) 874-2276. Tuesday–Sunday, 10 A.M.–4 P.M. Adults, $2; teenagers and students, $1.50; under 12, $1.

In 1913, Cecil B. DeMille established Hollywood's first major film studio in a barn on the corner of Selma and Vine streets. Today the restored (and relocated) barn serves as a museum dedicated to the silent film era in Hollywood. To the right as you enter is a re-creation of DeMille's first office in the barn, with his boots under the desk. (The boots were quite necessary because he shared the barn with a horse.)

A twenty-minute video presentation on the museum and the history of Hollywood is shown in a small screening room. (If your children are young, ask to skip the film. It would not interest them.) Exhibits that would interest children include early motion-picture cameras, projectors, and stud lights; costumes, including Roman shields; models of the Spanish galleons used in early pirate movies; and the chariot from *Ben Hur*.

You might want to combine this museum with a visit to the nearby Hollywood Bowl Museum.

Hollywood Bowl Museum
2301 North Highland Avenue, Hollywood. (On the Hollywood Bowl grounds, next to the Patio Restaurant.) (213) 850-2058. September 14–June 29; Tuesday–Saturday, 9:30 A.M.–4:30 P.M. June 30–September 13: Daily, 9:30 A.M.–8:30 P.M. on concert days, until 4:30 P.M. on other days. Free.

The Hollywood Bowl Museum offers changing exhibits on the performing arts and the Hollywood Bowl. (Exhibits change yearly, usually around November. The one that I saw was a fascinating display of musical instruments from around the world.) There are two small listening rooms where you can hear music tapes pertaining to the exhibit. Just up from the museum is a picnic area.

Mid-Wilshire

Bob Baker Marionette Theater
1345 West First Street. (213) 250-9995. Reservations required. Saturday and Sunday, 2:30 P.M.; extra performances scheduled on weekdays. $7 per person. Admission includes performance, workshop tour, and refreshments. Phone Tina at the theater in the morning for information.

One of the oldest continuing theaters in Los Angeles is a puppet-marionette theater for kids. Children sit on the floor close to the stage and watch the Bob Baker Marionettes perform in wonderful fast-paced productions. After the show, kids are given a tour of the puppet studio to see how marionettes are made and then are served ice cream, cookies, and punch. (There's coffee for grownups.) The whole experience takes about two hours, and even very young children can appreciate it. The Bob Baker people are not only serious about the art of puppetry, but they also genuinely enjoy kids. Three different birthday party packages are also available.

Grier-Musser Museum
403 South Bonnie Brae Avenue (two blocks east of Alvarado Street, just north of Third Street). (213) 413-1814. Wednesday–Saturday, 11 A.M.–4 P.M. Adults, $3; ages 5–15, $1.50; under 5, free.

A restored Victorian home serves as a reminder of a slower, earlier time in this urban neighborhood. The house is furnished in the period, with nineteenth-century personal and household items, including toys. A little girl's room contains old-fashioned dolls. On Saturdays, antique postcards are displayed.

La Brea Tar Pits/George C. Page Museum of La Brea Discoveries
5801 Wilshire Boulevard, Hancock Park. (213) 857-6311 or 936-2230 (tape). Tuesday–Sunday, 10 A.M.–5 P.M. Adults, $3; seniors and students, $1.50; ages 5–12, 75¢; under 5, free. Free the second Tuesday of the month. Joint admission for the museum and the Los Angeles County Museum of Art: Adults, $4.50; seniors and students, $2.25; ages 5–12, $1.

For thousands of years, prehistoric animals were trapped in these tar pits when they mistook the shiny black pools for water and got stuck in the ooze. The heavy asphalt, however, was a superb preservative. Since 1905 when archaeologists began exploring the tar pits, more than 500,000 specimens of plants, reptiles, insects, birds, and mammals have been recovered. Today, life-sized fiberglass reproductions of some of the ancient animals—most notably, the imperial mammoths with their 12½-foot-long tusks—recreate a bit of the scene thirty to forty thousand years ago at the tar pits.

The skeletons of the creatures uncovered at the tar pits are on display in the beautiful George C. Page Museum on the park grounds. In a nicely laid-out exhibition space, you'll see the reconstructed skeletons of sabertooth cats, giant ground sloths, dire wolves, mastodons, a twelve-foot-high imperial mammoth, antique bison, and extinct varieties of camels and birds. (Dinosaurs, kids may be disappointed to learn, disappeared sixty-five million years before the La Brea tar pits were even formed.) An open-view paleontological laboratory gives children the opportunity to watch technicians as they clean, repair, and sort the many fossils still being prepared for research.

Children will especially enjoy the museum's "Asphalt Is Sticky" exhibit where they can actually experiment with the La Brea ooze. Murals and three-dimensional dioramas of the prehistoric beasts serve as a lively backdrop for the exhibits. Twin theaters show a continuous fifteen-minute documentary outlining the story of the tar pits. The museum also boasts a lovely interior garden. Kids will enjoy climbing the stairs to the museum rooftop for an overhead view.

Craft and Folk Art Museum
5814 Wilshire Boulevard. (213) 937-5544. Tuesday–Sunday, 11 A.M.–5 P.M. Adults, $1.50; students and seniors, $1; children, 75¢.

Across the street from the Los Angeles County Museum of Art is a fine small museum of ethnic and folk art. The changing exhibitions, which have included "Traditional Toys of Japan" and "Wind and Weathervanes," often are of interest to children. A bright exhibition of Mexican folk art, for example, included piñatas and imaginative animal sculptures.

The museum also offers a monthly program on Sunday evenings for children and their parents, called Sunday Family night. The programs, which are for ages four and up, include a lively story-telling session followed by a craft workshop. The cost per session is $4 for adults and $2 for children. Check with the museum for the schedule; reservations are required.

Los Angeles County Museum of Art
5905 Wilshire Boulevard. (213) 857-6000. Tuesday–Friday, 10 A.M.–5 P.M.; Saturday and Sunday, 10 A.M.–6 P.M. Adults, $3.00; students and senior citizens, $1.50; ages 5–12, 75¢; under 5, free. Free second Tuesday of the month. Joint admission for the museum and the George C. Page Museum is $4.50 for adults; $2.25 for seniors and students; $1 for ages 5–12.

The collections in the Los Angeles County Museum of Art range from ancient treasures to the very latest in modern art. The museum, the largest in the western United States, is composed of four main buildings: the Ahmanson Gallery on the west, the Hammer Building on the north, the Bing Center on the east, and the 1986 Robert O. Anderson Building in the front. There is also a new pavilion for Japanese art. The buildings are united by a court and a stunning new museum entrance.

Children will probably find the ancient artifacts displayed in the Ahmanson Gallery the most interesting. Many of these pieces are at their eye level. The ethnic art and pre-Columbian galleries are located on the plaza level; the Egyptian, ancient west Asian, ancient Iran, and Greek and Roman galleries are on the second level. Children will probably also enjoy seeing the costumes displayed on the third level and the impressionist art hanging on the second level of the Hammer Building. Baby carriages and strollers are permitted in all galleries except for crowded special exhibitions.

The Bing Theater in the Bing Center offers excellent film series, including many family films. Call the museum for the schedule. The Bing Center also holds a pleasant cafe. You can eat inside or out.

The museum offers art classes year round for children and adults. Children aged 3½ to five participate with their parents in a variety of gallery experiences that include story telling, games, and art activities. Classes for first through third graders feature story telling, sketching from artworks in the galleries, and other art activities. Fourth- through sixth-graders study works of art in the galleries and do a variety of art activities. Classes generally meet once a week for five weeks. For more information, phone the art-class registrar at (213) 857-6139.

Special school tours are also available for the fourth through twelfth grades. For more information, call the Docent Office at (213) 857-6108.

Farmers' Market
6333 West Third Street (at Fairfax). (213) 933-9211. Monday–Saturday, 9 A.M.–6:30 P.M. (until 7 P.M. in summer); Sunday, 10 A.M.–5 P.M. (until 6 P.M. in summer). Closed holidays.

The Farmers' Market originated during the Depression when a group of farmers set up stalls on a large vacant field to sell their produce. The market has come a long way from its humble beginnings. Today it is a sprawling tourist attraction with some 160 shops, stores, stalls, and outdoor restaurants.

The market is very crowded and touristy, so I would not plan a long visit with children. On a brief visit, however, kids will enjoy watching the candy makers and bakers at work behind glass, and seeing peanut butter being made in a large machine. There is also a pet store that is fun to visit.

You can have a wonderful meal at the market. There are twenty-six different kitchens selling all sorts of American and international food. Many of the eating places are close together, so it is possible to sample items from more than one restaurant and enjoy them at an outdoor table.

Beverly Hills and West Los Angeles

Beverly Hills Public Library Story Hour
444 North Rexford Drive, Beverly Hills. (During remodeling of the Rexford Drive building, the library is located at 338 North Foothill, at the corner of

Third Street, Beverly Hills.) (213) 285-1083 or 285-1101 (children's librarian). Free.

The Beverly Hills Public Library holds a forty-five-minute story hour for children aged three through five on Saturday mornings at 10:30 A.M. The children hear stories, sing songs, and play games. (Parents are not allowed in the room.) A story hour for kindergartners and above is held on Saturdays at 4 P.M.

Children must be registered to attend the story hour. To register, bring proof that the child is at least three years old and fill out a registration card at the library. You need not be a Beverly Hills resident to attend.

Beverly Hills Recreation and Parks Department
450 North Crescent Drive, Beverly Hills. (213) 550-4864.

The Beverly Hills Recreation and Parks Department has a fine recreation program for children from the ages of infants and up. Babies as young as three months can participate with their parents in classes designed to stimulate their senses, coordination, and flexibility. A tiny-tots series provides two- to three-year-olds with an opportunity to socialize with others and participate in art and music. Children from 2¾ to five can enroll in up to five days of a preschool program of art, drama, music, exercise, and socialization. Available to older children are a number of after school and Saturday workshops, including instruction in gymnastics, art, puppetry, and dance. Family field trips are scheduled throughout the year. The Recreation and Parks Department also offers a day-care program for children from five to nine years old. Non–Beverly Hills residents may apply for the programs.

William O. Douglas Outdoor Classroom
Franklin Canyon Ranch. (Just north of Beverly Hills. From the intersection of Beverly Drive and Coldwater Canyon Drive, follow Beverly Drive north for 1.2 miles. Turn right on Franklin Canyon Drive. Continue 0.8 mile to Lake Drive. There is a stone house on the right. Make a sharp right. Follow Lake Drive for 0.7 mile to ranch. Park along Lake Drive.) (213) 858-3834. Free.

Located in Franklin Canyon, a pocket wilderness area north of Beverly Hills, the William O. Douglas Outdoor Classroom is a nonprofit environmental-education organization serving the people of Los Angeles. The organization offers a number of programs for children and their parents, including family nature hikes. There is a nature center, open every day from 9 A.M. to 5 P.M., which, among other exhibits, houses a king snake called Chaka. The center has brochures for a self-guided nature trail, and you can picnic in the park.

One gem of a program sponsored by the William O. Douglas Outdoor Classroom is Babes in the Woods, docent-led nature hikes for children aged two months to three years and their parents. Babies may ride in strollers, Snuglis, or backpacks, or toddle along. The paths are easy, the pace is slow, and there are rest stops for feeding and diapering during the two-hour walks. Tykes on Hikes is a similar program for children ages four to six. There is also a Babes at the Beach nature walk at Malibu Lagoon State Beach for children three months to six years. Reservations are required, usually weeks in advance, for all three programs.

Treepeople Tours
12601 Mulholland Drive (at Coldwater Canyon Road). (818) 769-2663. Sunday, 11 A.M. Free.

TreePeople is a nonprofit organization dedicated to planting smog-resistant trees in areas damaged by air pollution. You can take a free guided tour of the headquarters in Coldwater Canyon Park on Sundays at 11 A.M. You'll learn some things you probably didn't know about trees as a guide leads you along trails through the park. You'll also see the organization's tree nursery, gardens, and beehives. Before heading out to the park, telephone to make sure there is a tour that day.

Junior Programs of California
1230 Comstock Avenue. (213) 271-6402.

Junior Programs of California is a nonprofit organization that provides children's plays, musicals, and cultural events at various locations throughout the county, including West Los Angeles (at UCLA), Santa Monica, Culver City, Lakewood, San Gabriel, La Mirada, and Fontana. Three to six events are given in each area from September to May. The programs, which take place on weekends, last an hour and are geared to elementary-school-age children. The prices vary from $2 to $3 for children and from $2 to $5 for adults. The newspaper may announce the programs, but it is best to call the organization and ask to be put on their mailing list.

Century City Playhouse
10508 West Pico Boulevard. (213) 839-3322. Saturday, 1 P.M. $3 per person.

The Burbage Theater Ensemble presents a varied repertoire of children's plays at the Century City Playhouse on Saturday afternoons. The plays are designed so that children can participate. Facilities for birthday parties are also available.

Santa Monica, Pacific Palisades, and Malibu

Children's Book and Music Center
2500 Santa Monica Boulevard, Santa Monica. (From Los Angeles, take the Santa Monica Freeway [I-10] west to the Cloverfield–Twenty-sixth Street off ramp. Take Cloverfield north to Santa Monica Boulevard and turn right.) (213) 829-0215. Monday–Saturday, 9 A.M.–5:30 P.M.

This excellent store has an outstanding collection of books and records for children. Bookshelves are arranged by age group and by subject matter. There are shelves devoted to fairy tales, Dr. Seuss, easy readers, children's reference books, animal stories, bedtime stories, transportation, science, feelings and emotions, and many other topics, including death, divorce, birth, and sex. The record selection is equally broad, and there are record players with headphones so you can listen before buying. The store also boasts a fine selection of books and records relating to Black, Hispanic, Jewish, and other ethnic cultures. Videotapes and a broad range of children's musical instruments are also sold. The large staff is extremely knowledgeable and helpful. A story time is held at 10 A.M. on the first and third Saturday of the month. Other special events include Saturday morning sing-alongs and frequent autograph parties. A mail-order catalog is also available.

Westside Arts Center
2320 Arizona Avenue, Santa Monica. (213) 453-3966.

The Westside Arts Center is a private, nonprofit organization that is dedicated to providing creative arts experiences for children of all incomes, cultures, and abilities. The Center's studio arts program offers a variety of classes for children aged two through twelve. Two- and three-year-olds and their parents can participate in classes in music and art. Three- to five-year-olds may take classes in music, art, drama, ceramics, and Native American folk art. Among the classes for older children are book making, video, and guitar, as well as other art, drama, and music classes. The classes, which are taught by professional artists experienced in working with children, average about $55 for an eight-week (one-a-week) session. Scholarships are available.

The Center also offers family workshops, special-event workshops, field trips, parent education seminars, and a birthday party program. There is also an outreach program that goes to schools, and an annual Arts Fair.

Douglas Park

1155 Chelsea Avenue, Santa Monica. (One block west of Twenty-sixth Street, between California and Wilshire.) (213) 828-9912.

Families with young children will particularly enjoy this lovely small park. The landscaping is very pretty, with green rolling lawns, streams, and a little duck pond. On the California Avenue side of the park is a busy playground, with a separate and fair-sized toddler play area. (There are even a couple of swinging benches for parents.) The playground is separated from the rest of the park by a large oval recessed track (once a wading pool) that is perfect for bike riding. There are public phones and restrooms in the park.

Westside Children's Museum

1302 Eleventh Street, Santa Monica. (213) 451-5524. Phone for hours. Adults, $5; children, $2. Family membership: $35 per year.

The Westside Children's Museum is a new exploratory hands-on museum for kids. Initially the museum operated as a "museum without walls" offering special events and workshops on selected weekends. By the time you read this, the museum should be open full time with their permanent exhibits installed. The museum promises to be a place where children aged two through twelve can participate in a variety of exhibits designed for both learning and fun.

Santa Monica Playhouse

1211 Fourth Street, Santa Monica. (213) 394-9779. Performances: Saturday and Sunday, 1 P.M. and 3 P.M. All seats $5. Call for workshop schedule and costs.

The Santa Monica Playhouse presents children's plays or musicals every Saturday and Sunday afternoon. The programs, which change every three to four months, are recommended for ages three to ninety. Birthday party arrangements can be made. The playhouse also offers a summer theater workshop for children four to fifteen. The workshop introduces children to improvisation, scene study, make-up, costumes, music, diction, and live performance.

Angel's Attic

516 Colorado Avenue, Santa Monica. (213) 394-8331. Thursday–Sunday, 12:30–4:30 P.M. Adults, $3; senior citizens, $2; under 14, $1.

The oldest house in Santa Monica, an 1875 Queen Anne Victorian, has been restored to serve as Angel's Attic, a museum of antique dollhouses, dolls, and toys benefiting autistic children. The house, with its gingerbread trimming and wicker-furniture porch, seems like a giant dollhouse itself. Inside are the real things. Among the most interesting dollhouses are an exact replica of Ann Hathaway's cottage and a 1923 dollhouse from Puebla, Mexico, in the style of a well-to-do Mexican home of that era. Antique toys and miniatures are displayed on a track just below the ceiling. Old-fashioned dolls are displayed upstairs. There is also a small boutique selling dollhouse-related items.

After seeing the museum, adults can have tea, and children can enjoy lemonade and cookies, at one of the wicker tables on the front porch or in the Victorian-style garden in the back. The museum, which is very much a "no touch" experience, would be best enjoyed by school-age children.

Santa Monica Pier

At the foot of Colorado Avenue, Santa Monica. (213) 458-8900.

The highlight of the Santa Monica Pier is its 1922 Philadelphia Toboggan Company carousel. The carousel and the pavilion housing it have been painstakingly and lovingly restored to their original splendor. Each of the

Don't miss the bumper cars at the Santa Monica Pier.

forty-six hand-carved horses is different from the others, and all ride to the merry strains of one of the oldest Wurlitzer organs in the country.

The pier, which has been severely damaged by storms, is undergoing restoration. A new extension to the south of the carousel has added a fun zone with children's rides.

Santa Monica Heritage Square Museum
2612 Main Street, Santa Monica. (213) 392-8537. Thursday–Saturday, 11 A.M.–4 P.M.; Sunday, 12–4 P.M. Closed holidays. Free, but donation appreciated.

The city of Santa Monica worked for years to preserve, relocate, and restore the elegant nineteenth-century home that now serves as the Santa Monica Heritage Square Museum. The downstairs rooms of the house have been decorated to look as they would have in the late nineteenth and early twentieth centuries. The room that will interest children most is the kitchen with its old-fashioned stove and hot-water heater. Off the kitchen is a pantry with a 1920s beehive motor refrigerator that is still working.

Upstairs are changing exhibits that relate to the history of Santa Monica. Past exhibits have included sports, the beach, and even boats. Perhaps the best time to visit with children is the holiday season when the exhibits are often playful and the house is decorated for Christmas with a ten-foot tree hung with handmade old-style ornaments.

Burton Chace Park
End of Mindanao Way past Admiralty Way, Marina del Rey.
(213) 305-9596.

Located at the tip of the Mindanao jetty in the Chace Harbor at Marina del Rey, this park is a good place to watch boats, see airplanes (LAX is nearby), fly a kite (there is almost always a breeze), or just play. (The park is very crowded on Sundays, however.) There are picnic tables and barbecues. Free public concerts and other activities frequently take place in the park. Check with the park or the Marina Chamber of Commerce (phone: 213-821-0555) for the current schedule.

Marina Beach
Along Admiralty and Via Marina ways, between Palawan and Panay ways, Marina del Rey.

This is an excellent beach for children because there are no big ocean waves. In addition to a sheltered surface, the inland beach has a shallow bottom.

Fisherman's Village
13763 Fiji Way (off Admiralty Way), Marina del Rey. (213) 823-5411.
Daily, 10 A.M.–9 P.M. (open until 10 P.M. in the summer).

A replica of a Cape Cod fishing town, Fisherman's Village is a shopping and restaurant complex along the waterfront in Marina del Rey. In the main square is an Orange Julius snack bar in a replica of a lighthouse. Nearby is an old-fashioned red wagon selling popcorn. One shop here that children may enjoy is Let's Fly a Kite (13755 Fiji Way), which sells every imaginable type of kite.

Two Mississippi riverboat replicas, the *Marina Belle* and the *Showboat*, give regularly scheduled forty-five-minute narrated cruises of the harbor; tours leave the village boathouse at 13727 Fiji Way. Phone (213) 822-1151 for information on the cruises.

Will Rogers State Historic Park
14253 Sunset Boulevard, Pacific Palisades. (213) 454-8212. Park open daily, 8 A.M.–5 P.M. (until 7 P.M. during daylight savings time). House open 10 A.M.– 5 P.M. daily. Parking, $3.

Will Rogers lived on this 187-acre rustic estate from the 1920s until his death in a plane crash in 1935. Everything in this ranch house is maintained as it was when he lived there. (In the living room, the clock is stopped at 8:17, the time registered on his pilot's watch when his plane crashed.) Kids will appreciate that the famous humorist was also a former cowboy, and the house looks like a cowboy lived there. Even a stuffed calf that Rogers used to lasso is in the living room. Next to the house is a little museum that shows a continuous free movie about Rogers.

You can picnic on the large lawn area surrounding the house. Hiking trails wind through the hills above the house, some leading to excellent views of the city, mountains, and ocean.

Rogers was also an avid polo player who installed his own polo field on the estate. Games are still played on the field on Saturday at 2 P.M. and Sunday at 10 A.M. (weather permitting; call the park to make sure the games are being played). The games are great fun to watch.

Rustic Canyon Recreation Center
601 Latimer Road (from Sunset Boulevard just south of Will Rogers Park, take Brooktree Road east to park). (213) 454-5734.

The Rustic Canyon Recreation Center offers children classes in ballet, drama, creative movement, ceramics, art, and other subjects. Classes generally meet once a week, and fees range from about $16 to $20 per eight-week session. Student artwork is often exhibited at the center, which is located in a lovely glade.

Nursery Nature Walks
Palisades-Malibu YWCA, 821 Via de la Paz, Pacific Palisades. (213) 454-5591. Optional donation, $3 per family.

Nursery Nature Walks offers families with young children an opportunity to enjoy gentle docent-led nature walks in a variety of locations. The volunteer nonprofit organization, sponsored by the Palisades-Malibu YMCA, specializes in walks for families with infants, toddlers, and preschool children—although older children are also welcome. Babies can ride in Snuglis, backpacks, or strollers, and older children can join on foot. The pace is slow, and the emphasis is on helping children to discover nature. A wonderful feature of the program is that walks take place in parks and mountain areas across Los Angeles County. (To find out about walks in Orange County, phone 714-859-3496.) In addition to a variety of locations in West Los Angeles and Santa Monica/Malibu, walks take place in Griffith Park, Arroyo Seco Park in Pasadena, El Dorado Nature Center in Long Beach, Thousand Oaks Botanic Gardens, and Caballero Canyon and Chatsworth Park in the San Fernando Valley. Some sites are wheelchair accessible. Nursery Nature Walks also has a training program for parents who wish to become docents.

J. Paul Getty Museum
17985 Pacific Coast Highway, Malibu. (Take the Santa Monica Freeway west; it merges with Pacific Coast Highway.) (213) 458-2003. Tuesday–Sunday, 10 A.M.–5 P.M. Free; however, you must write or call the museum at least one week in advance for a parking reservation, which serves as your entrance to the museum.

Sitting high on a cliff overlooking the Pacific, the Getty museum building is an authentic re-creation of a first-century B.C. Roman seaside villa. All the colors and architectural details are like those used in ancient Rome. The gardens even contain the same type of trees, shrubs, and flowers that grew two thousand years ago in southern Italy. The museum's collections consist of Greek and Roman antiquities, western European paintings and drawings from the thirteenth through the twentieth centuries, eighteenth-century French decorative art pieces, illuminated manuscripts, and classic photographs. Children will probably be most interested in the ground-floor Greek and Roman antiquities, which include many sculptures of animals.

Santa Monica Mountains Recreation Area
Visitor Information Center: 22900 Ventura Boulevard, Woodland Hills. (818) 888-3770. Monday–Saturday, 8:30 A.M.–4:30 P.M. Free.

The Santa Monica Mountains stretch almost fifty miles across Los Angeles from Griffith Park to Point Mugu. In 1978, fifteen years of effort to protect this resource culminated in the creation of the Santa Monica Mountains National Recreation Area, a new part of the national park system. The area encompasses a variety of mountain parks, as well as the public beaches between Point Mugu and Santa Monica.

The Santa Monica Recreation Area offers a wide range of outdoor programs for families. Families can take easy ranger-led hikes through trails in a number of the parks in the area. Special programs for children have included an early evening hike to learn about nocturnal animals, a look at the special qualities of birds, an introduction to the Indians who once lived in the Santa Monica Mountains, and hikes through the woodlands to study the animals living there. The Visitor Information Center will supply you with a current schedule of activities.

South Bay and Beach Cities

Sand Dune Park
Thirty-third Street at Bell Avenue, Manhattan Beach. (213) 545-5621 (Manhattan Beach Parks and Recreation Department). Daily, dawn to 11 P.M. Free.

A steep sand dune that kids can climb and slide on is the outstanding feature of this park. The top of the sand dune can be reached by climbing the dune or by taking a winding path of steps. (Most kids will get worn out and slide down before they make it to the top.) If your children want to, they can bring a large piece of cardboard to slide on. The park has an enclosed young children's playground and play area for older kids. There is a tree-shaded picnic area, tables, barbecues, sinks, and restrooms. The only drawback is that parking is limited to crowded street space.

Old Town Mall
19800 Hawthorne Boulevard, Torrance. (From the San Diego Freeway, take the Hawthorne Boulevard exit and drive south 4 miles.) (213) 542-1506. Open daily. Merry-go-round operates Monday–Saturday, 10 A.M.–9 P.M., Sunday, 11 A.M.–5 P.M.

A carousel and puppet shows provide entertainment for children at this South Bay shopping mall.

Wonderworld Puppet Productions
Torrance Community Theater, 1522 Cravens Avenue, Torrance. Wonderworld phone: (213) 542-9349 or 532-1741. Admission, $4 per person.

Wonderworld Puppet Productions presents puppet shows for children on selected Saturday mornings at the Torrance Community Theater. The puppets are not threatening to young children, and the shows are imaginative and entertaining. After the show, the puppeteers demonstrate how the puppets work, and audience members can hold the puppets. Wonderworld also gives shows in other locations. Telephone for the schedule.

Lomita Railroad Museum
2135–37 250th Street, Lomita. (Go south on Harbor Freeway to Pacific Coast Highway exit. Go west on PCH to Narbonne Avenue, then turn right to 250th Street.) (213) 326-6255. Wednesday–Sunday, 10 A.M.–5 P.M. Admission, 50¢.

The large train mural at the corner of Pacific Coast Highway and Narbonne Avenue in Lomita will signal kids that they are near the Lomita Railroad Museum. It's still a great surprise, though, to turn the corner on 250th Street in this ordinary residential neighborhood and see a replica of a nineteenth-century Wakefield, Massachusetts, train depot with a shiny black 1902 Southern Pacific locomotive looming beside it. Kids can climb aboard the locomotive (all the valves and handles in the engine's cab are labeled with explanations of their purpose, but they cannot be touched) as well as a 1910 wooden caboose. Also on the tracks outside are a Southern Pacific tender used for hauling water and fuel oil and a velocipede handcar—a three-wheeled, one-man car used by track inspectors.

Inside the depot are an old-style ticket office, telegraph equipment, a hand-lantern collection, a calliope, train models, a button collection from trainmen's uniforms, and much more. The whole museum is meticulously well kept. Across the street is a grassy annex with a fountain and large red boxcar where you can have a picnic lunch.

Point Vincente Interpretive Center
31501 Palos Verdes Drive West, Rancho Palos Verdes. (213) 377-5370. Daily, 10 A.M.–7 P.M. Adults, $1; children, 50¢.

Whales are the focus of this small museum overlooking the ocean on the Palos Verdes Peninsula. Outside is a beautiful site for whale watching, picnicking, or just plain ocean gazing. Inside the center are exhibits on geology, natural history, and marine life. There are some touch exhibits for children, including an assortment of seashells to handle. You can also view a twenty-minute film on whale watching.

South Coast Botanic Gardens
26300 Crenshaw Boulevard, Palos Verdes Peninsula. (Take the Harbor Freeway to Pacific Coast Highway. Go west on PCH to Crenshaw Boulevard, south on Crenshaw.) (213) 377-0468. Daily, 9 A.M.–4 P.M. Adults $3; senior citizens and students, $1.50; ages 5–12, 75¢. Free third Tuesday of the month.

Kids who are learning about recycling will be especially impressed with the South Coast Botanic Gardens. These lovely gardens were recycled from a trash dump. The eighty-seven-acre site includes a manmade lake inhabited by ducks; a winding stream; and acres of flowers, plants, and trees. There are picnic tables on the lawn outside the gardens.

Los Angeles Harbor Area, Catalina, and Long Beach

Cabrillo Marine Museum
3720 Stephen White Drive, San Pedro. (Take the Harbor Freeway south until it ends. Turn left on Gaffey, then turn left on Twenty-second Street. Go two blocks and turn right on Pacific, then left on Thirty-sixth Street, which

becomes Stephen White Drive. Bear left past the large black anchors.) (213) 548-7546. School year: Tuesday–Friday, noon–5 P.M.; Saturday and Sunday, 10 A.M.–5 P.M. Summer: Tuesday–Sunday, 10 A.M.–5 P.M. Free. Parking, $4.

The Cabrillo Marine Museum, on the beach in San Pedro, has long been a favorite of kids. Devoted to the sea life and marine environment of Southern California, the museum includes more than thirty aquariums where children can watch the interaction of sea creatures. Perhaps the most fascinating aquarium is the fourteen-foot-long shark tank containing a variety of small sharks. (The biggest is just two feet long.)

Museum displays cover local habitat settings such as the Los Angeles Harbor, the open ocean, offshore kelp beds, sandy beaches, and mud flats. A colorful tide pool "touch tank" (open at posted or announced times) gives kids the opportunity to feel sea hares, sea cucumbers, urchins, and other sea life under the supervision of a marine expert.

Outside are tide pools that can be explored. There is also a grassy picnic area and a playground adjacent to the museum.

The museum also sponsors whale-watching boat trips and other marine-related activities. Call the museum for their program schedule. School (and preschool) tours of the museum are scheduled throughout the year.

Ports O' Call Village/Whaler's Wharf

Berth 77, San Pedro. (Take the Harbor Freeway south to the Harbor Boulevard exit, turn right for half a mile, and follow the signs to the village entrance.) (213) 831-0287. Daily, 11 A.M.–9 P.M. Free admission and parking.

Nineteenth-century California and New England seaport villages are simulated in this restaurant and shopping complex at the Port of Los Angeles. Ports O' Call Village, complete with cobblestone streets and gas lamps, aims to give the impression of an Early California seaport. Whaler's Wharf is a replica of a New England town with its fishmarkets and steepled courthouse.

Harbor tours are also available from Ports O' Call. The Village Boathouse (phone: 213-831-0996) offers one-hour fully narrated cruises afternoons daily ($6 for adults and $3 for kids). Buccaneer/Mardi Gras Cruises (phone: 213-547-2833) has one-hour cruises on the weekends on *Buccaneer Queen*, a replica of an old-fashioned pirate ship, and on the *Princess*, a replica of a Mississippi River paddlewheeler. Cruise prices are $6 for adults and $3 for children. Check with the companies for times.

Korean Friendship Bell/Angel's Gate Park
Gaffey Street between Thirty-second and Shepard streets, San Pedro. Daily, 8 A.M.–6 P.M. Free.

The largest bell in the United States hangs in a pagoda in Angel's Gate Park. The nineteen-ton Korean Friendship Bell was given to the United States by the Republic of Korea in 1976 to commemorate our nation's bicentennial. It sounds only three times a year: on New Year's Day, July Fourth, and Korean Liberation Day (August 15). The surrounding park offers a magnificent view and a good place to watch hang gliders sailing through the air.

Los Angeles Maritime Museum
Berth 84, San Pedro. (Take the Harbor Freeway south to Harbor Boulevard exit, turn right to Harbor Boulevard and Sixth Street.) (213) 548-7618. Tuesday–Sunday, 10 A.M.–5 P.M. Free.

The Maritime Museum is dedicated to ships and seafaring. Completed in 1978, the museum is housed in a remodeled ferry building in Los Angeles Harbor. Among the exhibits are navigation instruments, the bridge deck from the cruiser *Los Angeles,* wooden ships' wheels from World War I and II, early navy diving helmets, ships' bells, and scale models of historical ships such as the U.S.S. *Chesapeake.* The museum is bright and cheery, and the deck offers a good view of the harbor.

Princess Louise Restaurant
Berth 94, Los Angeles Harbor Main Channel. (Take the Harbor Freeway south to Harbor Boulevard exit. At the stop light, continue straight ahead into the Catalina Terminal parking lot under the Vincent Thomas Bridge.) (213) 831-2351; from Los Angeles, phone (213) 775-2341. Monday–Thursday, 11 A.M.–3 P.M. and 5 P.M.–10 P.M. (until 11 P.M. on Friday and Saturday); Sunday, 10 A.M.–3 P.M. and 4 P.M.–10 P.M. Reservations recommended.

Launched in 1921, the S.S. *Princess Louise* was known as the Queen of the Northern Seas, sailing from Vancouver, British Columbia, to Skagway, Alaska. Retiring, she entered a second career as a restaurant. The fun of eating here is that you are visiting a real ship; as soon as you ascend the gangplank, you feel her slight list. She has wooden railings, worn carpeting, heavy old-fashioned drapes, and pipes overhead in the restrooms. Ask for a table overlooking the channel so you can watch the ships in the water.

After dinner or while waiting for your table, you are free to browse through the ship. On the top deck (above the cocktail lounge) you can see the captain's and first and second mates' quarters, furnished with dummies and authentic-looking shipboard accessories of the 1920s. You can also see the radio room with its Marconi wireless. A few steep stairs take you up to the wheelhouse, where there is a real ship's wheel to turn.

Most lunch choices are $4.25. Dinner ranges from about $8.25 to $21.95. There is no children's menu, except at Sunday brunch when children are $6.50 and adults $11.50. The meals are more enjoyable for the setting than for the food.

Catalina Island
Catalina Visitors Information Center, P.O. Box 737, Avalon, CA 90704. (213) 510-2000 or (800) 428-2566. Catalina Cruises (boat service from San Pedro and Long Beach), phone (213) 775-6111. Catalina Express (boat service from San Pedro), phone (213) 519-1212. Catalina Passenger Services (boat service from Newport Beach), phone (714) 673-5245. Helitrans (four-passenger jet helicopter service from San Pedro), phone (213) 548-1314. Island Express (six-passenger jet helicopter service from San Pedro and Long Beach), phone (213) 491-5550.

Once a hideout for smugglers and pirates, Catalina Island still has natural areas where wild boar, wild goats, cattle, and buffalo roam. (The buffalo are the descendants of a small herd imported to the island for the filming of a 1924 movie.) On a day trip to Catalina, your visit will probably be confined to Avalon, the island's only city. Strict legislation limiting the number and size of cars in the city makes it a pleasure just to walk there.

Catalina offers a variety of activities for families. One of the most interesting is the glass-bottom-boat cruise. Through the windows in the boat's bottom, you see all sorts of fish, including giant saltwater goldfish, as well as waving kelp and sea ferns. Another boat cruise takes you to the eastern tip of Catalina, where you can often see seals frolicking; or it may explore the cove-dotted coastline to White's Landing. If you are there in the evening from May through September, take the flying-fish boat trip; the boat's searchlights spot the fish flying up to seventy-five yards through the air. (The fish sometimes even land in the boat.)

On an overnight or longer stay on Catalina, you might want to take a tour of inland Catalina. The Inland Motor Tour is a 3¾-hour trip through the island's beautiful mountainous interior. (You may even see buffalo, deer, goats, or boars wandering free.) The tour includes a stop at El Rancho Escondido to see a performance of the Arabian horses raised there. Shorter motor tours and other boat tours are also available. You might also want to take a tram from Avalon to see the Wrigley Memorial and Botanical Garden filled with native trees, cacti, succulent plants, and flowering trees.

Catalina also offers hiking, camping, picnicking, skindiving, fishing, and horseback riding; swimming in clear, surf-free waters; and boat and bicycle rentals. On the Pleasure Pier, the Chamber of Commerce has brochures, maps, and information on the island's activities. The Visitors Information Center, a very short walk from the Chamber of Commerce, handles sightseeing tour tickets. (For camping information [permits are required], phone the Los Angeles County Department of Parks and Recreation, 213-510-0688).

Ships to Catalina depart from Long Beach and San Pedro year round. Catalina Cruises offers cruises aboard triple-deck, seven-hundred-passenger vessels. The trip takes two hours each way, and round-trip tickets are $24 for adults and $12.70 for children ages two to eleven. Catalina Express offers service from San Pedro aboard 60- and 145-passenger boats with airplane-type reclining seats. The trip takes ninety minutes each way and round-trip tickets are $27.40 for adults and $20.20 for children. Service from Newport Beach is offered by Catalina Passenger Service on a five-hundred-passenger catamaran on weekends from January to April and daily from April through October. Several companies, including Helitrans and Island Express, offer jet helicopter service to Catalina. (The round-trip fare averages about $100 per person.) Reservations are required by all the companies.

Harbor Regional Park
25820 Vermont Avenue, Harbor City. Free.

This lovely 231-acre park contains a large lake for fishing, sailing, or duck feeding. Attractive, modern children's play areas are built in a sort of marina style and include nets for climbing. There are picnic facilities.

Banning Residence Museum and Park
401 East M Street, Wilmington. (Take Harbor Freeway south from Los Angeles to the Pacific Coast Highway exit. Turn left and go 1 mile east. Turn right on Avalon Boulevard for two blocks. Turn left on M street for two

blocks to the park.) (213) 548-7777. *The park is open daily, 6 A.M.–10 P.M. Free. Conducted tours through the house: Tuesday, Wednesday, Thursday, Saturday, and Sunday, at 12:30, 1:30, 2:30, and 3:30 P.M. Adults, $2 donation; children, free.*

Gen. Phineas Banning, the founder of Wilmington, built this showcase mansion in 1864 and landscaped the grounds with lovely gardens. Constructed during the Civil War, adjacent to the headquarters of the United States Army of the Southwest, the home was a center for rallies and meetings supporting the cause of the Union. You can take a conducted tour of the twenty-four-room mansion Tuesday, Wednesday, Thursday, Saturday, and Sunday afternoons; the park surrounding the house, however, is open daily. The park has children's playgrounds; picnic facilities; and lovely eucalyptus, giant bamboo, and jacaranda trees.

The *Queen Mary* and *Spruce Goose*

Pier J, Long Beach Harbor. (Take the Long Beach Freeway [710] south to the Queen Mary exit. The Spruce Goose *is next to the* Queen Mary.) *(213) 435-3511. Daily, 10 A.M.–6 P.M. (box office closes at 4 P.M.). From July 4 to Labor Day, 9 A.M.–9 P.M. (box office closes at 8 P.M.). Adults, $14.50; ages 5–11, $8.50; under 5, free. Parking, $2.*

The famed ocean liner, *Queen Mary,* and Howard Hughes's enormous "flying boat" are now side by side in the same entertainment complex in the port of Long Beach. One ticket admits you to both attractions.

The first sight of the dramatically showcased, 400,000-pound *Spruce Goose* is breathtaking. The world's largest aircraft, with a wingspan larger than a football field, the wooden *Spruce Goose* looks like no other plane. A viewing platform adjacent to the plane allows visitors to see the flight deck and cockpit. You can actually enter the cargo hold, where the aircraft's interior is exposed from nose to tail.

The line to get on the plane can be very long (an hour or more). However, there are a number of interesting displays to look at while a family member holds a place in line. Sharing the dome with the *Spruce Goose* is Time Voyager, a video and special-effects attraction in which passengers board a flight module to experience time travel.

After seeing the *Spruce Goose,* you'll board the *Queen Mary* for a self-guided tour that can take up most of the day. You'll see areas of the ship that her former passengers never got to see, such as the engine room—complete with boilers and forty-thousand-horsepower turbines—and the

Howard Hughes's legendary Spruce Goose has a wingspan longer than a football field.

emergency steering station. A light and sound show in the engine room excitingly recreates what a near-collision at sea would have been like. Children will also be impressed by the propeller chamber, a specially created chamber outside the ship's hull that enables visitors to see one of the ship's giant propellers in the water.

On the upper decks you'll see replicas of the original staterooms, crew's quarters, gymnasium, children's playroom, and the wheelhouse and radio room. Children should especially enjoy seeing the lifeboat demonstration and the exhibits that depict the *Queen Mary*'s role as a troop carrier during World War II.

A day aboard the *Queen Mary* involves considerable walking and therefore may be too tiring for preschool children. For other children, however, there is plenty of room to be active. Kids seem to particularly like climbing on the World War II anti-aircraft gun on the middle deck. There are a number of restaurants and snack bars aboard the ship, and a lot of places to rest.

Long Beach Harbor Cruises
Departures from the bow of the Queen Mary. *(213) 547-0802. Summer: Daily, 11 A.M., 12:15, 1:30, 2:45, 4, and 5:15 P.M. Phone for winter schedule (usually weekends only). Adults, $5.95; children 5–11, $3.95.*

You can see the *Queen Mary* from a different perspective on a cruise of the Long Beach Harbor. The forty-five-minute cruise also takes you past the *Spruce Goose*, Shoreline Village, and the other sights along the harbor.

Shoreline Village
Off Shoreline Drive at the foot of Pine Street, just south of the Convention Center. (Take the Long Beach Freeway to Shoreline Drive.) (213) 590-8427. Daily, 10 A.M.–9 P.M. Free.

Shoreline Village is a shopping, dining, and entertainment complex in the fanciful style of a turn-of-the-century beachside village. The top attraction here for children is the beautiful 1906 Charles Looff carousel with sixty-two hand-carved horses—and camels, giraffes, and rams. The carousel operates Sunday through Thursday from 10 A.M. to 9 P.M. and until 10 P.M. on Friday and Saturday. Clowns, mimes, jugglers, and other entertainers frequently perform weekends on an outdoor stage called the Off-Boardwalk Theater. Shoreline Village is adjacent to a marina; it's fun to walk along the wooden boardwalk and look at the boats. Snack food, as well as more substantial fare, is sold in a variety of eating establishments, and there are plenty of places to sit outside. The village is surrounded by grassy park areas.

Long Beach Children's Museum
445 Long Beach Boulevard, Long Beach. (At Fourth Street in the Long Beach Plaza. There is no mall entrance; the entrance is on the street.) (213) 495-1163. Thursday, Friday, and Saturday, 11 A.M.–4 P.M.; Sunday, 12–4 P.M. $1 per person.

Children as young as infants can have a wonderful time at this hands-on museum for kids. An infant-toddler area, partitioned with soft blocks, gives babies a variety of floor coverings to crawl across, low mirrors to watch themselves in, and a basket full of playthings to experience.

Of course, older children will find all sorts of exciting exhibits for themselves. "Gone Fishing" gives kids a chance to climb into a boat and catch fish using a fishing pole and Velcro bait. In "Granny's Attic" children have the opportunity to sort through clothes and dress themselves as fire fighters, police officers, society women, or whatever they imagine. An art center called the Creative Cafe provides kids with what they need to make their own art creations. In other exhibits, children can explore a hospital room, sit behind the wheel of a racing car, build a city of Legos, and fit themselves for glasses. Children are assisted, when they need it, by an excellent staff of museum interpreters.

Birthday parties are available for museum members. (Membership costs $35 a year and includes free admission and other benefits.) School field trips can be arranged by appointment.

Independent Press-Telegram Tour
604 Pine Avenue, downtown Long Beach. (213) 435-1161. Tours: Monday–Friday, 10 A.M., 2 P.M., and 3:30 P.M. during the school year. Reservations required one month in advance. Children need to be in at least the third grade.

All aspects of newspaper production—from the editorial to the advertising departments, from the wire room to the presses—are shown on this hour-long tour. A minimum of ten people are needed to take the tour.

Long Beach Firefighters Museum
1445 Peterson Avenue, Long Beach. (213) 597-0351 (ask for Herb). Parking inside gates. Second Saturday of each month, 10 A.M.–3 P.M. Free.

The old Long Beach Fire Station No. 10 serves as the home for a number of antique fire-fighting vehicles, including two horse-drawn steamers. You can see the equipment and watch pumping demonstrations on the second Saturday of every month from 10 A.M. to 3 P.M.

Rancho Los Cerritos
4600 Virginia Road, Long Beach. (Take the San Diego Freeway to Long Beach Boulevard. Go north on Long Beach Boulevard to San Antonio Drive, turn left, then go right one block on Virginia Road.) (213) 424-9423. Self-guided tours: Wednesday–Friday, 1–5 P.M. Guided tours: Saturday and Sunday, 1, 2, 3, and 4 P.M. Free.

Maybe it's because Rancho Los Cerritos is slightly off the beaten track, but this beautifully restored Spanish hacienda provides a real sense of the past. Built in 1844 around a central patio, the two-story hacienda is made of adobe brick with three-foot-thick walls and redwood beam ceilings.

The house has been meticulously furnished in the style of the period: Antique hairbrushes are arranged on a heavy wood bureau in a bedroom, and an old foot-treadle sewing machine is in the sewing room. Youngsters will appreciate the children's room, where antique toys and dolls are casually placed. You can take a self-guided tour of the rancho Wednesday through Friday. On weekends you can only see the rancho on a forty-five-minute guided tour.

Rancho Los Alamitos
6400 Bixby Hill Road, Long Beach. (From the San Diego freeway, take the Palo Verde Avenue exit south to the security gate of the walled residential community of Bixby Hill. The security guard will direct you to the rancho.) (213) 431-3541. Wednesday–Sunday, 1–5 P.M. (Tours are every half hour. The last tour is at 4 P.M.) Free.

In 1896, Juan José Nieto built an adobe ranch house on this hill. His ranch was part of a vast Spanish land grant—stretching from San Gabriel to the sea—which had been given to his father, a soldier in the Portolá expedition exploring California. Today all that remains of that vast rancho is 7½ acres, including five acres of gardens, the original ranch house, and six farm buildings.

On a sixty- to ninety-minute guided tour of the rancho, which was a working ranch from 1784 into the 1950s, you see the ranch house furnished with family possessions (including a vintage Edison Graphophone) that span many generations, the blacksmith shop, and the barns, which contain some restored farm equipment. The grounds are lovely and peaceful, but because of the length of the guided tour, a visit here is best made with older children.

El Dorado Park and Nature Center
7550 East Spring Street, Long Beach. (Take I-605 south to the Spring Street/Cerritos exit and go west on Spring Street.) El Dorado Park East and Nature Center phone: (213) 425-8569. El Dorado Park West phone: (213) 425-4712. West Park hours: Daily, 9 A.M.–5 P.M. Free. East Park hours: Daily, 7 A.M.–8 P.M. Nature Center trails: Daily, 8 A.M.–4 P.M. Nature Center Mu-

seum: *Weekdays, 10 A.M.–4 P.M.; weekends, 8 A.M.–4 P.M. Parking at El Dorado Park East: $2 weekdays; $3 weekends.*

El Dorado Park is an eight-hundred-acre recreation area that includes two parks and an eighty-acre semiwilderness nature reserve. El Dorado West City Park (south of Spring Street and west of the San Gabriel River) includes a duck pond, a children's playground, roller-skate rentals, and a number of game courts and ball diamonds. El Dorado East Regional Park (north of Spring Street and east of the San Gabriel River) includes several lakes where fishing is permitted, a large lake with paddleboat rentals, open meadows, and bicycle and roller-skating paths.

El Dorado Nature Center, located in the east park, is an eighty-acre forested nature sanctuary. There are two lakes, marshes, meadows, a stream, and miles of soft-bark hiking trails. The area is inhabited by raccoons, weasels, foxes, and other small animals. The Nature Center building, on an island in one of the lakes, has maps for self-guided tours and a museum that houses living and stuffed specimens of the area's animal inhabitants.

The San Fernando Valley

Universal Studios Tour
Universal City (located just off the Hollywood Freeway at either the Universal Center or Lankershim Boulevard exit). (818) 508-9600. Open daily, except Christmas and Thanksgiving. Summer and holidays: 9 A.M.–5 P.M. Rest of year: Weekdays, 10 A.M.–3:30 P.M.; weekends, 9:30 A.M.–3:30 P.M. Adults (12 years old and older), $17.95; ages 55 and older, $12.50; ages 3–11, $12.95; under 3, free. Parking, $3.

A tour of Universal Studios gives you amusement attractions and a behind-the-scenes look at a busy movie studio. The tour consists of a two-hour guided portion and as many free shows and exhibits before or afterward as you care to see. Most of the guided tour is by tram. You'll see the back lot, where the buildings have only fronts. You can see a New York street, a European street, and a western town that are used in film after film. You'll also visit a sound stage complex where kids selected from the audience will be asked to participate in displays of special effects.

There are enough exciting diversions on the tram ride—such as "alien

You may get a chance to act in a mini-episode of Star Trek on the Universal Studios Tour.

creatures" who order the tram inside a space ship, a bridge that appears to collapse when you cross it, and a dramatic assault by a thirty-foot King Kong—to keep children delighted. During the summer, the tour has a midway rest stop at Prop Plaza, where kids can play on top of giant props such as an outsized telephone or a Model T Ford that bounces on springs.

After the tour, you can visit the studio's Entertainment Center, which offers exhibits and a number of live, action-packed shows. (The shows last fifteen to twenty minutes; kids will enjoy any or all of them.) In the stunt show, for example, skilled stuntmen demonstrate how not to get hurt when they fall off buildings or punch each other. In the Star Trek Adventure, members of the audience, including children, participate in a special-effects-filled mini-Star Trek Adventure and then see the results on a large screen. There are also a couple of spectacular live-action shows that are themed after popular Universal television shows and movies. The Entertainment Center includes four new sets that visitors can walk through: Sherlock Holmes's Baker Street, the Moulin Rouge of Paris, a Parisian back street, and a 1950s American street.

McGroarty Arts Center
7570 McGroarty Terrace, Tujunga. (818) 352-5285.

Monsters do their best to make you feel at home at the Universal Studios Tour.

A former private home now serves the public as an art center for children and adults. Children three years old and older can select from classes that may include—depending on their age—ballet, ceramics, music, drawing, paintings, arts and crafts, guitar, and other subjects. The ten-week sessions of once-a-week classes cost about $15. A small park with a children's play area adjoins the arts center. The center is accessible to disabled children.

Van Nuys Airport Tour

6950 Hayvenhurst Avenue, Van Nuys. (818) 785-8838. School year: Monday–Friday, 9:30 and 11 A.M., plus one Saturday a month. Summer: Monday–Friday at 10 A.M. Reservations must be made at least a month in advance. Minimum age is 6. Free.

Van Nuys Airport, one of the busiest general-aviation centers in the nation, offers free tours of its facilities and of some of the aircraft stationed there. To take the tour, however, you must get together a group of at least ten people, and all children must be in the first grade or above. Your group boards an airport bus for the one-hour tour. You'll see aircraft ranging from Air National Guard C-130 cargo carriers to Fire Department and Highway Patrol helicopters. You'll also be able to board one of the aircraft.

Los Encinos State Historic Park
16756 Moorpark Street, Encino. (The park is one block north of Ventura Boulevard, just east of Balboa Boulevard. The entrance is on the south side of the street a few yards from the corner of Moorpark and La Maida streets.) (818) 784-4849. Grounds: Wednesday–Sunday, 10 A.M.–6 P.M. Free. House tours: Wednesday–Sunday, 1–4 P.M. Adults, $1; ages 6–16, 50¢; under 6, free.

A short distance from the bustle of Ventura Boulevard is a serene and lovely five-acre park containing the San Fernando Valley's first rancho. Gaspar de Portolá's Spanish exploration party camped here in 1769 after finding water on the site. In 1845 Governor Pio Pico gave the site and 4,460 surrounding acres to Vincente de la Osa, who built the nine-room ranch house that is still standing here.

You can take a guided tour of the ranch house, but the tour's appeal for children depends on the docent giving it. Some of the docents give the tour by rote and are not able to accommodate the interests or questions of children. Others are more understanding. Children would enjoy seeing some of the things on the tour, such as several antique saddles and a huge stagecoach lunch box. Outside are a pond with ducks, some old farm equipment, and a blacksmith's shop. There are three lovely shaded areas for picnicking.

On the park's Living History Days, docents dress in 1870s-style clothes, and there are special activities for visitors. Check with the park for the schedule.

Pages Books for Children and Young Adults
18399 Ventura Boulevard (in Tarzana Square), Tarzana. (818) 342-6657. Monday–Saturday, 10 A.M.–5 P.M.

Books for children from infancy through high school are carried in this children's bookstore. Pages also has a good selection of books on parenting, books in Spanish, and book-related toys and tapes. The staff all have backgrounds in teaching and are very knowledgeable about helping parents select appropriate books. If they cannot help you find the book you want, they will special order it for you.

Pages has a story hour for children aged three through eight on Saturdays at 11 A.M. The story hours, which last forty-five minutes, generally include crafts or dramatic activities relating to the books that have been read. No reservations are needed. A story hour for two- and three-year-olds is held during the week. (Check with the store for the schedule.) The store also publishes a newsletter four times a year with articles on book-related topics, reviews of new books, announcements of author appearances, and a calendar for the story hours.

The Enchanted Forest
20929 Ventura Boulevard, Woodland Hills. (818) 716-7202.

The Enchanted Forest combines creative arts classes for children with a toy store and a ninety-nine-seat puppet theater. Puppet shows take place on Saturday and Sunday (call for the prices and schedule). The classes include creative dramatics, costumed fantasy dance, magic, crafts, and—for the very young—creative play. (Classes are offered for children as young as eighteen months through junior-high school age.) Quality toys, puzzles, and puppets are sold in the toy shop. The Enchanted Forest also offers birthday party packages that include puppet shows or helping children put on their own play.

Reseda Park
18411 Victory Boulevard (at Reseda Boulevard), Reseda. (818) 881-3882. Open daily. Free.

The highlight of this thirty-six-acre park is a lake with an assortment of sociable ducks to feed. The park includes picnic areas, children's playgrounds, and huge shade trees.

The Farm/Rent-a-Pony
8225 Tampa Avenue (at Roscoe Boulevard), Reseda. (818) 341-6805. Saturday, Sunday, and holidays, 10 A.M.–5 P.M. (May open extra days during summer and school vacations.) Admission, $1.50 per person. Pony rides, $2.

It wasn't all that long ago that this part of the San Fernando Valley was out in the country. Kids can get a taste of those days at this combination small farm and pony corral. There is a weather-beaten 1915 red barn with a horse inside. Turkeys, chickens, and kid goats wander around the farmyard. Other animals—including sheep, goats, a cow, and even a llama—are in pens, and there are cages of smaller animals, such as bunnies. Bales of hay are stacked at one end of the yard, old farm equipment is lying around to be examined, and there are tractors to climb. Feed is available for the animals, and there are also some picnic tables.

The pony corral has tracks for slow- and faster-paced riders. The young people who work in the corral are very good with small children, and anyone old enough to sit up can find a pony to suit his or her pace. The Farm is a marvelously low-key place to visit.

Pierce College Farm
6201 Winnetka Avenue, Woodlawn Hills. (Take the Ventura Freeway to the Winnetka exit and go north on Winnetka.) (818) 719-6425. School Year: Tours Saturday at 10 A.M. and 2 P.M. (school groups only, Tuesday and Thursday at 10 A.M.). Summer: Tours Monday–Friday, 9 A.M. Reservations required. 50¢ per person.

City kids can see how a farm works without going farther than the San Fernando Valley. Pierce College offers children tours of the working farm it maintains for its agriculture department. They'll see two thousand hens in the egg farm; cattle grazing in the pasture; and sheep, goats, and baby pigs feeding in the pig pen. The walking tour of the farm takes an hour and a half. Since the farm is a working one, this is a watching experience for children; they won't be able to touch the animals. The tour is recommended for kids four years old and up, and there is a picnic area where you can have lunch or a snack.

Chatsworth Park South
22360 Devonshire Street, Chatsworth. (Go west on Devonshire Street past Topanga Canyon Boulevard to park.) (818) 341-6595. Open weekdays until 10 P.M., weekends until 7 P.M. Free.

Chatsworth Park South has a spectacular setting, with acres of green lawn spreading against the rugged red Simi hills. On the right as you enter there is a small shady playground with nearby picnic tables. Straight ahead is a vast expanse of lawn, perfect for frisbee throwing. You can bring bikes or hike in the rocky hills.

Orcutt Ranch Horticulture Center
23600 Roscoe Boulevard, Canoga Park. (818) 833-6641. Daily (except holidays), 7 A.M.–5 P.M. Free.

Once part of a large private estate, Orcutt Ranch offers a lovely site for picnicking and strolling. The ranch is surrounded by citrus groves, and kids can see picking equipment displayed next to the big red barn in the parking area. A nature trail leads from the rose garden in front of the ranch house through lush foliage down to a small picnic grove beside a stream.

Orcutt Ranch is quiet and uncrowded. On weekdays it is possible to be the only family there.

Leonis Adobe
23537 Calabasas Road, Calabasas. (Take Ventura Freeway to Mulholland Drive/Valley Circle Boulevard exit and go toward Mulholland Drive. Just south of freeway, turn right on Calabasas Road.) (818) 712-0734. Wednesday–Sunday, 1–4 P.M. Free.

Once the home of Miguel Leonis, a successful nineteenth-century rancher, this two-story house has been restored to look the way it did in the late 1800s. You can take a self-guided tour of the house, which is furnished with period items. Children probably will be most interested in the grounds where they can see ranch animals such as horses, sheep, goats, and turkeys, and examine old farm equipment. There is also a barn and a blacksmith shop. The Plummer House, which was the first house built in Hollywood, has been relocated on the grounds and serves as a museum displaying period photographs, clothing, and other items.

The town of Calabasas retains an Old West flavor that children may enjoy. Next door to the Leonis Adobe, the Sagebrush Cantina has the look of a cowboy saloon and serves Mexican food on a pleasant patio.

Mission San Fernando Rey de Espana
15151 San Fernando Mission Boulevard, Mission Hills. (Take the Golden State Freeway [I-5] north to San Fernando Mission Boulevard west.) (818) 361-0186. Daily, 9 A.M.–4:15 P.M. Adults, $1; ages 7–15, 50¢; under 7, free.

Founded in 1719, this mission once served as a Butterfield Stagecoach stop. A self-guided tour takes you through the church (reconstructed in 1974 following damage sustained in the 1971 Sylmar earthquake), the workshops, residence quarters, wine vats, and lovely gardens. Across the street from the mission is Brand Park, which features a statue of Father Serra and special plants from the other missions.

Andres Pico Adobe
10940 Sepulveda Boulevard, Mission Hills. (818) 365-7810. Wednesday–Sunday, 1–4 P.M. Weekdays by appointment. Free.

One of the oldest homes in the Los Angeles area, the Andres Pico Adobe was built by Mission San Fernando Indians around 1834. In 1853 the adobe (and half the San Fernando Valley) was purchased by Andres Pico, brother of Governor Pio Pico. The adobe, completely restored and furnished in the style of the era, is surrounded by a landscaped twenty-acre park.

Saugus/Newhall and Valencia Area

William S. Hart Park
24151 Newhall Avenue, Newhall. (Take I-405 or I-5 north to the Lyons Avenue off ramp at Newhall. Take Lyons Avenue east to Newhall Avenue and turn right.) (805) 259-0855. The park is open daily, 9:30 A.M. to one hour before dusk. Tours of the house: Wednesday–Sunday, 11 A.M.–3:30 P.M. Free.

On a trip to Newhall, youngsters can visit a real ranch: the former home of silent-movie cowboy star William S. Hart. Hart willed his 259-acre Horseshoe Ranch to the County of Los Angeles when he died. An old ranch building is filled with saddles and Hart's western gear. Children can climb the bars of the corral to pet the retired old horses grazing there. Farm animals such as pigs, cows, goats, chickens, and ponies are kept at the ranch. You can even see a herd of buffalo here, donated by Walt Disney. Hart's Spanish-style home is now a museum housing his original furniture and displays of western art, weapons, and Indian artifacts. There are barbecues, picnic tables, and wonderful old shade trees to eat under.

Placerita Canyon State and County Park and Nature Center
19152 West Placerita Canyon Road, Newhall. (Take I-405 or I-5 north to State Highway 14 [Antelope Valley Freeway] to the Placerita Canyon Road exit. Follow that road about 1½ miles east to the park.) (805) 259-7721. Daily, 9 A.M.–5 P.M. Free.

Gold in California was first discovered on the site of this park. A shepherd fell asleep under an oak tree here and dreamed of finding gold—or so the story goes—and when he awoke, he found gold flakes clinging to the roots of a wild onion that he dug up to eat. The park is a good place to hike. Eight miles of flat and hilly trails wander through oak woods and brush and along a stream. One of the trails is paved for wheelchair and stroller access. A free pamphlet describes what's alongside the park's half-mile ecology trail. Signs lead the way to the Oak of the Golden Dream, the picturesquely weathered coast live oak under which the sheepherder had his prophetic dream. The park's handsome nature center houses a museum with exhibits on ecology and park wildlife and often offers special activities for children and families. There is a large picnic area.

Vasquez Rocks County Park
10700 West Escondido Canyon Road, Saugus. (From Los Angeles, travel north and east via I-5 and Highway 14, left on Agua Dulce Road, and east on Escondido Canyon Road.) (805) 268-0991. Free.

The strange slanted rock formations in this 754-acre park make ideal climbing for children. Even very small children can find a rock to climb at their level. The park is named for Spanish-California bandit Tiburcio Vasquez, who is said to have hidden from the law here. The area is often used as a set for cowboy westerns.

Magic Mountain
Magic Mountain Parkway, Valencia. (From Los Angeles, take I-5 northwest and exit at Magic Mountain Parkway.) (805) 255-4100 or 255-4111 (tape), or (818) 992-0884 or 367-5965 (tape). Open daily from late May through early September; rest of the year, open weekends and school holidays. Always opens at 10 A.M., but closing hours vary. Admission covers all rides, attractions, and shows. Adults, $20; seniors, $10; children under 48 inches tall, $10; 2 and under, free. Parking, $3.

Magic Mountain is one of Southern California's "big attractions." Its much-publicized thrill-type rides appeal most to teenagers. However, the park also offers less-publicized attractions aimed at younger visitors. Bugs Bunny World is a six-acre children's park that includes a play area with imaginative equipment and a ride area with gentle, scaled-down versions of the park's rides. There is also a dolphin and sea lion show, an animal show, and

Bugs Bunny World at Magic Mountain has rides just for young children.

an animal farm where kids can pet and feed such animals as sheep, goats, and llamas. A restored 1912 carousel offers rides near the entrance to the park.

Pyramid Lake Recreation Area
About 35 miles north of San Fernando. (Take I-5 north to Hungry Valley road and follow the signs to the park.) (805) 257-2790. Open daily, 6 A.M.–8:30 P.M. Parking, $3.

Pyramid Lake is an easy drive from Los Angeles. The 1,300-acre lake is both rural and beautiful. The park offers excellent fishing and boating, and a swimming beach. There are roadside picnic tables and barbecues. Outdoor motorboats are available for rent.

Burbank, Glendale, Pasadena, and the San Gabriel Mountains

NBC Television Studio Tour
3000 West Alameda Street, Burbank. (818) 840-3557. Weekdays, 8:30 A.M.–4 P.M.; Saturday, 10 A.M.–4 P.M.; Sunday, 10 A.M.–2 P.M. Adults, $6; ages 5–14, $4; under 5, free. Free parking.

A tour of NBC takes you backstage through a giant broadcasting complex. On the seventy-five-minute walking tour, you'll be taken through the studios by a young page who will answer your questions. You'll see (depending on availability) the news studio, production studios, the wardrobe department, set construction, and several sets. There are video demonstrations on makeup and news gathering. You'll see yourself on television in a special ministudio that helps visitors understand the technology of television production. Kids will particularly enjoy the special-effects set, where a member of the tour group is chosen to fly like Superman over Los Angeles. Tours are taken in small groups and they are completely unstaged—you see exactly what's happening on that day. You may wait forty-five minutes to an hour to take a tour, so it's best to arrive early in the day, when waits are generally shorter.

George Izay Park Maze
111 West Olive Street, Burbank. (818) 953-9715. Open daily. Free.

Behind the Olive Recreation Center in George Izay Park is an amazing play structure. It's a huge yellow and white metal maze, complete with tunnels, slides, catwalks and bridges, that appears to offer endless climbing possibilities. Ramps are integrated into the structure so that children in wheelchairs have access to the maze bars, slides, and raised sandbox. There is also a seasonally operated wading pool incorporated into the maze that is accessible by wheelchair.

The maze is not shaded, so the play area can get hot. There are restrooms and shaded picnic benches close by.

Brand Park/Brand Library and Art Center
1601 West Mountain Street, Glendale. (From I-5, take Western Avenue north through Glendale.) (818) 243-8177. Daily, 8 A.M.–10 P.M. Free. Library and Art Center phone: (818) 956-2051. Tuesday and Thursday, 12:30–9 P.M.; Wednesday, Friday, and Saturday, 12:30–6 P.M.; closed Sunday and Monday. Free.

When you first catch sight of Brand Library perched high above the street, you may think you have chanced upon the palace of an Indian rajah or Moorish prince—certainly not a public library and park. The mansion was built by Leslie C. Brand in 1904. Called El Miradero, it was inspired by the East Indian Pavilion at the 1893 Chicago World's Fair, visited by Brand. The Brands later willed the property to the city to be used as a public park and library.

The library, housed in the mansion, is devoted to art and music. There are no children's books. The interior of the library, although very beautiful, is a no-touch affair. Adjoining the library is a new addition, which houses an art gallery that exhibits local artists in a beautiful environment. Although the library and art center are more for adults, children will love the huge grassy park overlooked by a palace. A children's playground is on the east side of the park.

Family Film Festival/Glendale Young People's Library
Glendale Central Library, 222 East Harvard Street, Glendale. (818) 956-3035. Saturday, 2:30 P.M. Free.

A free film program for children is offered year round by the Young People's Library of Glendale. The films screen on Saturday from 2:30 to 3:30 P.M. at the Central Library. During the summer, films are also shown on Friday from 10:30 to 11:15 A.M. On Wednesday and Thursday from 10:30 to 11 A.M., there is a story hour for children aged three through five.

Verdugo Park
1621 Canada Boulevard (near Verdugo Road), Glendale. (818) 956-2000. Open daily. Free.

Behind a stone-fence border is the pleasant and shady Verdugo Park. The park has a very nice play area for toddlers, including a miniature slide and horse swings. A playground for older children is next to the toddler yard. Another playground, with a space ship motif, is on the north side of the park. The park's thirty-five acres include some good trees for climbing and lots of pleasant picnic space.

Descanso Gardens
1418 Descanso Drive, La Canada. (Take the Glendale Freeway [2] north to Verdugo Boulevard, go right to Descanso Drive, and turn right again.) (818) 790-5571. Daily, 9 A.M.–4:30 P.M. Adults, $3; senior citizens and students, $1.50; ages 5–12, 75¢. Free on the third Tuesday of the month.

It's hard to believe, but this flower-filled 165-acre area was formerly a private residence. The owners, a Los Angeles newspaper publisher and his wife, began planting the gardens shortly after they purchased the place in 1937. Today, visitors to Descanso Gardens can enjoy one of the world's largest camellia gardens, year-round blooming flowers, a section of native California plants, and a native California oak forest.

Although *descanso* means "rest" in Spanish, there are plenty of ways for children to be active here. There are nature trails, open grassy areas to play in, picnic facilities, and squirrels and ducks that children can feed. A Japanese teahouse serves refreshments from 11 A.M. to 4 P.M., Tuesday through Sunday, in a Japanese garden setting that features ponds and a flowing stream. Tram tours of the gardens are available Tuesday through Friday at 1, 2, and 3 P.M.; Saturday and Sunday at 11 A.M., 1, 2, and 3 P.M. ($1.50 per person).

Pacific Asia Museum
46 North Los Robles Avenue, Pasadena. (From Los Angeles, take the Pasadena Freeway north until it ends at Arroyo Parkway; continue north on Arroyo Parkway to Colorado Boulevard; turn right on Colorado Boulevard and continue east; turn left on Los Robles Avenue. The museum is on the right.) (818) 449-2742. Wednesday–Sunday, noon–5 P.M. Adults, $2; senior citizens and students, $1.50; under 12, free.

In the middle of downtown Pasadena is an elegant and authentic Chinese imperial palace courtyard-style building complete with green roof tiles from China and bronze dragons. The building houses the Pacific Asia Museum, which is devoted to the arts and cultures of the Pacific and Asia. The shows, which feature special effects such as music and fragrant aromas, may include such items of interest to children as costumes, headdresses, saddles, and swords. A special children's gallery includes items such as puppets, toys, dolls, and costumes that relate to the main exhibit.

Younger children who would not get anything out of the exhibits might enjoy seeing the museum building and the magnificent central courtyard featuring a goldfish pond and Oriental figures and landscaping. For children five to ten, the museum offers summer workshops in the arts of Asian and Pacific cultures, such as Indonesian theater masks or Japanese clay.

Kidspace
390 South El Molino Avenue, Pasadena. (From Los Angeles, take the Pasadena Freeway [110] to its end. Go straight on Arroyo Parkway to California Street and turn right. Go three blocks to El Molino and turn left.) (818) 449-9143. School year: Wednesday, 2–5 P.M.; Saturday and Sunday, noon–4:30 P.M. Summer: Tuesday–Friday, 1–4 P.M.; Saturday and Sunday, noon–4:30 P.M. $2.50 per person; seniors, $2.25; under 2, free.

Kidspace invites children to be whatever they would like to be. Indeed, the participatory exhibits at this private, not-for-profit children's museum are all designed to stimulate a child's imagination, as well as to spark learning. In the "Grown-Up Tools" exhibit, for example, children can learn about adult professions by trying on the uniform of a fire fighter and climbing on the back of fire truck. Or, they can put on a Grand Prix race car driver's helmet, climb into a real racing car, and zoom off in their imaginations.

Children can learn about insects by observing a real ant colony, then they can pretend to be an ant by crawling through a large, carpeted structure that is built like an anthill. Kids can learn about human anatomy in the museum's "Outside/In" exhibit, which includes the opportunity to examine X-rays and to handle the bones pictured. Other exhibits include a working kid-sized television newsroom and a radio broadcasting station.

Kidspace also offers a continuing program of workshops and special events including puppet shows, storytelling, and film festivals. Most workshops and events are free with admission. You can also arrange to have your child's birthday party at the museum. Kidspace is housed in a former junior high school auditorium, and everything in the museum is touchable.

Pasadena Arts Workshops
390 South El Molino Avenue, Pasadena. (818) 792-5101.

The Pasadena Arts Workshops offer instruction in the arts for children aged three through sixteen. Recent classes have included dinosaur art, origami animal stories, musical instrument construction, doll making, animal masks and folklore, and mime, magic, and juggling. Tuition is about $55 per seven-week session. Some scholarships are available. The classes are accessible to disabled children. Free art programs are also held in parks and community centers throughout Pasadena. (Plans call for the Pasadena Arts Workshops to move into new quarters at the California National Guard Armory Building, 145 North Raymond, Pasadena, at some point in the near future.)

Norton Simon Museum of Art
411 West Colorado Boulevard (at Orange Grove Boulevard, at the junction of the 210 and 134 freeways, Pasadena). (818) 449-6840. Thursday–Sunday, noon–6 P.M. Thursday–Saturday: Adults, $2; students and senior citizens, 75¢; under 12, free. Sunday: $3 for all patrons over 12; under 12, free.

The Norton Simon Museum houses one of the finest art collections in the country. The collection includes European paintings from the fourteenth through the twentieth centuries, one of the finest collections of Indian and Southeast Asian sculpture outside of Asia, an extensive collection of Picasso graphics, and an impressive array of nineteenth- and twentieth-century sculpture. Children may enjoy the Degas gallery downstairs with his paintings and sculptures of ballet dancers and paintings of horses at the races. They should also enjoy the sculpture garden with its fountain, reflecting pool, and monumental sculpture.

Eaton Canyon County Park and Nature Center

1750 North Altadena Drive, Pasadena. (Take the Altadena Drive exit north from eastbound I-210.) (818) 794-1866. Nature Center hours: Monday–Saturday, 9:30 A.M.–5 P.M.; Sunday, 1–5 P.M. Free.

Almost all of this 184-acre park at the base of the San Gabriel Mountains has been left in its natural state. You will see a wide variety of plants and animals here, and the park is a good place for bird-watching. There are three self-guided nature trails, including one designed primarily for preschoolers. Some of the wildlife you'll observe along the trails are wood rats nesting in the laurel sumac, California legless lizards, yucca moths and yucca flowers, white sage, and California sagebrush. Warblers and flycatchers are some of the birds that may be seen along the park's running stream.

The Nature Center houses ecological exhibits on the park's wildlife. There is someone on duty to answer questions, and trail maps are available in the office. Shaded picnic tables and cooking facilities are near the Nature Center.

Huntington Library, Art Gallery, and Botanical Gardens

1151 Oxford Road, San Marino. (From the Pasadena Freeway: Continue north from the end of the freeway on Arroyo Parkway to California Boulevard. Turn right and drive 2 miles to Allen Avenue, then right to Huntington Gardens. From the 210 Freeway west: Take Hill Street exit south, then turn right on California and continue as above. From the 210 Freeway east: Take the Allen off ramp.) (818) 405-2100. Tuesday–Sunday, 1–4:30 P.M. Advance reservations required on Sunday; phone: (818) 405-2273. Suggested donation, $2 per adult.

Millionaire art collector Henry E. Huntington willed this estate—including his art collection, a priceless library, and the two-hundred-acre garden—to the public. On display in the library is a Gutenberg Bible, a first printing of Shakespeare's plays, and George Washington's genealogy in his own handwriting. The Huntington Gallery was originally the Huntington residence, and many of the works of art are displayed in furnished rooms. Probably the most famous paintings here are Gainsborough's *Blue Boy* and Lawrence's *Pinkie*. The Virginia Steele Scott Gallery for American art, which opened in 1984, displays American paintings from the 1730s to the 1930s. The library and art galleries will probably interest only older children and adults.

If your kids are younger, they'll enjoy a visit just to the Botanical Gardens. Each of the twelve gardens has a separate identity. The most interesting one for children is the Japanese garden, a quarter-mile west of the main entrance. This is a lovely landscaped canyon of five acres with Japanese plants, stone ornaments, an old temple bell, *koi* ponds, a drum bridge, and a furnished Japanese home.

A cafeteria open from 1 to 4 P.M. serves lunch and snacks.

Lacy Park
3300 Monterey Road, San Marino. (The park entrance is on Virginia Road.) (818) 304-9648 or 300-0700. Monday–Saturday, 6:30 A.M.–sunset. Closed Sunday and holidays. Free on weekdays. On Saturday there is a fee of $3 per person to use the park.

Lacy Park is one of the most beautiful city parks imaginable. Surrounded by trees and encompassing acres of immaculate rolling lawns, you feel as if you are on a private estate. A pleasant playground in the center of the park includes an old red fire truck to climb aboard. Opposite the playground are a number of picnic tables shaded by sycamore trees. (No barbecuing is permitted.) You can take your kids on a stroll to the rose garden, and there are broad cement paths for bike riding.

The big drawback of Lacy Park is that non-San Marino residents must pay to use the park on Saturdays ($3 per person, which can make a simple family outing to the park rather expensive). On Sunday and holidays, the park is closed to non-residents.

San Gabriel Mountains
For information and details contact Angeles National Forest, 701 North Santa Anita Avenue, Arcadia, CA 91006. (818) 574-5200. Office open weekdays, 8 A.M.–4:30 P.M.

The San Gabriel Mountains, a part of the Angeles National Forest, sit at the back door of Los Angeles. Just a short distance from the city are opportunities for hiking, riding, camping, and picnicking in scenic wilderness areas. There are hundreds of miles of rivers, eight lakes, and more than five hundred miles of hiking and riding trails. The quiet trails are seldom crowded, and the terrain changes are dramatic: One moment you may be walking in a fern dell or looking at a waterfall, and a few minutes later you find yourself in a dry chaparral landscape. Although the nicest areas of wilderness must be reached on foot, you can still tour the mountains by car.

Mount Wilson
East end of Mount Wilson Road, Angeles National Forest. (Take the Glendale Freeway [2] north to Foothill Boulevard and east to Angeles Crest Highway. Or take I-210 to Angeles Crest Highway [State Route 2] and go north to Mount Wilson Road.) (818) 449-4163. Open daily, 10 A.M.–5 P.M. (weather permitting). Free.

Located on a crest of the San Gabriel Mountains above Pasadena, Mount Wilson provides spectacular views of Los Angeles. It is also the site of the renowned Mount Wilson Observatory. Although the observatory itself is not open to the public, the grounds are open, and there is a museum with photographs of the heavens and models of the planets on display.

Mount Wilson Skyline Park, nearby, offers picnicking and three hiking trails leading down the southern slope of the mountain to the valley below. There is also a concession stand where you can buy food.

Chilao Visitors Center
Angeles National Forest, State Highway 2 (located about 27 miles north of the Angeles Crest Highway off ramp from I-210). (818) 796-5541. Daily 9 A.M.–5 P.M. Free.

The Chilao Visitors Center, located about thirteen miles north of Mount Wilson, offers a variety of indoor exhibits on the forest, and self-guided nature walks on easy trails. Picnic areas and campgrounds are nearby. Day visitors can purchase food and drinks at Newcomb's Ranch Cafe.

San Gabriel Municipal Park
Take the San Bernardino Freeway to the Del Mar Avenue exit and go north to Wells Avenue. Turn west and proceed two blocks to the park. (818) 308-2875. Daily, 7:30 A.M.–10 P.M. Free.

This is an ideal park for families with small children. A Kiddie Korral solely for children six and under has pony swings, animal and car-shaped jungle gyms, a little boat, and other playground equipment scaled for preschoolers. In another area, a playground for bigger kids features a rocketship slide and traditional swings, slides, and jungle gyms.

The best part of the park (located behind the baseball diamond) is a colorful zoo of concrete animals to climb on and slide down. Children climb up the arms of a big purple octopus and slide out the mouth of a blue whale. There are dragons to bump down, porpoises to ride, and a half-sunken pirate ship to play on. Nearby, a sea serpent stares at a ten-foot-high snail that doubles as a slide.

There are benches for the old folks and covered tables for birthday parties. The park also has a number of barbecues and picnic tables.

Los Angeles State and County Arboretum

310 North Baldwin Avenue, Arcadia. (Take the Baldwin Avenue off ramp from the 210 Freeway and go south about a quarter of a mile on Baldwin.) (818) 446-8251. Daily, 9 A.M.–4:30 P.M. Adults, $3; seniors, $1.50; students age 13 and over, $1.50; ages 5–12, 75¢; under 5, free.

It's easy to spend a whole day enjoying the Los Angeles State and County Arboretum. Once the estate of millionaire E. J. "Lucky" Baldwin, it is now 127 acres of beautifully landscaped public gardens where peacocks wander freely. The area kids will enjoy most is to the left as you enter the park. Palm trees over a hundred feet tall surround a huge lagoon that was used as a set for many Tarzan films. Children can play Tarzan in the thick jungle path around the lagoon. (Wear old clothes and tennis shoes for your visit.) Ducks and geese will run up for a handout at the sound of coins being dropped into the poultry-feed dispensers on the shore of the lagoon.

By following the curve of the lagoon you come to a restored adobe, originally built in 1839. You can look through the windows to see the rooms furnished in the original manner. Beside the adobe is a reconstruction of an Indian village. The reed huts are open and children can play in them.

Nearby is the Queen Anne Cottage, built in 1881 by Lucky Baldwin. Through the windows of the cottage you see life-sized mannequins in rooms furnished in the style of the era. Each room has a bouquet of fresh flowers and lovely stained-glass windows. The Coach Barn offers interesting displays of old tools and coaches. Tram rides through the park are available for $1.50, from 12:15 P.M. weekdays and 10 A.M. weekends. The trams start at the tram station near the entrance.

Santa Anita Workouts

Santa Anita Park, 285 West Huntington Drive, Arcadia. (Take the Santa Anita Avenue exit south from I-210, or north from I-10, to Huntington Drive. Or take the Baldwin Avenue exit south from I-210, or north from I-10.) (818) 574-7223. Hours: Wednesday–Sunday, 7:30–9:30 A.M. during racing season (about December 26 to April 22). Free.

You can stand at the rail during morning workouts at Santa Anita Park and watch the thoroughbred horses go through their paces any racing day (weather permitting). At the peak of the exercise period, several dozen horses will be on the track at the same time. The practicing horses drill counterclockwise; those finished working out walk clockwise, along the outer rail, back to their barns. A public-address commentary gives the names of the horses and their workout times.

During workout time on Saturday and Sunday, the track offers free tram rides around the track facilities and stable area. A knowledgeable guide points out famous horses and explains about their care. The tram often stops to let you see the stable's pet goats and chickens. Each tour lasts fifteen minutes.

You may want to take your children to see an actual race. Children under seventeen are admitted free with an adult; adults pay $2.75. You may picnic in the infield during the race, where a fully supervised children's playground, called Anita Chiquita, is also located.

Whittier Narrows Nature Center
1000 North Durfee Avenue, South El Monte. (Take the Pomona Freeway to the Rosemead exit.) (818) 444-1872. Daily, 9 A.M.–5 P.M. Free.

Along the San Gabriel River is a 277-acre wildlife sanctuary protecting more than 150 species of plants and animals. Four lakes, totaling twenty-six acres, attract hundreds of migratory birds each year. There are several miles of self-guiding nature trails where you can sometimes spot rabbits and raccoons.

The wildlife sanctuary is part of the 1,092-acre Whittier Narrows Dam Recreation Area, which features a large lake for boating and fishing, hiking and equestrian trails, sports fields, children's play areas, and picnic facilities.

Heritage Park
1918 North Rosemead Boulevard, El Monte. (Take the Rosemead exit north from Pomona Freeway [60]. Go north on Rosemead about 1¼ miles to the museum.) (818) 442-1776. Weekends, noon–4:30 P.M. Adults, $2; ages 10–15, $1; ages 5–9, 50¢; under 5, free.

Located on 7½ acres within the Whittier Narrows Recreation Area, Heritage Park displays more than eighty military vehicles, including American

You can pet the goats at Santa Anita Park.

and foreign jeeps, trucks, and tanks. Other displays in this museum of military equipment include ship propellers, radar screens, and cannons.

Pio Pico State Historic Park

6003 South Pioneer Boulevard, Whittier. (213) 695-1217. Wednesday–Sun-

day, 9 A.M.–5 P.M. Free.

Although the home of the last Mexican governor of California, Pio Pico, has been closed due to the damage it suffered in the October 1987 earthquake, you can still picnic here on the grounds.

Mrs. Nelson's Toy and Book Shop
1355 North Grand Avenue (located in the shopping center on the southwest corner of Arrow Highway and Grand Avenue), Covina. (818) 339-9914. (After early fall 1989, the store will be located at 1030 Bonita Avenue, La Verne. Check for new phone number.) Monday–Saturday, 9 A.M.–6 P.M.

This well-stocked children's book and toy shop features about eight thousand book titles ranging from board books for babies to young adult titles. There is also a large selection of books on topics for parents. A story hour is held at 11 A.M. on Saturdays during the school year. (No pre-registration is necessary.) The store also offers an Eager Reader program for children in the first through eighth grades, with special discounts on books. Other store-sponsored activities include workshops, author signings, and concerts. If you can't find the book you want, they will special order it. The staff is knowledgeable about children's books, and everyone working in the store is a parent. Mrs. Nelson's also publishes a book-review newsletter five times a year.

The store offers a good selection of high-quality toys, and toys are out where children can examine them. Children's videotapes, musical instruments, and science materials are also sold. The store provides free gift wrapping.

Hacienda Heights Youth Science Center
Located at the Wedgeworth Elementary School, 16949 Wedgeworth Drive, Room 8, Hacienda Heights. (From the Pomona Freeway [60], exit Azusu Avenue south to Pepper Brook Way. Turn right to Wedgeworth Drive.) (818) 968-2525 Saturday, 10 A.M.–2 P.M. Telephone for weekday schedule. Free.

The Youth Science Center is a nonprofit organization dedicated to science education; it operates two museums (the other is in Fullerton). Both museums offer children fascinating science exhibits and hands-on experiments. The Youth Science Center also sponsors a variety of classes and field trips. Science classes at Hacienda Heights have included model rocketry for ages ten and up; "talking rocks," a geology class for kindergarten through third grade; and stargazing for the entire family. Field trips have included excursions to hospitals, manufacturing sites, and science laboratories, as well as nature outings.

Claremont, Pomona, and Vicinity

Raging Waters
111 Raging Waters Drive (Via Verde), San Dimas. (714) 592-8181 or 592-6453 (tape). (Located in Frank G. Bonelli County Regional Park, near the intersection of Freeways 210, 10, 71 and 57. Exit I-210 at Raging Waters Drive [Via Verde] and drive east to the park.) Open weekends May to mid-June and mid-September to mid-October. Open daily mid-June to mid-September. Hours vary, but open at least 10 A.M.–6 P.M. Adults (over 48 inches), $12.95; seniors, $6.95; children (42–48 inches), $8.95; children under 42 inches, free. There are reduced weekday rates for adult nonparticipants with paying children and discounts after 5 P.M.

Covering forty-four acres in Frank G. Bonnelli Regional Park, Raging Waters is a combination swimming lagoon, water-slide adventure, and aquatic playground. The park is designed for the whole family. For the daring there are several steep slides, as well as hundreds of feet of twisting, curving water slides. A special attraction, called Raging Rivers, offers a quarter-mile of inner-tube rapids, with four separate channels ranging from mild for younger children to wild for the foolhardy. A large family swimming lagoon, called the Wave Cove, features manmade waves and activity islands where kids can climb across rope nets, swing on tires, and perform lots of other feats. The lagoon is surrounded by sunbathing beaches. Small children have their own imaginatively designed play pool. There are picnic facilities, as well as a variety of snack bars. Dressing rooms and lockers are available. Bring your own beach towels and chairs, and don't forget sunscreen.

Raging Waters has more than a hundred lifeguards; however, you should still keep close watch on your children. For safety, the park maintains a maximum-admission limit. Therefore, if you are coming on a busy weekend, plan to arrive early or after 5 P.M.

Kellogg's Arabian Horse Center

Kellogg Campus, California State Polytechnic University, Pomona. (Go east on I-10, take the Cal Poly off ramp near Pomona, and follow the signs.) (714) 869-2224. Center open daily, 9 A.M.–4 P.M. Horse shows: First Sunday of the month, October–June at 2 P.M. Adults, $1.50; seniors, $1; children, 50¢.

A splendid herd of Arabian horses lives on this campus. The Arabians are used by students studying horse husbandry and training. On various Sundays during the year, the horses demonstrate their intelligence for the public in an hour-long show. They rock baby carriages, do arithmetic, and even open a cash register and put money into it.

Although the horse show is a lot of fun for everyone, you don't have to attend it to see the horses. You can visit the horses any day, without charge, and even go right up to them and pet them. In the spring, the mares will have their newborn colts by their sides.

Adobe De Palomares

491 East Arrow Highway, Pomona. (Take the Garey Avenue—Orange Grove exit from I-10. Go north on Orange Grove to Palomares Adobe.) (714) 620-2300. Tuesday–Sunday, 2–5 P.M. Free.

Built in 1854, the thirteen-room Adobe de Palomares has been restored to look the way it did a hundred years ago, with authentic furniture, cooking utensils, tools, clothing, and toys from that era. Picnic facilities are available in Palomares Park directly behind the adobe.

Griswold's Smorgasbord

555 West Foothill Boulevard, Claremont. (Intersection of Indian Hill and Foothill boulevards.) (714) 621-9360. Monday–Saturday, 6:30–11 A.M., 11:30 A.M.–4 P.M., and 4:30–8:30 P.M. (until 9 P.M. on Friday and Saturday). Sunday, 6:30 A.M.–1 P.M. and 1:30–8:30 P.M.

The Griswold's complex includes a hotel, several restaurants, and a number of shops, many of which are housed in the former Claremont High School. Griswold's Smorgasbord is a fine family restaurant serving a wide selection of hot and cold smorgasbord items for all three meals. In addition to the fun of selecting from a smorgasbord, kids enjoy looking through the restaurant's large bakery window to see cakes being decorated.

A few of the shops in the schoolhouse complex might interest children, including the Trading Card Co. (phone: 714-621-0660), which deals solely in baseball cards. Also, on weekends from about 9 A.M. to 5 P.M., a colorful crafts fair takes place on the lawn with as many as 150 craftspeople participating.

Rancho Santa Ana Botanic Garden
1500 North College Avenue, Claremont. (From Los Angeles, take I-10 east to Indian Hill Boulevard, then turn north on Indian Hill.) (714) 625-8767. Daily, 8 A.M.–5 P.M. Free.

The main blooming period of this eighty-three-acre garden is from late February to the middle of June. Then the mazanitas, California lilacs, and tree poppies are especially striking. Most of the plants are grouped according to natural association, such as the chaparral community. The garden isn't for all kids, as it is a walking and observing experience.

Raymond M. Alf Museum
1175 West Base Line Road, Claremont. (714) 626-3587. Monday–Friday, 9–11 A.M. and 1–4 P.M. Closed in summer. Free.

Located at the Webb School of Claremont (a college preparatory school for boys), this museum houses the findings of Dr. Alf and his students from their paleontological digs. The findings include thousands of bones, fossil footprints, a fifteen-million-year-old peccary skull, and fossils showing the history of mammals. There are related exhibits of Indian relics and ancient Egyptian artifacts. You need to make an appointment to tour the museum, which even preschool children can enjoy.

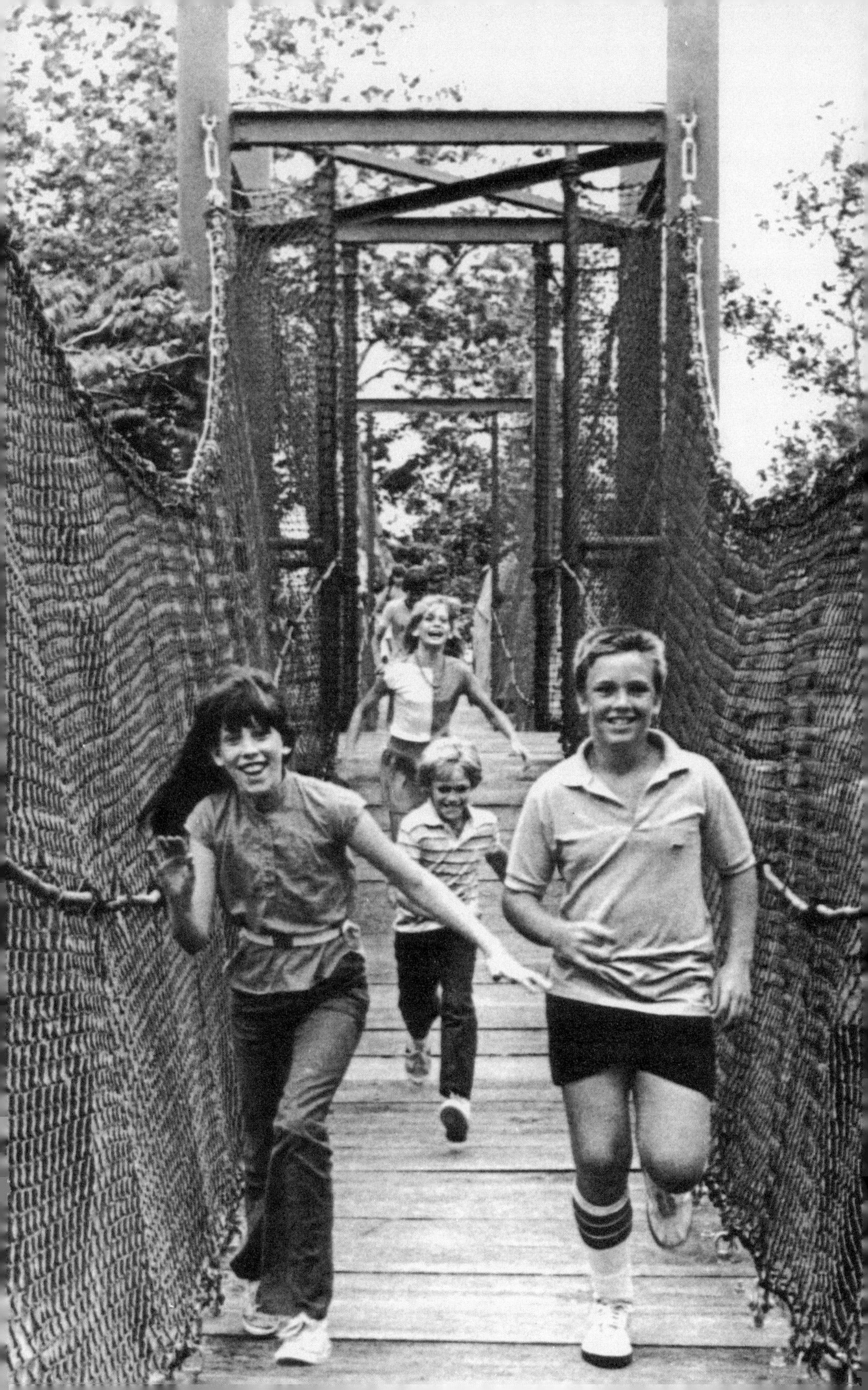

Orange County

The citrus groves for which this county was named have given way to the greatest concentration of amusement parks and entertainment attractions anywhere. Yet, impressive as Disneyland and Knott's Berry Farm may be, there is a great deal more to Orange County than amusement parks.

Orange County boasts miles of beautiful beaches, wonderful harbors, big green parks with imaginative play areas for children, a famous artists' colony, and several wildlife sanctuaries. Every year, right on schedule, flocks of swallows return to their nests in one of the state's loveliest missions. A number of fine museums are located in the county, including several just for children.

Orange County's public transit system offers extensive service throughout the county. The OCTD telephone number is (714) 636-7433. The Southern California Rapid Transit District (213-626-4455) also has service to Orange County.

Suspension bridges are part of the outdoor fun in Camp Snoopy at Knott's Berry Farm.

Buena Park/Anaheim

Knott's Berry Farm
8039 Beach Boulevard, Buena Park. (Exit at Knott Avenue from the Santa Ana Freeway and follow the signs.) (714) 827-1776 or 220-5200 (recorded information). Summer: Sunday–Thursday, 10 A.M.–11 P.M. Open until midnight on Friday and 1 A.M. on Saturday. Winter: Monday–Friday, 10 A.M.–6 P.M.; Saturday, 10 A.M.–10 P.M.; Sunday, 10 A.M.–7 P.M. Unlimited-use ticket: Adults, $17.95; seniors, $12.95; ages 3–11, $13.95. Parking, $3.

Those of us who grew up in Southern California remember Knott's Berry Farm as a recreated Old West ghost town where kids could play all day for no more than the 25¢ train-ride fare. In the years since that time, Knott's has developed into one of the nation's best-attended amusement parks.

In addition to an expanded Old West section with an exciting Calico Mine ride, the park now includes a Fiesta Village with rides and attractions in an Early California theme, as well as big thrill rides, and a Roaring '20s

Snoopy presides over the activities at Knott's Berry Farms' Camp Snoopy.

section depicting an amusement park of the twenties and offering big thrill rides. The Roaring '20s area is also home to Kingdom of the Dinosaurs, a seven-minute indoor ride that takes you back in time to encounter some twenty-one fully animated moving and screeching dinosaurs. (The experience is too frightening for small children.)

If your children are young, head immediately for Camp Snoopy, a six-acre scenic area of attractions for children, including a petting farm, opportunities to be physically active, and old Snoopy himself.

The fifth and newest area of the park is the 3½-acre Wild Water Wilderness. The highlight here is the Bigfoot Rapids, which offers guests an exhilarating and very wet ride down a whitewater river.

Knott's Berry Farm has the most relaxed feeling of all the Southern California amusement parks, and it can be the most enjoyable park for families with small children. There are several reasonably good eating places at Knott's, but by far the best is the old-fashioned Chicken Dinner Restaurant. There is no charge to enter the Knott's outside shopping and dining area.

Movieland Wax Museum

7711 Beach Boulevard, Buena Park. (From I-5 or Artesia Freeway 91, exit Beach Boulevard, south.) (714) 522-1154. Open daily, including holidays. Summer: 9 A.M.–11:30 P.M. Rest of year: 10 A.M.–10:30 P.M. The box office closes 1½ hours before the museum. Adults, $9.95; ages 4–11, $5.95.

The spookiness of so many wax museums is completely avoided in this lavish place. Wax replicas of movie and television stars are displayed on individual sets that recreate their famous roles. Most sets include original costumes and props. Laurel and Hardy sit on the running board of an old Model T; Ben Hur is in his chariot pulled by four horses. Special animation, lights, and sound effects enliven the displays.

Children above the age of five will find enough characters they recognize—such as Superman, Mr. T., the crew from "Star Trek," and Michael Jackson—to enjoy the museum.

Medieval Times

7662 Beach Boulevard (across the street from Movieland Wax Museum), Buena Park. (714) 521-4740 or (800) 438-9911 (toll free in California). Performances nightly with a Sunday matinee. (Phone for times; reservations required.) Admission, including dinner, show, beverages, and tax: Adults,

There are a lot of opportunities to be active in Camp Snoopy at Knott's Berry Farm.

$26 ($28 on Friday and Saturday; $24 for Sunday matinee); ages 12 and under, $18 ($16 for Sunday matinee).

Medieval Times is an eleventh-century-themed dinner and entertainment complex one block north of Knott's Berry Farm. Knights on horseback parade, joust, sword fight, and engage in games of skill on a sand-covered ring while the audience eats dinner. Each pavilion in the theater has its own knight to root for, and the audience gets into the act with hissing, cheering, and table banging. The horses, Andalusian stallions, are beautiful; the knights are skilled; and the show is exciting. It also gets very loud and boisterous. (Kids in upper elementary school probably have the most fun.) The food, at best, is fair, and the evening is expensive. You can, however, tour the castle on your own, Monday through Saturday, from 9 A.M. to 4 P.M., free of charge.

Museum of World Wars
8700 Stanton Avenue (off Beach Boulevard), Buena Park. (714) 952-1776. Daily, 11 A.M.–6 P.M. Adults, $1; children, 50¢.

Not everyone's cup of tea perhaps, but the Museum of World Wars claims to be the largest privately owned military museum in the United States. It houses military field equipment and vehicles—including five tanks and a German field marshal's car—uniforms, armor, headgear, weapons, swords, and other historical relics dating from antiquity to 1945.

Los Coyotes Regional Park
8800 Rosecrans Avenue, Buena Park. (Take the Beach Boulevard exit from either the 91 Freeway or I-5 and go north to Rosecrans Avenue.) (714) 522-4660. October 1 to March 31: Open daily, 7 A.M. to sunset. April 1 to September 30: Open daily, 7 A.M.–10 P.M. Parking, $1.

Los Coyotes Regional Park rests on a rich prehistoric fossil site. The park was created to preserve the fossil beds, as well as to provide a recreational facility. The developed area of the park, encompassing forty-eight acres, includes a lagoon with an island playground that is reached by crossing a bridge. There are a number of picnic areas with nearby play equipment, three softball fields, a baseball diamond, four tennis and two volleyball courts, and a bike trail.

Hobby City Doll and Toy Museum
1238 South Beach Boulevard, Anaheim. (714) 527-2323. Daily, 10 A.M.–6 P.M. Adults, $1; children and senior citizens, 50¢.

This doll and toy museum is housed in a half-scale replica of the White House as it appeared in 1917. More than two thousand rare, antique, and collectible dolls and toys are on display. The dolls, ranging from a five-thousand-year-old doll from ancient Egypt to modern troll dolls, are arranged chronologically as you go through the museum. Each group from a particular time and place is displayed in a separate glass case with appropriate background and accessories. The dolls are from all over the world;

some of the most interesting are from ancient China. The owner of the museum, Mrs. Bea DeArmond, started collecting dolls when she was four years old.

Disneyland
1313 Harbor Boulevard, Anaheim. (Take the Santa Ana Freeway to Anaheim, exit at Harbor Boulevard, and follow signs.) (714) 999-4000 or (213) 626-8605. Winter: Monday–Friday, 10 A.M.–6 P.M.; Saturday, 9 A.M.–midnight; Sunday, 9 A.M.–9 P.M. (Hours can vary, so phone ahead.) Summer: Sunday–Friday, 9 A.M.–midnight; until 1 A.M. on Saturday. Admission and unlimited use of attractions: Adults, $21.50; seniors, $17.25; ages 3–11, $16.50; under 3, free. Parking, $3.

Everyone knows about Disneyland. A day spent here can be expensive and exhausting, but it's always memorable. If possible, schedule your visit for the winter months, when the park is much less crowded. If your visit is in the summer, aim for a weekday and come early. With children in the summer, it's best to get to the park when it opens in the morning.

Go first to the park's most popular attractions, such as Star Tours, Captain EO, Splash Mountain, Space Mountain, and the Matterhorn Bobsleds. That way you can see them before midday when the waits can reach an hour. If you have older children, you might want to come later in the day during the summer and stay into the evening when it's cooler, the lines are shorter, and there are special entertainments and fireworks. (Try not to miss the Main Street Electrical Parade.)

One of the best places for families in the park is Frontierland's Tom Sawyer Island. Kids can spend an hour here crawling through tunnels, forts, and mining shafts; running across a barrel bridge; and playing on a teeter-totter rock. Meanwhile their parents can sit and rest. Big Thunder Ranch in Frontierland features a petting farm and is a calm area of the park. Fantasyland has the most rides for small children. For older children and hardy adults, Space Mountain can compete with the scariest of thrill rides anywhere.

Disneyland Hotel
1150 West Cerritos Avenue, Anaheim. (714) 778-6600.

The Disneyland Hotel is a world of its own. Sitting on sixty acres across the street from Disneyland—and connected to it by monorail—the Disneyland Hotel is the largest hotel in the county. In the backyard of the hotel is a freshwater marina with docks, bridges, ramps, and paddleboat rentals. The marina is surrounded by Seaports of the Pacific, a waterfront bazaar featuring shops, artisans at work, restaurants, and displays of marine equipment.

You don't have to be a hotel guest to stroll around the marina or rent a paddleboat (available daily during summer and on weekends the rest of the year). In the evening there is a Dancing Water spectacle produced by lighted fountains; and visitors have a view of Disneyland's fireworks in the summer.

The many restaurants in the complex range from full-course Continental to casual pantry type; all are accommodating to children and reasonably priced for what they serve.

If you decide to stay at the hotel, double accommodations begin at $116, plus $14 per extra person. (Special family discounts are sometimes available.) In the off chance that you might lapse into boredom at the hotel, there is a full-time activities director to assist you.

Anaheim Stadium Tours
Katella and State College, Anaheim. (714) 937-7333. Recorded event information: (714) 937-6750. Tour daily, each hour on the hour, 10 A.M.–3 P.M. (There are no tours on the days of daytime home games or events. The tour ends at 2 P.M. when there are night games.) Adults, $3; children, $2; under 5, free.

This forty-five-minute-to-an-hour tour takes you behind the scenes at Anaheim Stadium. You'll tour home plate, the locker rooms, the press box, and other areas you would ordinarily not see close up.

Garden Grove, Santa Ana, and Orange

Garden Grove Park/Atlantis Play Center
9301 Westminster Avenue, Garden Grove. (Take the Garden Grove Freeway to Magnolia Street, go south about half a mile to Westminster Avenue, and east about a block to the park.) Park phone: (714) 638-6711. Free. Atlantis

Play Center phone: (714) 892-6015. Summer: Tuesday–Saturday, 10 A.M.– 4 P.M.; Sunday, noon–4 P.M. School year: Tuesday–Friday, 11 A.M.–4 P.M.; Saturday, 10 A.M.–4 P.M.; Sunday, noon–4 P.M. Admission 50¢.

Garden Grove Park is the home of the Atlantis Play Center, a nicely landscaped, four-acre fenced area where children accompanied by adults can slide down a colorful sea serpent, climb on Stelly Starfish, and enjoy playing on many other outsized concrete aquatic creatures. Picnic tables are available in the play center. The rest of the forty-acre park is neat and clean. There is ample and imaginative play equipment, softball and football fields, and a volleyball court.

Discovery Museum of Orange County
3101 West Harvard Street, Santa Ana. (714) 540-0404. Saturday and Sunday, 11 A.M.–3 P.M. (The museum is open Tuesday–Friday for school, scout, and youth group tours.) Adults, $1; children, 50¢. (Telephone for school and youth group prices.)

A gabled Victorian mansion serves as the centerpiece of an exciting museum designed to show children what life was like in Orange County at the turn of the century. The mansion—the historic 1898 Kellogg house—has been restored and furnished with period items such as an antique piano. But unlike most other museums in historic houses, kids can touch the exhibits here. They can dress up in Victorian clothing, roll up their sleeves, and do laundry with a scrub board and wooden ringer. They can also try out a handcrank telephone, operate a telegraph key, use a butter churner, and handle all sorts of other implements from the past. Docents are on hand to explain the exhibits. Outside the house are a rose garden and a citrus orchard where kids on school tours can pick fruit.

A different theme—such as transportation or old-time games—offering additional activities is featured each month. Victorian birthday parties also can be arranged for children four to twelve. Centennial Park adjacent to the museum offers picnicking and play before or after the museum visit. The Discovery Museum is highly recommended.

Charles W. Bowers Museum
2002 North Main Street, Santa Ana. (Take the Main Street exit from the Santa Ana Freeway [5]. The museum is located just south of the exit on

Main Street.) (714) 972-1900. Tuesday–Saturday, 10 A.M.–5 P.M.; Sunday, noon–5 P.M. Free.

Housed in a pretty mission-style building, the Bowers Museum contains exhibits on California and Orange County history, southwestern Indian artifacts, natural history, archaeology, and California art. An Ethnic Gallery presents artifacts from Africa, New Guinea, and from pre-Columbian times. Children should enjoy the history exhibits, which include costumes, old-fashioned schoolchildren's things, old kitchen items such as a butter churn, and a fancy old cash register.

Other exhibits that kids will like include a whale's skull and other whale bones, a fascinating collection of African masks, and a giant totem pole. Outside in the museum's patio area is a collection of old buggies, a logger's wagon, an old fire ladder-wagon, a 1904 Cadillac, and a large *metate* used by Indian women for grinding acorns. The museum also offers art workshops for children; check with the museum for the schedule.

Santa Ana Zoo
1801 East Chestnut Avenue (in Prentice Park), Santa Ana. (Take the First Street exit from the Santa Ana [5] Freeway.) (714) 835-7484. Daily, 10 A.M.–5 P.M. (until 6 P.M. in summer). The ticket booth closes one hour before the zoo. Adults, $2; seniors and ages 3–12, 75¢.

This small zoo contains about a hundred species of animals. The highlight is the fairly extensive monkey collection, which includes an unusual group of black-capped capuchins. Other exhibits include a nicely landscaped waterfowl pond and a moated enclosure for alpacas. There is a good petting zoo for children that houses a variety of farm animals. The zoo has picnic areas and a playground. Educational programs, including tours and a summer zoo camp, are also offered.

Dwight D. Eisenhower Park
Orange. (Take the Newport Freeway to the Lincoln Avenue exit. Go west about ¼ mile, turn north on Ocean View Avenue, and follow the signs to one of four small parking lots.) (714) 532-0383 (park information for city of Orange). Daily, daybreak–10 P.M. Free.

Twenty acres of grass, a four-acre lake, ducks to feed, and a two-hundred-yard stream in which children may play help to make this an enjoyable park. There are two play-equipment areas for small children, one of which—Astro City—is an intriguing complex of slides. Picnic tables and barbecues are found throughout the park.

Santiago Oaks Regional Park
End of Windes Drive, Orange. (Take Katella east from the 55 Freeway. Katella becomes Santiago Canyon Road. Go north on Windes Drive to the park.) (714) 538-4400. Park: Daily, 7 A.M.–8 P.M. Nature center: Daily, 7 A.M.–5 P.M.

A few miles east of downtown Orange is a 125-acre wilderness park. The park includes a creek and a pond where kids can fish. The nature center, located in a rustic cottage that was once a private residence, offers trail maps, mounted wildlife exhibits, and special programs. There is a small playground and picnic tables among the coast live oaks.

Irvine Regional Park
21501 East Chapman Avenue, Orange. (Located in Santiago Canyon, 6 miles east of the city of Orange. Take the Newport Freeway [55] to the Chapman off ramp. Go east on Chapman for approximately 5 miles to the park entrance.) (714) 633-8072 October 1 to March 31: Daily, 7 A.M.–sunset. April 1 to September 30: Daily, 7 A.M.–9 P.M. $1.50 per vehicle.

Irvine Regional Park is a lovely 477-acre park located in the hillsides of Santiago Canyon. The park, which dates from an 1897 gift to the county from James Irvine, Jr., contains both beautifully landscaped and wilderness areas. Among the features of the park are five children's playgrounds, two softball diamonds, a paved bicycle path, a nature trail, and a pretty lake where rowboats may be rented. Picnic areas with tables, barbecues, and nearby restrooms and parking are situated throughout the park.

The park also contains a small zoo that features animals native to the area. The zoo includes a petting area where children can make friends with goats and sheep. There is no charge to visit the zoo, which is open daily from 10 A.M. to 4 P.M. Another highlight of the park for children is the pony rides, which are available on weekends and holidays from 10 A.M. to 6 P.M. If your visit to the park is on a weekday, children can still see the ponies grazing in front of their stables.

Park rangers sponsor nature hikes, lectures, and workshops throughout the year. (Check with the park for the schedule.) Irving Regional Park is extremely well kept and peaceful. It is well worth a day's outing.

Fullerton/La Habra

Fullerton Museum Center
301 North Pomona Avenue (one block east of Harbor Boulevard between Chapman and Commonwealth Avenue), Fullerton. (714) 738-6545. Tuesday, Wednesday, Saturday, and Sunday, 11 A.M.–4 P.M.; until 9 P.M. Thursday and Friday. Adults, $2; students, $1; under 12, free.

The Fullerton Museum Center features changing exhibits in science, history, and the cultural arts. The recently renovated museum is housed in the former Fullerton Public Library, a historic W.P.A. building. Past exhibits have included Tinker Toy creations, teddy bears, and the history and science of holography.

Fullerton Youth Science Center
1700 East Wilshire Avenue, Room 26, (located at Ladera Vista Junior High School), Fullerton. (714) 526-1690. Saturday, 10 A.M.–noon. Telephone for weekday schedule. Free.

This is one of two museums—the other is Hacienda Heights—operated by the Youth Science Center, a nonprofit organization dedicated to science education. Both museums offer fascinating science exhibits, hands-on experiments, and helpful curators. The Youth Science Center also sponsors a variety of science classes, field trips, and nature hikes. Science classes at the Fullerton location have included kaleidoscope-making, the chemistry of fireworks and rockets, and the behavior of bees. Field trips have included a fossil dig, as well as excursions to hospitals, science labs, and manufacturing sites. There are also small museum stores at both locations.

La Habra Children's Museum

310 South Euclid Street, La Habra. (From the Orange Freeway [57] exit at Lambert Road and go west. Turn right on Euclid to museum.) (213) 905-9793. Tuesday–Saturday, 10 A.M.–4 P.M. Adults, $1.50; ages 3–16 and over 55, $1.

La Habra's 1923 Union Pacific railroad depot is now the home of the La Habra Children's Museum. The station has been restored as closely as possible to its original condition, and retired railroad cars are displayed on the tracks outside. You pay to enter at the old railroad ticket window. The former waiting room houses the nature-walk exhibit: an array of stuffed wild animals—including a bear, a mountain lion, a deer, an opossum, and many others—in a natural setting. The animals are out in the open at children's eye level and can be touched and petted. A special touch table in the corner includes such items as a dinosaur knuckle bone, a giant crab shell, and birds' nests. In the bee observatory, you can see a working beehive behind glass.

Operating in the former baggage room is an elaborate model train and village. Another permanent exhibit is a restored caboose with historic artifacts and a dummy conductor inside. The museum includes a play space—with tables and chairs, floor pillows, a piano, bookshelves, and a dollhouse—where younger children can look at books, draw, play games, try out the 1920s piano, present their own puppet shows, and ride a real Dentzel carousel.

Two large connecting galleries house the museum's changing exhibits. Temporary exhibits have included "Another Way to Be," in which nondisabled children explored what it is like to be handicapped; "The Musical Express," in which kids could put on costumes and perform in a dance studio; and "Building the Future," in which children created their own worlds from thousands of pieces of construction toys. A birthday party package is available from the museum. Parties are held Tuesday through Saturday from 4 to 6 P.M., after the museum closes to the public. The La Habra Children's Museum also sponsors a children's arts festival each spring with art workshops and exhibits, food, and special performances. The museum is located in Portola Park, which includes a children's playground.

Huntington Beach, Fountain Valley, and the Newport Beach Area

Huntington Central Park
Golden West and Talbert, Huntington Beach. (Take the San Diego Freeway to the Golden West Avenue off ramp and drive south about 3 miles to the park.) (714) 960-8847. Free.

An outstanding feature of this park for kids is Adventure Playground, a shallow, muddy lake where they can slip, slide, and raft. There are inner-tube swings, ropes to climb, and a muddy hill to slide down. Kids are also given wood, nails, and tools to hammer together forts, rafts, clubhouses, or whatever. The result is a child-built village that changes with the whims of young carpenters. Adventure Playground is open only during the summer, Monday–Saturday from 10 A.M. to 5 P.M. Admission is $1. (Adventure Playground is located near the library in the park. Turn east on Talbert from Golden West and park in the library parking lot. The telephone number for Adventure Playground is 714-842-7442.) You should dress your children in old clothes and bring a change of clothing. There is an outdoor shower.

The lushly beautiful Central Park also offers fishing in a fifteen-acre lake, six miles of paved bike and walking trails, and three children's playgrounds. There is a nature center (located on the west side of Golden West) where you can pick up a pamphlet for a one-mile nature walk.

Mile Square Park
Warner and Euclid streets, Fountain Valley. (Take the San Diego Freeway to Euclid Street and go north about a mile.) (714) 962-5549. Free.

This park offers two lakes (one for fishing), two children's playgrounds, picnic tables, and barbecues. There are paved paths for biking and skateboarding; and weekend activities, such as fishing derbies, are often scheduled.

The Children's Book Shop offers a huge selection of children's books and a well-trained staff of former teachers and librarians, who know how to help children find the right books for their reading levels and interests. The owner of the store, Sara Brant, was a reading specialist in the public schools for many years. In addition to the large hardback collection, the Children's Book Shop has a separate room stocked with paperbacks for children and young adults.

The store is bright and cheery, with stuffed bears, special decorations, small rocking chairs, a rocking horse, and small tables with toy and book baskets. They will special-order, gift-wrap, and mail books for you. A special service of the Children's Book Shop is their individual book club. You tell them the age and interests of the child to whom you are giving bookclub membership, and they will make an appropriate selection and mail it to him or her every month.

The Children's Book Shop hosts special children's-book-related parties, such as a summer Pooh party with stories and other activities throughout the day for different age groups. The store also offers a story hour program for three- to five-year-olds (which requires pre-registration). On Saturdays at 10 A.M., they offer a special story hour for five- to eight-year-olds; no pre-registration is necessary.

Newport Dunes Aquatic Park
Pacific Coast Highway and Jamboree Road, Newport Beach. (714) 644-0510. Daily, 9 A.M.–10 P.M. (Lifeguard on duty until 7 P.M.) Adults, $2; ages 11 and under, $1.

The calm, lifeguarded waters of this fifteen-acre lagoon make it an ideal place to take small children to swim. There are large stationary "whales" in the water to play on. Sailboats, kayaks, and paddleboats are available for rent. During the summer, it's best to come here on a weekday when the crowds are thinner.

Balboa Island Ferryboat Ride and Fun Zone
Take Pacific Coast Highway to Balboa Boulevard. The ferry is at the foot of Palm Street, off Balboa Boulevard on the Balboa Peninsula near Main Street. The ferry operates continuously throughout the day, and 24 hours a day during the summer. Pedestrians ride for 20¢ each way.

One of the few remaining ferries in California crosses the one thousand feet of water that separate Balboa Peninsula from Balboa Island in Newport Harbor. The short trip is fun for kids, and grownups love the view. The Fun Zone at the ferry's terminal on the peninsula side has been largely rebuilt. There is a Ferris wheel next to the water, a merry-go-round, bumper cars, and game arcades. Shiny new restaurants and snack places fit in comfortably with the old hot dog and frozen banana stands. At the foot of Main Street, the Balboa Pavilion, still looking much like it must have when it opened in 1905, houses the Tale of the Whale Restaurant (phone 714-673-4633), a good, moderately priced seafood restaurant with children's plates available.

Harbor cruises leave from the dock between the ferry landing and the Pavilion from 11 A.M.–6 P.M. during the summer, and hourly from noon to 3 P.M. the rest of the year. The cruises, which are narrated, last forty-five minutes. For more information, contact the Fun Zone Boat Company at (714) 673-0240. You can also cruise the harbor aboard the *Pavilion Queen* (phone: 714-673-5245), a double-deck Mississippi-style riverboat that leaves from the Balboa Pavilion from 11 A.M. to 5 P.M. on the hour in summer, and from noon to 3 P.M. the rest of the year. Newport Landing Sportfishing (just west of the ferry landing at 503 Edgewater; phone: 714-675-0550) offers half- and three-quarter-day fishing trips.

A few short blocks along Main Street from the Pavilion is the Balboa Pier, a good vantage point for watching the surfers in action. Ruby's at the end of the pier is a cute 1940s style cafe that also has a takeout window.

Sherman Library and Gardens
2647 East Coast Highway, Corona del Mar. (714) 673-2261. Gardens open daily, 10:30 A.M.–4 P.M. Adults, $2; ages 12–16, $1; under 12, free. Free to everyone on Mondays.

More than 850 different kinds of flowers and plants grow on this beautiful two-acre garden. There's a temperature-controlled conservatory that includes ferns, orchids, and carnivorous plants. Children will enjoy the touch-and-smell garden.

The Museum of Natural History and Science
2627 Vista del Oro, Newport Beach. (Exit I-405 at Jamboree Road. Go south to Eastbluff, turn right, then right again on Vista del Sol to Vista del Oro. Turn right. The museum is located in the former Eastbluff Elementary

School.) (714) 640-7120. *Tuesday–Saturday, 10 A.M.–5 P.M.; Sunday, 12–5 P.M. Adults, $2; children, $1; under 7, free.*

In the early 1970s, extensive Ice Age fossil beds were unearthed during excavations for new homes in the Eastbluff area of Newport Beach. Meanwhile, more fossils, including ancient camels and a totally preserved mammoth, were uncovered by other developers in Orange County. In 1974, the Natural History Foundation of Orange County was formed to help ensure the preservation of the fossils being uncovered.

The Museum of Natural History and Science is the Foundation's new museum. The museum, which includes a working fossil lab, is housed temporarily in a former elementary school. Eventually, the museum plans to have a site of its own.

The museum's approach is hands-on and experience oriented. Children are invited to gently touch a display of whale vertebrae or the model head of a tyrannosauras rex. In addition to fossils, exhibits cover insect, animal, bird, and marine life; rocks and minerals; and Southern Indian artifacts. Special activities for children include a December Dinosaur Party and Micro Pals, a program that introduces older children to microscopic study.

Irvine and South Orange County

A Kid's Place Annex

14775 Jeffrey Road (in Arbor Village Center), Irvine. (714) 551-1464. Monday–Thursday, 10 A.M.–8 P.M.; Friday, 10 A.M.–9 P.M.; Saturday, 10 A.M.–8 P.M.

This marvelously well-stocked bookstore has books for children from babies through the teenage years. There is also a large, excellent selection of books on being a parent and on every sort of trauma that parents and children might face. The staff is composed of former teachers and librarians, and every book in the store has been read by at least one of the staff. A special children's area features a castle that kids can enter with their books. A Kid's Place Annex also has story hours for ages three and up (advance sign-up is necessary), and author discussions for older children.

Turtle Rock Nature Center

Turtle Rock Community Park, Turtle Rock Drive at Sunnyhill, Irvine. (Take Culver Drive south from I-405. Go south on Culver Drive to Bonita Canyon, turn east on Bonita Canyon to Sunnyhill, and go north to park.) (714) 854-8151. Monday–Thursday, 2–5 P.M.; Saturday and Sunday, 12–5 P.M. Free.

A five-acre wilderness area within the Turtle Rock Community Parks gives native plants and animals—as well as children—a refuge from the surrounding suburban bustle. Children can walk through the nature center on paved walkways, catching sight of squirrels and other small animals. There is a stream that leads into a duck-inhabited pond. Other animals, including snakes, turtles, rabbits, and raccoons—as well as nature exhibits—can be seen at the nature-center building.

Heritage Hill Historical Park

25151 Serrano Road, El Toro. (From I-5 south of Irvine, take the Lake Forest Drive exit. Go east on Lake Forest Drive about 2 miles, then turn left on Serrano Road to the entrance and parking area.) (714) 855-2028. Open daily, 8 A.M.–5 P.M. Tours of the historical structures: Tuesday–Friday at 2 P.M.; Saturday, Sunday, and holidays, 11 A.M. and 2 P.M. Free.

Heritage Hill is Orange County's first historical park. The park's four acres were once a small part of a 10,688-acre land grant awarded to Don José Serrano in 1842. His adobe, which still stands, is one of four restored historic structures in the park. The others are El Toro's 1890 grammar school, complete with wooden desks and a pendulum clock; the 1891 St. George's Episcopal Church, with original stained-glass windows; and the 1908 Bennett Ranch House. You can see the buildings, which all have period furnishings, on a sixty- to ninety-minute free guided tour. Children need to be about ten or older to find the tour interesting.

    The park includes a visitors' center with exhibits on the county's history from the rancho period to the beginning of the citrus industry. Picnic tables are available, although shade can be limited. There is a children's playground in the adjacent Serrano Creek Park, which also includes picnic areas and hiking trails.

Tucker Wildlife Sanctuary

29322 Modjeska Canyon Road, Modjeska Canyon. (Take the El Toro exit from I-5 in El Toro, south of Irvine. Go left on El Toro road 11 miles to Mod-

jeska Canyon Road. Turn right and go about 2 miles to the sanctuary.) (714) 649-2760. Daily, 9 A.M.–4 P.M. Admission, $1.50.

Children interested in birds and animals can sit on benches and watch the birds as they come to feed from the bins of seed arranged in a row facing the special observation porch. The sanctuary is most famous for its many hummingbirds, although at least twenty-six other kinds of birds make year-round homes here. A naturalist is on duty to explain the types of birds you'll see. You and your children can also explore the sanctuary's ten acres where, in addition to birds, you can spot frogs, salamanders, snakes, and other small animals.

Wild Rivers
8800 Irvine Center Drive (adjacent to Irvine Meadows Amphitheater), Laguna Hills. (Exit I-405 at Irving Center Drive in Irvine and go south.) (714) 768-9453. Mid-May–early June and mid-September–early October: Open weekends and holidays, 11 A.M.–5 P.M. Mid-June–early September: Daily, 10 A.M.–8 P.M. Ages 10 and older, $13.75; ages 3–9, $10.75; senior citizens, $6.75; 2 and under, free. After 4 P.M. (and for spectators during the day), $6.75. Parking, $2.

Wild Rivers is an African-themed water park on the old Lion Country Safari site. The park has three water-attraction areas: Thunder Cove features two large wave-action pools for body-boarding and inner-tubing. The high-speed slides and water thrill rides appealing to teenagers and young adults are located on Wild Rivers Mountain. The third area, Explorers' Island, caters to children and families. There's a lagoon with scaled-down rides for children under fifty-four inches tall. A separate pool, less than a foot deep, features a gorilla swing and an elephant slide. There is also a pool for adults and a quarter-mile loop for slow-moving inner tubes.

Life vests are available at no extra charge. Lifeguards are stationed throughout the park, although parents should still keep a close eye on young children. Food service is available. (You are not permitted to bring your own food, beach chairs, inner tubes, etc.). Rates are reduced significantly for people entering the park after 4 P.M.

Laguna Art Museum
307 Cliff Drive (at the intersection of Pacific Coast Highway), Laguna Beach. (714) 494-6531. Tuesday–Sunday, 11 A.M.–5 P.M. Adults, $2; seniors and students, $1; under 12, free.

Sitting on a hill by the ocean, the Laguna Art Museum features a special children's corner with rotating exhibitions of artwork created by children. The art is professionally framed and displayed like the other artwork in the museum. The attractive museum has a permanent collection of regional and contemporary art and changing exhibitions.

Mission San Juan Capistrano
San Juan Capistrano (one block off the San Juan Capistrano off ramp from I-5). (714) 493-1111. Daily, 7:30 A.M.–5 P.M. Adults, $2; under 12, $1.

Founded in 1776, Mission San Juan Capistrano is among the most beautiful of all the California missions. It is best known for the swallows that return to their nests here every year on St. Joseph's Day, March 19, and always depart on the day of the mission's patron saint, October 25. The majority of birds really do keep to this schedule, and it's well worth a trip here on March 19 to see them arrive.

The mission has two churches. One, a once-magnificent cathedral, was destroyed in an earthquake in 1812. You can explore its ruins and see the mud nests of the swallows in the broken arches. The other, a modest adobe, is believed to be the oldest church in California; Mass is still performed there daily.

The lovely mission grounds are full of flowers, shade trees, and rose-covered walls. Children will enjoy feeding the white doves that cluster on the grounds and eat right out of one's hand. Four bells ring out in a campanile each day at noon. Children will also enjoy the mission's tanning vat ruins, kitchens, padres' sleeping quarters, and small jail.

Orange County Marine Institute
24200 Dana Point Harbor Drive, Dana Point. (From I-5, take the Pacific Coast Highway/California 1 off ramp. Follow California 1 north to Dana Point, then go left at Dana Point Harbor Drive.) (714) 831-3850. Daily, 10 A.M.–3:30 P.M. Free.

Dana Point Harbor, a lovely natural cove surrounded by dramatic cliffs, was once the only major port between San Diego and Santa Barbara. Ships would anchor here to trade New England goods to the local ranchers and the mission at San Juan Capistrano in exchange for cowhides tossed from the cliffs. In 1835 the harbor was visited by Richard Henry Dana, a crewman aboard the sailing ship *Pilgrim,* who later wrote about his adventures in *Two Years Before the Mast.*

Today, you can see a replica of the *Pilgrim* anchored in the harbor below the Orange County Marine Institute. (The *Pilgrim* is owned by the Marine Institute and is used as a living-history laboratory to give groups of children aged nine to thirteen a sense of what it was like to be a nineteenth-century sailor.)

The Orange County Marine Institute is an educational facility for children. Inside the building are displays on marine life that are enriched by the active participation of museum docents and volunteer marine biologists. One laboratory room is devoted to whales and includes the skeleton of a gray whale. In the other room, a marine biologist is on hand to help kids explore the institute's tide pool.

The Marine Institute also sponsors a variety of educational programs for children and their parents. Parents and their children aged four to seven can explore the local marine environment together in a series of four classes, and older children can participate in summer sea camps. The whole family can enjoy a summer "expedition" on a marine research vessel, 10 there is much more. On the last two weekends in February and the first in March, the Institute holds a children's whale festival. The Institute also offers birthday parties that include a program with a marine biologist for children four to eleven years old.

A beautiful park is adjacent to the museum, with green lawns, picnic facilities, and a small swimming beach with a cordoned area for waders.

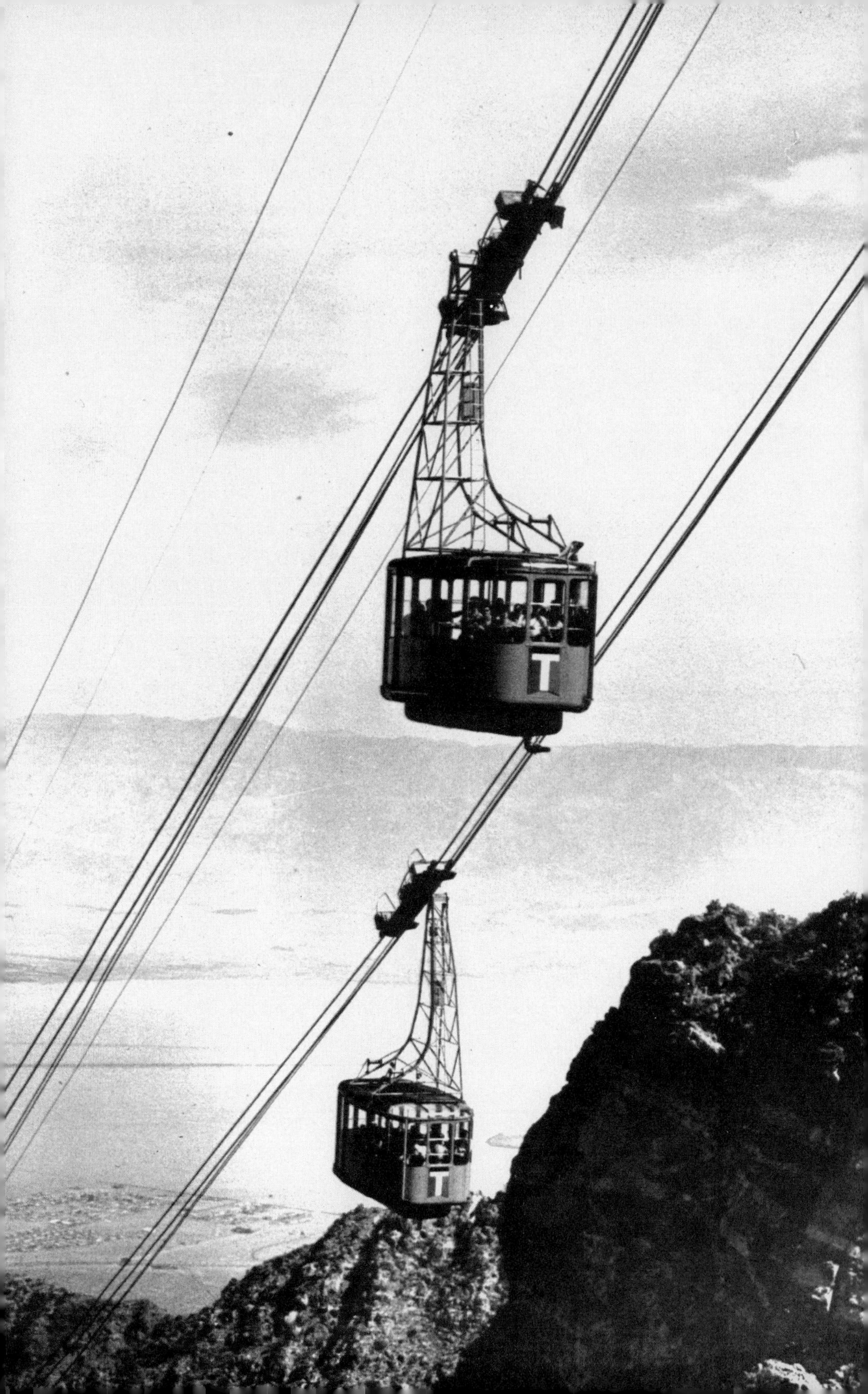
T
T

Riverside and San Bernardino Counties

Two great deserts, splendid mountain ranges, spectacular lakes, famous resorts, and large urban areas all come together in Riverside and San Bernardino counties. The San Bernardino Mountains, stretching fifty miles across, are the highest of the mountain ranges surrounding Los Angeles. Popular mountain-resort areas built around two beautiful lakes—Arrowhead and Big Bear—offer summer camping, hiking, fishing, and water sports; wintertime brings snow sports and activities. The less-well-known Crestline resort area offers families activities centered around Lake Gregory. Silverwood Lake, north of Crestline, is a relatively new state recreation area offering scenic picnic sites, swimming beaches, fishing, and boating. The San Jacinto Mountains to the south (both ranges are included in the San Bernardino National Forest) include the lovely resort area of Idlewild.

Adjacent to the San Jacinto Mountains, the Palm Springs area offers children an introduction to the wonders of the Colorado Desert. Usually thought of as a playground for adults, this famous resort area offers a number of fascinating adventures for children, including the Palm Springs Aerial Tramway's breathtaking ride up the face of San Jacinto Mountain.

The vast Mojave Desert can be explored from a base in Barstow. Among the attractions for families in the Barstow area is the restored 1880s Calico Ghost Town.

The urban areas of Riverside and San Bernardino also offer their share of enjoyable destinations: great parks, historical attractions, and museums housing everything from mounted birds to trolley cars.

Take the Aerial Tramway from the desert of Palm Springs to the top of 8500-foot Mount San Jacinto.

In and Around Riverside and San Bernardino

Riverside Art Museum
3425 Seventh Street, Riverside. (From Riverside Freeway south, exit at Seventh Street; going north, exit at University Avenue and turn west on Seventh Street.) (714) 684-7111. Monday–Friday, 10 A.M.–5 P.M.; Saturday, 10 A.M.–4 P.M. Free.

The Spanish Revival-style building housing the Riverside Art Center and Museum was originally designed as a YWCA in 1929 by Julia Morgan, the chief architect of Hearst Castle. Downstairs is a lovely lobby with a tile fireplace, and several galleries displaying the work of Southern California artists. Of special interest to children are the rooms upstairs, where they can see art created by children in the museum's art classes. The classes, available for children three and up, are taught by professionals and are geared to the children's age levels. In a recent session, children eight and older learned printmaking techniques, while five- through seven-year-olds created castles of clay, and preschool children experimented with a variety of mediums. Tuition for the classes averages about $40 for a ten-week session of weekly classes.

Lunch is served in the museum's courtyard (or by the fireplace on rainy days) on weekdays from 11 P.M. to 2 P.M. Kids are welcome.

Riverside Municipal Museum
3720 Orange Street (at Seventh Street), downtown Riverside. (714) 782-5273. Tuesday–Friday, 9 A.M.–5 P.M.; Saturday and Sunday, 1–5 P.M. Free.

Once Riverside's post office, this pleasant museum contains local history and natural history exhibits. There are displays of area wildlife, local Indian artifacts, guns and tools of early settlers, and—especially interesting—the skeleton of a sabertooth cat in a case on the floor, where it can easily be examined by children.

Heritage House
8193 Magnolia Avenue (about ten minutes south of downtown, between Adams and Jefferson), Riverside. (714) 689-1333. Tuesday–Thursday, noon–2:30 P.M.; Sunday, noon–3 P.M. Donation requested: Adults, $1; children, 50¢.

This marvelous-looking Victorian house was completed in 1891 for the family of a citrus grower. It is now owned by the Riverside Museum, and you can see the inside on a tour. Outstanding features of the home include a beautiful staircase, gas lamps (the house was one of the first in Riverside to have them), and tile fireplaces in every room. The house is furnished with period pieces, some of them original. Since you must see the house on a tour—where you may hear about the legend of a ghost who sometimes haunts the house—and since there is obviously no touching, a visit here is best appreciated by older children.

Sherman Indian Museum
9019 Magnolia Avenue, Riverside. (714) 359-9434. Monday–Friday, 1–3 P.M. Free, but donation appreciated.

The Sherman Indian Institute, established in 1902, was originally a school for Indians of Southern California. Later it expanded to include Indians from southwestern reservations. Today it is a boarding school for Native American high school students from the southwest, Oregon, and the Dakotas.

Housed in the last remaining building of the original Institute, this museum displays artifacts of the various Indian cultures represented at the Institute throughout the years. In addition to pottery, baskets, beadwork, and other artifacts, the museum contains dioramas of leading Indian cultures.

Fairmount Park
2624 Fairmount Boulevard (near intersection of Highway 60 and Market Street), Riverside. (714) 782-5301. Free.

This pleasant city park surrounds Lake Evans. You can boat on the lake and fish if you have a license, although there are no boat rentals. The 183-acre park has playgrounds, picnic facilities, and a rose garden. There is also a wilderness area with hiking trails and a nature study trail.

March Field Museum
March Air Force Base, Riverside. (Follow signs on I-215 or Highway 60 to March Air Force Base. Obtain a pass from the visitors' center at the main gate.) (714) 655-3725. Monday–Friday, 10 A.M.–4 P.M.; Saturday and Sunday, noon–4 P.M. Free.

March Field, established in 1918, is the oldest Air Force base in the western United States. Exhibits on display inside and around the museum depict the evolution of air power and the history of the base. Starting with World War I uniforms and artifacts, the history of the Air Force is traced to the present. (One exhibit lets you listen in on a recorded mission briefing for a World War II bombing run.) More than thirty historic planes are displayed, including bombers, fighters, and trainers from World War II through the Vietnam era. The museum runs a shuttle weekdays at 1 P.M. and weekends at 2 P.M. to take visitors to those planes parked on the flight line. Included are a U-2 spy plane, an F-100 supersonic fighter, and the B-52 bomber.

Lake Perris
On Ramona Expressway off I-15E, southeast of Riverside. (714) 657-0676. Daily, 6 A.M.–8 P.M. (open until 10 P.M. in summer). Day use, $4 per vehicle.

Lake Perris is a large manmade lake offering boating, swimming beaches, fishing, and picnicking. The picnic areas include tables and grills. There are also playgrounds, restrooms, hiking and bicycle trails, and a snack bar. Because the park is relatively new, the trees are still small. Facilities are available for recreation vehicles, and there are also boat-launching areas and a boat supply shop. Lake Perris is a popular recreation spot, so you may find a line to enter during the summer.

Orange Empire Railway Museum
2201 South A Street, Perris (just south of Riverside on I-15E). (714) 657-2605. Grounds open daily, 9 A.M.–5 P.M. Trains and trolleys operate Saturday, Sunday, and holidays, 11 A.M.–5 P.M. Grounds free. All-day train pass: Adults, $3.50; ages 6–11, $2; under 6, free.

In the late 1950s, as the last streetcar and interurban rail lines were closing in Southern California, a group of young men dedicated to preserving this passing technology founded the Orange Empire Railway Museum. Since then, a large number of cars have found their way to the museum, including steam locomotives and wooden passenger trolleys; freight, maintenance, and construction cars; and even an old Los Angeles funeral car. Museum members restored the cars and laid all the tracks.

The outdoor museum is the size of a small town, and it is a wonderful place for kids. Construction is constantly in progress. On a weekend visit, children can see the actual work of building and maintaining a railroad. They may see crews laying rails, setting poles, stringing trolley wire, or restoring an old train or trolley car. In addition to seeing the trains, children can wander around and see a variety of off-rail equipment and old trucks.

Best of all, they can ride the old cars. Several different streetcars and trolleys are usually running on a weekend. An all-day pass allows you to go from one to another, riding as many times as you wish. The old cars, which still have their original advertising posters above the seats, are staffed by uniformed volunteer motormen and conductors who are wonderfully serious about what they do.

The museum has a shaded picnic ground and a small children's playground. Dress for warm weather, wear old clothes, bring lunch, and plan to spend the day.

Prado Regional Park
16700 South Euclid Avenue, Chino. (From I-10, take Euclid Avenue south; or take Highway 71 north from the Riverside Freeway or south from the Pomona Freeway.) (714) 597-4260. Daily, 7:30 A.M.–dusk. $3 per car.

This 2,200-acre park is nestled in a rural area dotted with cattle and dairy farms. Kids can see the cattle grazing from the car window along Highway 71 (leading to the park from the Pomona Freeway), and you can smell the farms from the park. The park has a number of large grassy areas surrounding a central fifty-six-acre lake. Fishing ($3 permit for ages seven and over) is offered, and paddleboat and rowboat rentals are available. There are individual and group picnic areas with tables and grills, and several small attractive playgrounds. The park also has riding stables and trails and a well-equipped recreational-vehicle camping area.

Planes of Fame Air Museum
7000 Merrill Avenue, Chino. (Located at the Chino Airport. From the Pomona Freeway [60] take the Euclid Avenue exit [Highway 83] south to Merrill. The air museum is in the northeast section of the airport.) (714) 597-3722. Daily, 9 A.M.–5 P.M. Adults, $4.95; ages 5–11, $1.95; under 5, free.

More than fifty rare aircraft from the beginning of aviation to the space age are housed in two large hangars that make up the Planes of Fame Air Museum. You'll see a Japanese Zero, an M-109, a B-17, and many more planes in flyable condition.

San Bernardino County Museum
2024 Orange Tree Lane, Redlands. (From eastbound I-10, take the California Street exit, turn left on California Street, and go about two blocks to the museum.) (714) 825-4825. Tuesday–Saturday, 9 A.M.–5 P.M.; Sunday, 1–5 P.M. Free.

Located in a bright geodesic-domed building, the San Bernardino County Museum houses a remarkable mounted-bird exhibit and the world's largest display of birds' eggs. More than twenty thousand eggs are exhibited, as well as nests from all over the world. Other displays cover the prehistoric people of California, the California Indians, and the geological and fossil history of the local area. Specimens of local wildlife, such as snakes, lizards, birds, and small mammals are also on display. Kids will enjoy playing in the old army tank out in back.

Oak Glen Apple Farms/Oak Tree Village
Oak Glen Road, Oak Glen. (From Los Angeles, take I-10 past Redlands to the Yucaipa Boulevard exit. Take Yucaipa Boulevard east to Oak Glen Road and turn left. Oak Tree Village is about 5 miles up the hill.) (714) 797-4020. Daily, 10 A.M.–5 P.M.

Oak Glen, a mile into the foothills of the San Bernardino Mountains, is the Southland's largest apple growing region. Indeed, during a fall visit, when the air is crisp and the leaves are in vibrant color, you'll feel as if you have been transported to New England.

Most of the apples grown here are sold directly to the public; many of the orchard owners sell their apples in roadside stands. A few of the orchards—including Linda Vista Orchards, Riley's Log Cabin Farm and Orchard, and Apple Creek Orchard—will allow you to pick your own apples. Apple cider is made daily at some of the orchards, and there are places where visitors can watch the presses in action. Most of the orchards also have tree-shaded tables for picnickers.

Oak Tree Village, an area of restaurants and shops near the center of Oak Tree Road, offers children a small animal park where, for a quarter, they can see deer, peacocks, hens, and other small animals. Mountain Town, another group of shops near Oak Tree Village, offers kids a small nature museum containing a variety of stuffed wildlife. Another interesting stop along Oak Glen Road is the old schoolhouse, which contains historical displays and information on apple growing. Near the schoolhouse kids can see an old wagon and early apple farming equipment.

Apple harvest season lasts from September to December. You will want to schedule your visit for a time *other* than a weekend in October, when Oak Glen gets very crowded. Visits to Oak Glen are also enjoyable in the winter when snow may fall—the roads are kept cleared—and during the spring (mid-April through mid-May), when the apple trees are in blossom. If you come in the spring, you might want to combine the visit with a trip to nearby Cherry Valley where some of the farms permit you to pick cherries.

Santa's Village
Skyforest. (From San Bernardino, take I-215 north from I-10. Go about 4 miles to Mountain Resorts turnoff. Continue on Mountain Resorts Freeway to Waterman Avenue exit. Turn left on Waterman, which is Highway 18; the village is on Highway 18, 2 miles past the Lake Arrowhead turnoff.) (714) 337-2481. Mid-June to mid-September and mid-November through December: Open daily, 10 A.M.–5 P.M. Closed March 1 to Memorial Day weekend. Rest of year: Open weekend and holidays, 10 A.M.–5 P.M., weather permitting. Ages 3–16, $7.50; ages 17 and over, $6.60; under 2, free. Admission includes unlimited rides.

Children can visit Santa Claus year round at Santa's Village in the San Bernardino Mountains. The village is essentially designed for small children. Kids can pet and feed Santa's reindeer and other tame animals. There are a number of rides for young children, including a candy-cane sleigh ride, train and antique car rides, a bumblebee monorail, a merry-go-round, a Ferris wheel, bobsleds, and pony and burro rides. The rides are all old and slow, but small children seem to love them. Other attractions include a puppet theater and toy and doll shops. The village includes a pantry, a bakery, a candy shop, and snack bars, and there is gift-shop browsing for the grownups. Children's birthday-party packages are also available. Santa's Village is rather worn and old-fashioned, but it is absolutely charming to young children. The village, which is located in a spectacular mountain setting, gets very crowded on weekends between Thanksgiving and Christmas.

In and Around Palm Springs

Palm Springs Aerial Tramway
From Los Angeles, take I-10 to Highway 111 to Palm Springs city limits and Tramway Road. The tramway's valley station is 3½ miles from Highway 111. (619) 325-1391. Monday–Friday, 10 A.M.–9:15 P.M. Saturday and Sunday, 8 A.M.–9:15 P.M. Cars depart at least every half hour. The last car up to Mountain Station is at 7:30 P.M. (In summer, the last car up to Mountain Station is at 9 P.M., and the last car down the mountain is at 10:45 P.M.) Adults, $12.95 round trip; ages 3–12, $7.95. Free parking.

In eighteen minutes, an eighty-passenger car on the Palm Springs Tramway carries you safely up the side of Mount San Jacinto, from cactus and desert sand to the cool air and evergreen trees of 8,516-foot-altitude Mount San Jacinto State Park. The ride up is breathtaking. At times, the car heads directly into the jutting face of the mountain and then rises around it in a sharp uplift. The view of the valley below and the changing terrain is spectacular. (Try to be near the head of the line boarding the tram so you can find your children a place next to the window. You must stand on the tram ride, but there are benches next to the window where kids can stand to see out.)

At the San Jacinto Station are a restaurant, a snack bar, a game room, snow equipment rentals, and observation decks that provide a view of the entire valley, extending to the Salton Sea, forty-five miles away. The top of Mount San Jacinto is a six-mile hike from the tram station. Behind the station is a walkway leading to a recreation area; the walkway is heated in the winter to keep it free of snow. Picnic facilities are available in summer; in winter months there is a play area where toboggans and snow saucers can be rented.

Palm Springs Desert Museum
101 Museum Drive, Palm Springs. (From Palm Canyon Drive in downtown Palm Springs, turn west on either Andreas Road or Tahquitz-McCallum Way and go two blocks to the museum.) (619) 325-7186. Tuesday–Friday, 10 A.M.–4 P.M.; Saturday and Sunday, 10 A.M.–5 P.M.; closed Mondays and during summer. Adults, $4; seniors, students, and children aged 6–17, $2; 5 and under, free. Free (except for special exhibits) the first Tuesday of the month. Free parking.

Housed in a beautiful seventy-five-thousand-square-foot, split-level, cantilevered building, the Palm Springs Desert Museum is devoted to art, natural science, and performing arts. The art galleries feature constantly changing exhibitions from collections around the world. The museum gives art classes for local schoolchildren and frequently displays their work. There are also two lovely sunken sculpture gardens and a main-level sculpture court that children might enjoy seeing.

It is the museum's natural science galleries, however, that will impress children most. One particularly appealing exhibit is a long diorama of the desert's life by day and by night. It's out in the open and at children's eye level. They can activate the display by pushing a button to see animals such as a roadrunner, a coyote, and a bobcat in their daytime and nighttime environments. A button-activated desert wildflower exhibit, Cahuilla Indian dioramas and artifacts, a display of Salton Sea birds, and a self-activated desert slide show also invite exploration.

The museum's staff conducts nature field trips every Friday from the first Friday in October to the last in May. The trips, which vary in length and subject, leave from the museum's north parking lot at 9 A.M. Call the museum for information.

Village Green Heritage Center
221 South Palm Canyon Drive, Palm Springs. (619) 323-8297. Wednesday and Sunday, noon–3 P.M.; Thursday, Friday, and Saturday, 10 A.M.–4 P.M. Closed June to mid-October. Adults, $1; children, free.

The Village Green Heritage Center is a new grassy plaza containing Miss Cornelia White's House, the 1893 home of a pioneer Palm Springs woman, and the McCallum Adobe, the first house built by a white settler in Palm Springs. The McCallum Adobe features changing exhibits of local historical artifacts. Displays that would interest children might include an antique doll carriage and doll, a spinning wheel, an early typewriter, costumes, and toys from the early 1900s.

Miss Cornelia White's House, built from railroad ties, was the home of a remarkable woman who wore pants and boots long before it was acceptable dress for women and who taught political science, carpentry, and plumbing. The house has been extremely well kept. Inside you'll see an old-fashioned hand-crank telephone (the first phone in Palm Springs); the delightful old kitchen with its antique stove, charcoal iron, and original water pump on the sink; and the bedroom, where the chamber pot is visible under the bed.

Palm Springs Public Library
Main branch: 300 South Sunrise Way, Palm Springs. (619) 323-8291. Welwood Murray Branch: 100 South Palm Canyon Drive, Palm Springs. (619) 323-8296.

The Palm Springs Public Library system has a comprehensive collection that includes eighteen thousand children's books. The library has weekly programs for children; call for the schedule. In-library services are free. Borrowing privileges are $20 per year to Palm Springs visitors.

Moorten's Botanical Gardens
1701 South Palm Canyon Drive (two blocks south of East Palm Canyon Drive), Palm Springs. (619) 327-6555. Monday–Saturday, 9 A.M.–4:30 P.M.; Sunday, 10 A.M.–4 P.M. Adults, $1.50; ages 7–16, 50¢; under 7, free.

More than two thousand varieties of cactus and other desert plants from every desert in the world are arranged according to region in this botanical garden. Kids will enjoy picking out personalities in the cacti. Some even have names, such as the Bearded Grandfather. Rabbits, chipmunks, and other small animals live on the garden's four acres and can often be seen scurrying through the grounds. There are also displays of rocks, petrified wood, and a real dinosaur's footprint. Kids can climb on the wooden wagons on display, and they'll enjoy watching the live turtles.

Oasis Waterpark
1500 Gene Autry Trail (between Ramon Road and Highway 111; 6 miles south of I-10), Palm Springs. (619) 325-7873. Mid-March to early September: Daily, at least 11 A.M.–6 P.M. Early September through October: Weekends, at least 11 A.M.–6 P.M. Ages 12 and over, $12.95; ages 4–11, $9.95; under 4, free.

This twenty-one-acre water park in the desert offers seven slides of various configurations and speeds. There is a very large wave pool with waves of up to four feet for inland surfing. For a more relaxing time, you can float in a slow-moving inner tube along a six-hundred-foot loop. There is a rather small play area for young children, called Squirt City, that has little water slides. Plan to keep a close eye on young children.

Palm Springs Bicycle Trails

Palm Springs has more than thirty-five miles of bicycle trails, clearly marked by blue and white signs. A free bike-trails map is available at the Leisure Center in the Sunrise Park complex (bounded by Sunrise Way, Ramon Road, Baristo Road, and Pavilion Way; phone 619-323-8272). Bike rentals are available at Burnett's Bicycle Barn, 429 South Sunrise Way (at Ramon Road, in the shopping center, year round; phone 619-325-7844), and at most other Palm Springs bicycle shops.

Horseback Riding/Smoketree Stables
2500 Toledo Avenue, Palm Springs. (619) 327-1372.

Smoke Tree Stables rents horse to riders of all abilities. Miles of bridle trails provide adult riders and kids with wonderful views of the desert and plenty of fun. Guides are available, and overnight pack trips can be arranged.

Palm Springs Swim Center/Sunrise Park
Sunrise Park: Bounded by Sunrise Way, Ramon Road, Baristo Road and Pavilion Way, Palm Springs. Open daily. Free. Swim Center: Located in Sunrise Park. (619) 323-8278. Daily, 11 A.M.–5 P.M. Adults, $2; 12 and under, $1. Season passes are available.

The Palm Springs Swim Center features a fifty-meter, Olympic-sized public swimming pool with two 1-meter diving boards and one 3-meter board. There is a separate swimming section for children, as well as spacious lawns and a sun deck. Swimming instruction for children and adults is also given.

The Swim Center is located in Sunrise Park, a lushly landscaped thirty-eight-acre park complex that includes a large playground, the main branch of the Palm Springs public library, the Palm Springs Parks and Recreation headquarters, and the Palm Springs Angels Baseball Stadium and practice field, as well as picnic facilities. Organized activities for children, summer concerts and family film series, and Fourth of July fireworks are also held in the park. (Phone the Palm Springs Parks, Recreation, and Library Department at 619-323-8272 for the schedule.)

Palm Canyon/Andreas Canyon
Five miles south of Palm Springs. (From Palm Springs, take the toll road at the end of South Palm Canyon Drive.) (619) 325-5673. Daily, 9 A.M.–4 P.M. Closed from June to September. Adults, $3; ages 6–12, 75¢. Admission price includes both canyons.

The native Indian residents of the Palm Springs area still own and control large sections of land here. The Agua Caliente Indian Reservation comprises thirty-two thousand acres in and around Palm Springs. The tribal council has reserved a portion of the reservation south of Palm Springs, including two magnificent canyons, for visitors to see. Palm Canyon is lined for a distance of seven miles by more than three thousand Washington palms, estimated to be from fifteen hundred to two thousand years old. This splendid canyon can be seen from points on the rim or by hiking down into the canyon itself. There is a picnic area.

Living Desert Reserve
47-900 Portola Avenue, Palm Desert. (From I-10, take the Thousand Palms-Ramon Road exit and follow the signs to Palm Desert, traveling south on Bob Hope Drive to Highway 111 and east to the reserve.) (619) 346-5694. Daily, 9 A.M.–5 P.M. Closed June, July, and August. Adults, $3.50; ages 3–15, $1; 2 and under, free.

One thousand acres of beautiful California desert are set aside and protected from development in the Living Desert Reserve. The reserve is home to a wide variety of desert plants and animals. Tortoises, lizards, hawks, owls, and bighorn sheep are kept in enclosures. You can see other animals such as rabbits, roadrunners, and hummingbirds roaming freely on the reserve. Quail, doves, and other desert birds can be seen in a walk-through aviary. Acres of botanical gardens recreate different deserts of the world.

The Pearl McManus Center, through which you enter the reserve, has exhibits of small live animals in natural habitats. Especially interesting is the "Desert at Night" exhibit, a dark room where you can watch the nighttime activity of desert animals. (I couldn't take my eyes off the tiny deer mice scampering around in fast motion.)

The reserve has an excellent trail system with more than six miles of self-guided trails, permitting you to choose from walks of varied length and attractions. (The reserve eventually hopes to increase its trail system to a total of ten or fifteen miles.) There is a shaded picnic area, and there are water fountains and shaded areas throughout the grounds.

Lake Cahuilla
Located south of Indio, at the intersection of Jefferson and Fifty-eighth streets, 9 miles south of Highway 111. (From Palm Springs, take Highway 111 southeast to Jefferson Street outside of Indio and turn south.) (714) 787-2553. Daily, 6 A.M.–8 P.M. Picnics/swimming: $2 per vehicle (add 50¢ per person after the fourth person). Fishing: Adults, $3; ages 10–17, $2; under 10, free.

In the brilliant desert sun, Lake Cahuilla shimmers a cool, inviting turquoise. Surrounded by date trees, this huge (135-acre surface) lake offers an as-yet uncrowded desert escape. There is swimming in the lake and a special play area for children on the beach. Striped bass, channel catfish, and (in winter) rainbow trout can be caught in the fishing areas of the lake (license required). Picnic tables and barbecues are available, and there are a lot of grassy, shaded areas around the lake. There are hiking trails for those who want to explore the desert. Family campsites and RV hookups are available. (Phone 714-787-2553 during business hours for reservations.)

Shields Date Gardens
80-225 Highway 111, Indio. (619) 347-0996. Daily, 8 A.M.–6 P.M. Free.

The Coachella Valley is known as the date capital of the world. Many varieties of dates are grown here, packaged, and shipped all over the world. You can take a self-guided tour of the Shields Date Gardens to see the cultivation process. Inside their sales building are booths and a large old-fashioned counter where you can sample a date shake or some of their black-date ice cream. In an auditorium, they show a continuous, free, but dated (no pun intended) slide show on the romance and sex life of the date.

Jensen's Date and Citrus Gardens
80-653 Highway 111, Indio. (619) 347-3897. Daily, 9 A.M.–5 P.M. Free.

From the highway, Jensen's pink-walled gardens resemble the Garden of Allah. The gift shop is situated in a lovely garden with roses and fruit trees. It's a nice stop for children because it is an opportunity to see a variety of fruit-laden trees up close. Big grapefruits hang from one, blood oranges from another. There are date trees, of course, with the ladders used for gathering the fruit. The trees are all labeled, and the date-growing process is explained. Inside the gift shop you can enjoy date shakes or fresh citrus juice.

Cabot's Old Indian Pueblo and Museum

67-616 East Desert View Avenue, Desert Hot Springs. (Desert Hot Springs is just north of Palm Springs. Take Palm Drive north to Desert View Avenue and turn east.) (619) 329-7610. Saturday and Sunday, 9:30 A.M.–4 P.M. Weekdays by appointment. Adults, $2; seniors, $1.50; ages 6–16, $1; under 6, free.

At the age of sixty, Cabot Yerxa began building this thirty-five room Hopi-style pueblo by hand, using material he found in the desert. When he died twenty years later, in 1965, he was still building. Yerxa was an unusual man who sold tobacco in Alaska during the Gold Rush, traveled widely, lived with the Indians of the southwest, and came to live in the desert. His idea to build a pueblo for his home came from his affection for the Hopi Indians. One of the reasons for building it was to make the Hopis who visited him feel at home.

The pueblo, built out of the side of the mountain, is similar to that of the Hopis, except Yerxa did not use ladders as the Indians did. Instead he built narrow twisting staircases that go up from room to room. The structure is four stories high and contains 150 windows and sixty-five doors. The pueblo has been preserved and kept open to the public; you can see it on a guided tour.

You'll go through Yerxa's kitchen with its water pump and wash basin, the Hopi prayer room, and the living room with its dirt floor. You can climb the narrow stairs to his wife's quarters on the next floor. Some of the pueblo's rooms are used as a museum where you will see Indian headdresses, Geronimo's wristband, Kit Carson's money belt, Buffalo Bill's chair, and a 1914 Troy motorcycle. Many other things are also displayed, including tools and animal skins used by the Alaskan Eskimoes. (Yerxa lived with the Eskimoes in Alaska. Their treatment of his frostbitten hands left him with a deep affection for their people.) Other displays include desert animal traps, pack saddles, and pictures taken during the Gold Rush.

Kingdom of the Dolls

66071 Pierson Boulevard, Desert Hot Springs. (From Palm Springs or I-10, take either Indian Avenue or Palm Drive north. From Indian Drive, turn right on Pierson Boulevard. From Palm Drive, turn left on Pierson Boule-

vard.) (619) 329-5137. *Tuesday–Sunday, noon–6 P.M.; summer hours by appointment. Adults, $2.50; children, 75¢.*

Using small dolls, cardboard boxes, egg cartons, paint, Popsicle sticks, bits of cloth, clay, and other ordinary material, Betty Hamilton has created an extraordinary miniature diorama of four thousand years of man's history. Her hobby started some twenty-plus years ago when she entered a doll-dressing contest. She has been costuming dolls and constructing historical sets for them ever since.

Beginning with the Cretan-Mycenaean culture of 2000 B.C., Hamilton's richly detailed handcrafted sets depict the major periods in human history. Displays include a miniature temple of Solomon, Cleopatra in her castle, a remarkable Byzantine castle, and Henry VIII and his eight wives in their castle. There are Vikings in their ships, knights on horseback, and royalty dancing at the court of Versailles. A southern plantation with everything from cottonfields to the elaborately furnished mansion is there in miniature.

From a row of doll-inhabited houses dating from 1840 to 1940, kids can see the changing clothing and architecture of those years. The details are stunning—flowers grow in tiny window boxes and cakes line a baker's shelf in a street scene. Best of all are Hamilton's detailed knowledge and graphic descriptions of the daily life in each period represented. Perhaps a visit here will inspire children to go home and make their own models.

Whitewater Trout Farm

Whitewater Canyon Road, Whitewater. (Take the Whitewater turnoff from I-10 northwest of Palm Springs.) (619) 325-5570. Tuesday–Sunday, 9 A.M.– 5 P.M. $2 for pole and bait.

You can catch your own dinner in this pleasant, tree-shaded picnic area. The water is packed with trout, so you are virtually assured of catching one. Cleaned and packaged, the trout cost $2.35 a pound. There are barbecue areas where you can grill your fish, and running water is usually available.

Morongo Wildlife Reserve

Morongo Valley. (Take I-10 to Highway 62. Turn right on East Drive from Highway 62 in the town of Morongo Valley.) Daily, 8 A.M.–sunset. Free.

A well-known wildlife sanctuary, Morongo is home for more than two hundred species of birds and 150 varieties of plant life. Kept in its natural state so as not to disturb the wildlife inhabitants, the park appears less well maintained than other San Bernardino County parks—but this may add to its appeal for some. It's an ideal spot for nature study. There are shaded meadows for picnics and a good nature trail system.

Hi-Desert Nature Museum
57117 Twentynine Palms Highway, Yucca Valley. (Turn north on Dumosa Street from Route 62 in the city of Yucca Valley. The museum is located in the Community Center Complex just off Route 62.) (619) 365-9814. Wednesday–Sunday, 1–5 P.M. Free.

This small, well-kept museum has a fine collection of nature displays. Among them, you can see an extensive collection of butterflies from around the world, live reptiles, birds' nests and eggs, fossils, petrified wood, a fascinating display of insects, and an unusual collection of pine cones. There is also a fluorescent display of rocks and minerals. In addition to the regular exhibits, the museum has changing exhibits, such as a wildflower display in the spring. Everything is well lit and attractively displayed. Information about nearby nature trails can also be obtained from the museum.

Joshua Tree National Monument
The north entrances to the monument are off Highway 62 (take I-10 east from Los Angeles to Highway 62) at the towns of Joshua Tree and Twentynine Palms. The south or Cottonwood Springs entrance is 25 miles east of Indio on I-10. There are visitors' centers at the Cottonwood Springs and Twentynine Palms entrances. (619) 367-7511. Open daily all year. Monument headquarters, located near Twentynine Palms, is open daily, 8 A.M.–5 P.M. The Cottonwood Springs visitors' center is open daily, 9 A.M.–4 P.M. (may be closed at lunchtime). Free.

Two great deserts—the low Colorado and the high Mojave—come together at the dramatically beautiful 870-plus-acre Joshua Tree National Monument. If there has been enough rain, spring is the best time to visit, because then the desert blooms with wildflowers. The western half of the monument is dominated by Joshua trees—actually not trees at all, but giant desert lilies. With their thick, matted trunks and limbs stuck together at all sorts of odd, twisted angles, the trees (named by pioneer Mormons who thought they resembled Joshua raising his arms to heaven) have been known to grow as tall as forty feet.

Some areas of particular interest in the monument are the Fortynine Palms Oasis, a beautiful California fan palm oasis reached by a 1½-mile hiking trail; Hidden Valley, whose picnic facilities and trail system lie in a stunning area of massive boulders; the Geology Road Tour, an eighteen-mile nature tour that you take in your car through some of the monument's most fascinating terrain; and Cottonwood Springs, a manmade palm oasis noted for its birdlife and easily accessible by road.

The visitors' centers in Oasis of Mara (Twentynine Palms entrance) and Cottonwood Springs have maps and other information. There is also a small museum at the Twentynine Palms visitors' center.

Barstow, Victorville, and Vicinity

Barstow Way Station
831 Barstow Road, Barstow. (Take the Central Barstow exit from I-15 and go north one block.) (619) 256-3591. Daily, 9 A.M.–5 P.M. Free.

Barstow lies in the heart of the fascinating high desert. A former mining center and frontier town, Barstow is a booming city today. It is also a good base for exploring the surrounding Mojave Desert. Depending on your family's interests, you can explore caverns, drive or hike into lovely canyons, rock hunt, see the remains of ancient volcanic activity, visit a restored ghost town, and much more.

Your first stop in the area should be the Barstow Way Station. The way station is operated by the Bureau of Land Management and is staffed by friendly personnel trained to assist you in planning your explorations. They supplement their information with free maps, brochures, and current weather information.

The way station is also worth visiting for its displays. Kids will particularly enjoy the "Desert IQ" display where they can test their knowledge of the desert by pushing buttons that light up explanations of correct and incorrect answers. Other displays inform about desert hazards and where desert animals are located during the day and at night.

The way station also houses the 2¾-ton Old Woman Meteorite, the second largest meteorite ever found in the United States. It is out in the open where it can be touched and examined.

Barstow Station
1611 East Main Street (between I-15 and I-40), Barstow. (619) 256-0366. Daily, 9 A.M.–9 P.M.; weekends until 10 P.M. McDonald's: Sunday–Thursday, 6 A.M.–10 P.M.; Friday and Saturday, 6 A.M.–11 P.M.

A group of retired railroad cars form the framework of this shopping and eating area. The railroad cars turn what would otherwise be an ordinary fast-food stop and souvenir center into quite a charming area. Converted railroad cars serve as the dining rooms for a McDonald's restaurant. A bakery train with an adjacent dining car sells sandwiches and bakery goods. Also at the station are a large old-fashioned-style candy and souvenir store and a Baskin-Robbins ice cream parlor. Upstairs is a pinball and electronic game arcade.

Mojave River Valley Museum
270 East Virginia Way (corner of Barstow Road), Barstow. (619) 256-5452. Daily, 11 A.M.–4 P.M. Free.

This very small museum houses rock and mineral displays and Indian artifacts such as arrowheads. There are a few stuffed animals, including snakes, lizards, and a coyote; and some dried wildflower displays. Outside are a railroad car, which is locked up, and some old cagelike jail cells. A park across the street has grassy areas, picnic tables, and a spiral slide.

Calico Ghost Town
Located 10 miles northeast of Barstow via I-15, then 4 miles north on Ghost Town Road. (619) 254-2122. Daily, 7 A.M.–dusk. Closed Christmas. Parking and admission, $3 per car.

Calico Ghost Town is a restored 1880s silver-mining boomtown located beside the ore-filled Calico Mountains. Founded in 1881 as a result of one of the West's richest silver strikes, the town enjoyed a colorful heyday and then declined rapidly when the price of silver dropped dramatically at the turn of the century. Walter Knott, the founder of Knott's Berry Farm, worked in the camp as a youth. Years later he decided to restore the town as accurately as possible. The area was eventually deeded to San Bernardino County, which now operates it as a regional park.

Many of the buildings you will see in the town are original; you'll notice that they were built with a crude form of cement using the local dirt, which gives the buildings a reddish hue. There is a museum with exhibits such as a blacksmith's shop and an old barber shop that doubled as a dentist's office, complete with appropriate-looking dummies. The rails around the exhibits are very low, so it is easy for children to get a close look.

The town's old schoolhouse has an ancient teeter-totter and a swing kids can use. Everyone except claustrophobics will enjoy a walking tour of the Maggie Mine, which includes an opportunity to look deep into the shaft. Children will also enjoy a ride on the Calico-Odessa Railroad and a visit to the Mystery Shack, which seems to defy the laws of gravity. The town also includes a shooting gallery, a theater, shops, and places to eat.

A special combination ticket covering the shooting gallery, train, mystery shack, mine tour, and the short tram ride into the ghost town is $5.25 for adults and $3.25 for children on weekends. (On weekdays the price is $4.25 for adults and $2.50 for children). Camping sites are located near the town for $9 per unit per night. Call for reservations.

Calico has been carefully restored to its original condition as a silver mining town of the 1880s.

Rainbow Basin
Twelve miles north of the Barstow Way Station. (From the way station, take Barstow Road north to Main Street. Go left on Main and turn right on First Street. Take First Street across two bridges and turn left on Fort Irwin Road. Do not be alarmed by the "Not a Through Street" sign. From this sign, it is 4.8 miles to Fossil Bed Road. Turn left on this dirt road and follow the signs to Rainbow Basin Loop Road. Rainbow Basin Loop Road is narrow and impassable for vehicles larger than campers.) Open daily. Free.

Rainbow Basin was formed some 10 to 30 million years ago on lake beds now long gone. Over the years, erosion of the multicolored sedimentary layers has produced a panorama of vividly colored and wildly shaped rock formations. The four-mile drive around the Rainbow Basin Loop Road is beautiful and exciting. Richly colored rocks tower in wondrous formations over a narrow dirt road. It is a thrill produced by nature.

Roy Rogers-Dale Evans Museum
Seneca Road and Civic Drive, Victorville (off I-15). (619) 243-4547. Daily, 9 A.M.–5 P.M. Adults, $3; seniors, $2; ages 13–16, $2; ages 6–12, $1; under 6, free.

Here's old Trigger, the smartest horse in the movies, stuffed and on display along with the jeep Nelly and the costumes and other mementos of Roy Rogers and Dale Evans. While adults may find the museum somewhat peculiar (especially its displays of the sort of family relics most people keep in a box in the garage—if at all), kids seem to have a good time in the fortlike building. Kids will probably enjoy seeing Rogers's collections of guns, cowboy boots, animal trophies, and old cars. There is also a considerable selection of photographs from the couple's movies and television shows.

Mojave Narrows Regional Park
Two miles south of Victorville via I-15. (From I-15, take the Bear Valley turnoff east to Ridge Crest Road and go north to the park.) (619) 245-2226. Daily, 7:30 A.M.–dusk. Day use: $3 per car.

There is no better description of this park than the one the San Bernardino County Regional Parks people give: It's Huck Finn country. Lush and pastoral, this is a wonderful park with creeks, ponds, broad meadows, cottonwood patches, willow thickets, a marsh, and two lakes. The larger lake,

Horseshoe Lake, offers some of the finest fishing in the area. (Fishing licenses and bait are available at the boathouse and entrance station.) Pedalboats can be rented for a ride on the lake.

There are miles of hiking and horseback-riding trails, a wildlife area, a nature trail, and a specially designed paved nature trail for the handicapped. Picnic facilities with barbecue grills are available. The park is bordered by pasture land, so you will even see cows grazing, a silo, and bales of hay stacked about. Overnight camping is available in an eighty-seven-unit campground complete with hot showers and adjacent to Horseshoe Lake.

Providence Mountains State Recreation Area/Mitchell Caverns
About 40 miles west of Needles; about 113 miles east of Barstow. (From I-40, take the Essez Road off ramp and go north about 15 miles to the caverns.) For information, phone the Bureau of Land Management Office at Needles: (619) 326-3896. Tours weekdays at 1:30 P.M.; weekends at 10 A.M., 1:30, and 3 P.M. Closed in the summer.

These limestone caverns were once the homes of Indians. The caves, El Pakiva and Tecopa, were formed by water dissolving the mountains' limestone eons ago; you'll find stunningly intricate stalagmites and stalactites throughout. The caverns remain at a constant temperature of a cool 65 degrees. A manmade tunnel connects the two caves, and the trail through them is easily negotiated. The walking tour lasts about an hour and a half. Overnight camping is available in six primitive campsites. The caverns can be seen in a day trip, though, from headquarters in Barstow or the closer Needles.

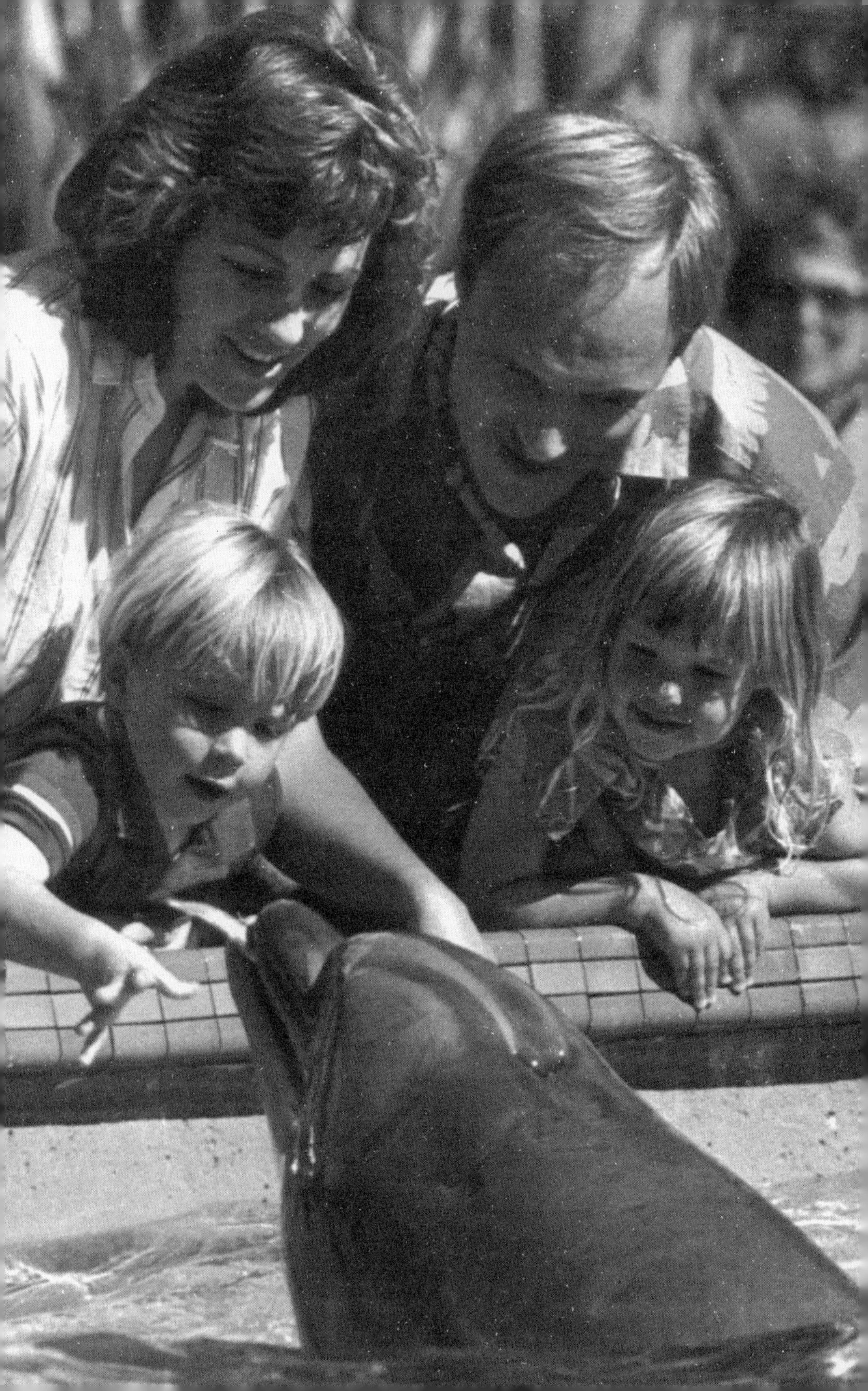

San Diego County

California history begins in San Diego. The first Europeans to discover California landed at Point Loma in 1546, and the Spanish made their first West Coast settlement at Mission San Diego de Alcala, on Presidio Hill. The chain of missions that the Spanish used to settle California led north from San Diego.

Today, San Diego is California's second largest city. It is a major commercial center and seaport, the home of the U.S. Navy's largest fleet, and, many believe, the best vacation destination in Southern California.

There is a belief that it never rains in Southern California. Well, it may rain in *some* places in Southern California, but it never rains in San Diego—or so it seems. The area is blessed with one of the world's most equable climates: temperatures average 70 degrees and humidity is low year round. On top of its weather, San Diego boasts a stunning natural beauty with lush vegetation, miles of shoreline, and one of the world's prettiest natural harbors. San Diego's Spanish heritage and close proximity to Mexico result in a Spanish-flavored lifestyle that adds to the area's charm.

Families will find a variety of memorable experiences here, many of them free. San Diego's history is preserved in its Old Town section, in its mission, and on Presidio Hill. The city boasts one of the world's finest zoos, one of the country's most interesting city parks, and one of the largest oceanariums in the world. There are a number of fine museums here, too, and countless water activities.

Make friends with a dolphin at Sea World.

But there is far more to San Diego County than just the city of San Diego. Nearly the size of Connecticut, San Diego County stretches from the Pacific to include foothills and mountain ranges, a national forest, and a great desert. A wild-animal park, a giant telescope, and a charming old mining town are just a few of the places that can be reached in a short jaunt or on an all-day tour up the coast or into the back country.

The excellent San Diego Convention and Visitors Bureau offers all sorts of information and assistance to visitors. The Visitor Information Center is located in the Horton Plaza shopping center at first Avenue and F Street in downtown San Diego (phone: 619-236-1212). The Mission Bay Visitors Information Center off I-5 at the end of the Claremont-Mission Bay off ramp provides a similar service. For recorded visitor information, phone (619) 239-9696.

San Diego

Balboa Park
Entrances at either Sixth Avenue and Laurel Street or Park Boulevard and El Prado. (From I-5, take Exit 163.) (619) 239-0512. Open daily. Free.

In the heart of San Diego is one of the country's prettiest and most interesting city parks. In addition to lovely green spaces, this 1,074-acre park holds most of the city's major museums, a Shakespearean and two other theaters, an artist's colony, sports facilities, the world's largest outdoor organ, and one of the world's best zoos. It is impossible to see all of this park in a day. If you can spend only one day here, see the zoo and the children's zoo first. If you have any energy left after that, you might visit either the Museum of Man or the Reuben H. Fleet Space Theater and Science Center. The park's information center, located in the House of Hospitality on El Prado, has free maps and information on the park.

Two playgrounds in Balboa Park feature a large variety of slides, swings, and other equipment. One is at the north end of Balboa Drive; the other is at the Pepper Grove Picnic Area. Children will also enjoy the miniature train and the merry-go-round, both located beside the zoo parking lot. There is a restaurant in the park, as well as several cafes and numerous food vendors. On Sundays at 1:30 P.M., the House of Pacific Relations sponsors free lawn programs of ethnic music and dance.

Balboa Park also offers an exciting variety of summer classes for children. Special programs are offered at the Museum of Man, the Aerospace Museum, the Natural History Museum, the Museum of Photographic Arts, the Reuben H. Fleet Center, the Museum of Art, and the zoo. There is also a theater arts program. Contact the park or the individual institutions for more information.

San Diego Zoo

Balboa Park. (619) 234-3153. Open daily. July–Labor Day; 9 A.M.–5 P.M. Post Labor Day–June: 9 A.M.–4 P.M. Adults, $8.50; ages 3–15, $2.50; under 3, free.

One of the world's largest collections of wild animals resides at the San Diego Zoo in a hundred-acre tropical garden. Instead of bars and cages separating animals from visitors, most of the zoo's 3,200 animals roam freely behind moats and low walls in habitats that resemble their home in the wild. In addition to the popular favorites—lions, tigers, elephants, and the like—the zoo is home to many rare and exotic species, including koalas, long-billed kiwis, pygmy chimps, and New Guinea tree crocodiles. A new attraction, "Tiger River," contains more than one hundred animals—including tigers, crocodiles, and tropical birds—in an environment that simulates a tropical rain forest.

A guided forty-minute bus tour covers most of the zoo. The fare is $2.50 for adults and $2 for children. An aerial tramway called the Skyfari gives an exciting overhead look at the zoo, and is also a shortcut from the front of the zoo to its outer exhibits. One-way fare for adults is $1 and for children, 75¢. Cameras, strollers, and wheelchairs are available to rent. The zoo also has free animal shows, several restaurants, a gift shop, snack bars, and shaded picnic areas.

Children's Zoo

Located in the San Diego Zoo in Balboa Park. (619) 234-3153. Daily, 9:30 A.M.–5 P.M. Ages 3 and up, 50¢; under 3, free.

This zoo-within-a-zoo is especially for small children. Everything in the zoo, including drinking fountains and benches, is scaled to the size of a four-year-old. All the exhibits are at a young child's eye level. The exhibit that is probably the most fun is the paddock where visitors of all ages can pet baby sheep, goats, and deer. It's like a minicircus, with children show-

Reach out to a goat at the San Diego Children's Zoo.

ering affection on animals, goats nipping at women's purses, and fathers trying to take it all in with their cameras. Other highlights of the Children's Zoo are the hatchery where you can watch baby chicks hatch, and the nursery for baby primates where the diapered babies play with their toys in playpens.

San Diego Museum of Man
1350 El Prado (west end of El Prado), Balboa Park. (619) 239-2001. Daily, 10 A.M.–4:30 P.M. Closed Thanksgiving, Christmas, and New Year's. Adults, $3; ages 13–18, $1; ages 6–12, 25¢; under 6, free. Free on the first Tuesday of the month.

The California Building in Balboa Park, designed to look like the Cathedral of Mexico in Mexico City, houses a fine anthropology museum. The emphasis is on the cultures of the western Americas, particularly Mexico and the Indians of the southwest. The changing exhibits are downstairs and often include demonstrations such as tortilla making or weaving. Permanent exhibits include life-sized models of prehistoric humans in various stages of evolution, models of cave dwellers inside their caves, early hunting implements, and a reconstructed Hopi Indian adobe, complete with dirt floor, fireplace, and models of a mother and her two children. Check the display board as you enter the museum to decide which of the many exhibits appeal most to you and your children.

Across the street in the museum's "Wonder of Life" exhibit. Prepared with the assistance of physicians, religious leaders, and educators, the exhibit introduces children to the facts of conception and childbirth in a clear and frank manner. Adults will also find it informative and neither uncomfortable nor embarrassing. You go first into a small theater for a ten-minute film presentation and then into the exhibit itself. The display includes models of babies in the womb at various stages of development. The models are at children's eye level and most kids pat the babies on the head as they pass.

San Diego Museum of Art
1450 El Prado, Balboa Park. (619) 232-7931. Tuesday–Sunday, 10 A.M.– 4:30 P.M. Adults, $4; seniors, $3; students, $2; ages 6–12, $1, under 6, free.

The museum features a fine collection of European masterworks, as well as Asian and American art. Some of the traveling exhibits—such as exhibits of youth art—may interest children, and children may enjoy seeing the museum's enclosed sculpture garden.

Botanical Building
Balboa Park. (Behind and to the right of the Museum of Art.) Thursday– Tuesday, 10 A.M.–4:30 P.M. Free.

This enormous lath building houses a vast array of tropical and subtropical plants, ferns, and flowers. The plants are all labeled, and the building is very pleasant to wander through. A lily pond is outside.

Timken Art Gallery
1500 El Prado, Balboa Park. (619) 239-5548. Tuesday–Saturday 10 A.M.– 4:30 P.M.; Sunday, 1:30–4:30 P.M. Closed Mondays, holidays, and the month of September. Free.

The Timken Art Gallery, next door to the San Diego Museum of Art, contains works by European masters, eighteenth- and nineteenth-century American paintings, and a collection of Russian icons.

Museum of San Diego History
1649 El Prado, Balboa Park (in Casa de Balboa). (619) 232-6226. Wednesday–Sunday, 10 A.M.–4:30 P.M. Admission prices vary; some exhibits are free.

The Museum of San Diego History is devoted to bringing the city's history to life. The changing exhibits use photographs, costumes, and artifacts to trace aspects of the city's history, such as women at work. A permanent display area for the museum is under construction.

Museum of Photographic Arts
1649 El Prado (located in Casa de Balboa), Balboa Park. (619) 239-5262. Friday–Wednesday, 10 A.M.–5 P.M.; until 9 P.M. on Thursday. Adults, $2; under 12, free.

The Museum of Photographic Arts is one of a small number of museums in the country devoted exclusively to photography. The museum features changing exhibits of the work of important artists such as Ansel Adams, Henri Cartier-Bresson, and Alfred Stieglitz. The museum will appeal primarily to older children and adults, although it is not difficult to visit here with small children.

San Diego Model Railroad Museum
1649 El Prado (in Casa de Balboa), Balboa Park. (619) 696-0199. Friday, 11 A.M.–4 P.M.; Saturday and Sunday, 11 A.M.–5 P.M. Adults, $1; under 16, free.

Working scale models of historic California train routes are on display in this museum founded by three San Diego model-railroad clubs. All the routes are authentically landscaped. The San Diego and Arizona Eastern route, for example, includes a model of downtown San Diego and a ride over a wooden trestle spanning the steep Carriso Gorge. The exhibits are not complete, and work on them is on-going. Small children will have to be lifted to see some of the trains.

San Diego Hall of Champions
1649 El Prado (in Casa de Balboa), Balboa Park. (619) 234-2544. Monday–Saturday, 10 A.M.–4 P.M.; Sunday, noon–5 P.M. Adults, $2; over 55 and students, $1; ages 6–17, 50¢; under 6, free.

The San Diego Hall of Champions honors San Diego's outstanding athletes, including Ted Williams, Bill Walton, Archie Moore, and Florence Chadwick. All the major sports are covered, even motorcycle racing and surfing. Exhibits include photographs, equipment, uniforms, computerized team records, and video displays. Continuous free sports films are shown in a small theater. The museum is bright and cheerful.

Natural History Museum
Corner of El Prado and Village Place (opposite the fountain), Balboa Park. (619) 232-3821. Daily, 10 A.M.–4:30 P.M. Adults, $3; ages 6–19, $1; under 6, free.

A forty-foot-long duckbilled dinosaur skeleton and the Foucault Pendulum—a 185-pound brass bob suspended on a forty-three-foot cable, which demonstrates the rotation of the earth—are among the highlights for children of this natural history museum. There are displays on whales, birds, plants, minerals, mammals, reptiles, shells, prehistoric animals, and ecology. The new Hall of Desert Ecology illustrates the evolution and adaptation of plants and animals to the environment of the southwestern deserts. Other interesting exhibits include the seismograph near the entrance and the Hall of Shore Ecology, which features a tide pool and other seashore exhibits. The museum's changing exhibits often feature hands-on displays. On weekends, nature films are shown at no extra charge.

Reuben H. Fleet Space Theater and Science Center
1875 El Prado (east end of El Prado, at the Plaza de Balboa), Balboa Park. (619) 238-1168 for details on the shows, starting times, and prices. Prices vary depending on show. Admission to the Science Center only: Adults, $1.50; ages 5–15, 75¢; under 5, free.

The Space Theater is a combination multimedia theater and planetarium. Seating accommodates 350 people, all facing the same direction (as opposed to the usual full circle). The screen itself is a hemisphere seventy-six feet in diameter and tilted twenty-five degrees. It's an impressive theater, giving the audience the sensation of sitting in space. The shows, which change from time to time, are uneven, however. For example, a fascinating presentation of the origins of astronomy, projecting the sky of thousands of years ago in front of you, can be coupled with a disappointing travelog. The programs are best for school-age children and older.

The Space Theater ticket also admits you to the Science Center across the hall, which is a great place for kids. All the exhibits are visitor-activated, encouraging the kids to touch and participate. Many of them are at children's height. You can play tic-tac-toe with an electronic brain that never loses, have your hearing tested, or have your age guessed by a machine. Children will be particularly intrigued by the large dishes that bounce a whispered conversation to the other side of the room.

Aerospace Museum
Aerospace Historical Center, 2001 Pan American Plaza, Balboa Park. (619) 234-8291. Daily, 10 A.M.–4:30 P.M. Adults, $3.50; ages 6–17, $1; under 6, free.

The history of aviation in our country from the dawn of flight to the age of space travel is excitingly depicted in the San Diego Aerospace Museum. You'll see early gliders, a replica of the plane flown by the Wright Brothers at Kitty Hawk, World War I planes, early barnstorming planes, the first airmail planes, and an exact flying replica of Charles Lindbergh's *Spirit of St. Louis*. Aircraft from World War II are on exhibit, as well as modern fighter planes and a NASA space capsule. Many of the planes are colorfully displayed within a surrounding exhibit, and there are a number of push-button displays.

Also in the Aerospace Historical Center is the International Aerospace Hall of Fame, which features memorabilia of the heroes of aviation and space history. A very interesting exhibit honors the contribution of women to aviation.

Firehouse Museum
1572 Columbia Street (corner of Cedar). (619) 232-FIRE. Open Thursday–Sunday, 10 A.M.–4 P.M. Free.

The Firehouse Museum is an old fire station now housing a dozen major pieces of fire-fighting equipment from the early days of San Diego up to the present. One of the most interesting pieces is the Metropolitan Steamer, built in 1903. Weighing ten thousand pounds, it used coal to operate the water pump. Lanterns, old hats, pictures, axes, hoses, and badges are displayed on the walls and other surfaces. An old telephone switchboard and the speaking trumpets through which the chief would shout his orders are other engaging relics from the past.

The Old Spaghetti Factory
Fifth Avenue at K Street. (619) 233-4323. Monday–Thursday, 5–10 P.M.; Friday, 5–11 P.M.; Saturday, 4:30 –11 P.M.; Sunday, 4–10 P.M.

This is one of those "you have to see it to believe it" kind of restaurants. Located in what was once San Diego's commercial center, the Old Spaghetti Factory really looks like a factory from the outside. The inside is something else. Decorated with a bright jumble of Tiffany lamps, stained glass, and Victorian couches, the restaurant offers an unusual assortment of eating arrangements. You can dine in an old streetcar in the middle of the restaurant or on a table set between the headboard and footboard of an antique bed.

The dinners—which include salad, spaghetti, bread, a beverage, and spumoni—start at $3.75. A child's dinner is available for $2.95. The restaurant is always packed with families, and the help is adept at moving around the small kids who are busy weighing themselves on an old scale or playing throughout the restaurant. There are plenty of highchairs and booster chairs for young children.

The only problem with this restaurant (which is part of a West Coast chain) is that there is always a wait, sometimes as long as an hour, and they don't take reservations. It's best to arrive around opening time.

Villa Montezuma Museum
1925 K Street. (Coming south on I-5, take the Imperial Avenue exit; go left on Imperial to Twentieth Street and left on Twentieth Street to K Street. Coming north on I-5, take the J Street exit, go right on J Street to Twentieth Street, and go right on Twentieth to K Street.) (619) 239-2211. Wednesday–Sunday, 1–4:30 P.M. Adults, $2; under 13, free.

If you visit just one restored old home in Southern California, it probably should be this one. Built in 1887 (during San Diego's land boom) for Jesse Shepard, a celebrated musician of the era, the Villa Montezuma was (according to the December 17, 1889, *San Diego Sun*) "the most ornately finished and artistically furnished house in the city."

The house is so unique and so lavish that it should interest everyone above the age of six or so. It is filled with brilliant stained-glass windows, which include portraits of Shakespeare and Goethe. The redwood music room contains, in addition to a piano and other furniture, an antique doll collection. Ask to see the downstairs kitchen, which has been restored as a typical turn-of-the-century townhouse kitchen, complete with spices in the spice rack, and hanging laundry.

Seaport Village/Marina Park
849 West Harbor Drive (at the foot of Pacific Highway). (619) 235-4013. Daily, 10 A.M.–10 P.M. Free.

Built on the site of the old Coronado Ferry landing on San Diego Bay, Seaport Village is a new waterfront complex of shops, restaurants, and family amusements.

The fourteen-acre village is the most enjoyable complex of this type that I have seen. Three plazas—designed to look like Victorian San Francisco, nineteenth-century Monterey, and old Mexico—front eight acres of parkland on the bay. The architecture is fun and includes a forty-five-foot-high lighthouse and a Victorian clocktower. The pleasant landscaping includes a lake.

The highlight of the village for children is the Broadway Flying Horse Carousel, a beautifully restored turn-of-the-century Coney Island merry-go-round with forty-six hand-carved wooden animals, each with its own leather reins. Rides on the carousel, which goes round at a good clip, are 75¢.

Adjacent to the merry-go-round is an electronic-games center. There is an old-fashioned popcorn wagon, and performers such as jugglers and mariachi bands are generally strolling around. Some of the stores may interest children, including a magic shop, a puzzle store, a kite shop, and a stuffed-bear store. There are also two toy stores: Fantasy World of Toys and the Apple Box, which specializes in wooden toys.

Marina Park is adjacent to Seaport Village, with a view of Coronado Bridge and Coronado Island on one side and the San Diego skyline on the other. It is a great spot for watching sailboats and navy ships, for flying kites, and for picnicking.

Maritime Museum
1306 North Harbor Drive (1 mile south of San Diego Airport on the north Embarcadero between Ash Street and Broadway). (619) 234-9153. Daily, 9 A.M.–8 P.M. Adults, $4; senior citizens and ages 13–17, $3; ages 6–12, $1; $8 maximum per family. One ticket provides admission to all the ships.

A fully rigged iron windjammer, an 1898 ferryboat, and a World War I-vintage yacht make up San Diego's Maritime museum. By far the most interesting of the three vessels is the *Star of India*, an 1863 merchant sailing vessel. The ship's keeper directs you first to the main deck, where the captain and first-class passengers slept and ate. The cabins are furnished in detail; old uniforms hang in the captain's closet; a chamber pot is near the bed. There is a children's cabin with toys and a small rocking horse. (The half-gates across the cabins have wide posts, so small children can see without being lifted.) At the other end of the main deck are the cramped bunks of the crew.

Between decks on the *Star of India* is a museum with photos of ships, displays of rope knots and old tools, and some interesting odds and ends like a doctor's medical saddlebag. Young children will probably enjoy standing behind the ship's wheel and playing on the poop deck.

The *Berkeley*, docked next door, is a propeller-driven ferryboat. She is much less engaging than the *Star*, and you'll probably want to spend less time here. The *Medea*, built in 1904, is an old English yacht with a colorful history. The yacht itself is not that interesting, but what is fun is crossing the gangplank to her from the *Berkeley*. You might not want to try it with small children, but kids six and over will love jumping onto the small ship from the narrow gangplank.

Navy Ships' Open House
U.S. Navy Pier, off Harbor Drive, near Broadway on the Embarcadero. (619) 235-3534.

You can tour a submarine, an aircraft carrier, a destroyer, or other naval craft most weekends between 1 and 4 P.M. when U.S. Navy ships hold open house for the public. (You need to make special arrangements, however, to tour an aircraft carrier.) At least one ship is usually shown each weekend. The navy guide will take you though the entire ship and patiently answer any questions.

San Diego Harbor Excursion
Foot of Broadway at Harbor Drive. (619) 234-4111. Daily. Two-hour cruise: Adults, $11; children, $5.50. One-hour cruise: Adults, $7.70; children, $3.85; under 3, free.

Pleasant excursion ships with sun decks, glass-enclosed cabins, and galley snack bars offer one- and two-hour cruises in the San Diego Harbor. A tour guide singles out and explains the points of interest over a clear public address system. The one-hour, twelve-mile cruise passes by the *Star of India* sailing ship, the Naval Air Station, and San Diego's shipyards. The fishing fleet, aircraft carriers, merchant vessels and the Coronado Bridge are some things the guide will point out to you. The two-hour, twenty-five-mile trip covers the same territory plus the Cabrillo National Monument.

For most children's attention spans, the one-hour cruise is probably best. There are cruises daily, with frequent departures during the summer; telephone for the schedule. In the winter, whale-watching cruises are offered. Even in the summer, it's a good idea for everyone to bring a sweater.

Cabrillo National Monument
At the tip of Point Loma, San Diego. (Take Highway 209 to its south end at the monument. The monument is approached through the gates of the Naval Oceans System Center.) (619) 557-5450. Daily, 9 A.M.–sunset. Admission, $3 per car.

Commemorating the European discovery of the West Coast by Juan Cabrillo, this national monument on the tip of Point Loma offers an unparalleled view of the city and the bay. The visitors' center shows films and has exhibits on Cabrillo—and the other Pacific Coast explorers—and on the gray whales. (The monument includes a whale-watching lookout.) A walkway leads uphill to the old Point Loma Lighthouse, which has been restored and furnished to look the way it did a century ago. A tape recording tells kids what life was like for the lightkeeper and his family. (The light from the lighthouse was often obscured by low-flying clouds, and in 1891 the lighthouse was abandoned for one on lower ground.)

You can also take a walk along a nature trail that winds through the chaparral along the bay side of Point Loma. (A guide to the trail is available at the visitors' center.)

Whale Watching

Every year more than ten thousand California gray whales make the five-thousand-mile migration from their summer feeding grounds above Alaska and Siberia to their winter mating and calving grounds in the warm lagoons of Baja California. The migration passes by Southern California from about mid-December to about mid-February. As many as eighty whales per day can be spotted off San Diego's coast during the height of the migration in January. You can actually see the whales from land at the free whale-watching station at Cabrillo National Monument on the tip of Point Loma. But for a closer look, you'll want to join one of the whale-watching excursions. These usually last a couple of hours, and sightings are almost certain. Among the companies offering whale-watching excursions are San Diego Harbor Excursions, phone (619) 234-4111; H and M Landing, phone (619) 222-1144; and Invader Cruises, phone (619) 234-8687.

Pier Fishing

The ocean off San Diego is one of the finest areas for catching fish along the Pacific Coast. Many companies operate half-day sportfishing boats out of San Diego. However, you don't have to take your children out on a boat to have a good day fishing: Perch, bonito, and barracuda can be caught off San Diego's piers. No fishing license is required, you won't get seasick, and what's more, it's free. The following piers are open daily and do not charge for fishing:

☐ Crystal Pier, located at the foot of Garnet Street in Pacific Beach.
Fishing is open to the public from 7 A.M. to 5 P.M. daily on this privately owned pier. (There is no fee, but children must be accompanied by an adult fisherman.) There is a bait house on the pier.

☐ Oceanside Pier, located at the foot of Third Street in Oceanside.
As the story goes, a thirty-five-pound yellowtail was once caught off this 945-foot pier. The bait house next to the pier will take care of your bait-and-tackle needs.

☐ San Diego Public Fishing Pier, located at the foot of Niagara Street in Ocean Beach, a section of San Diego city.
Built in 1966 at a cost of $3 million, this pier stretches 2,150 feet into the ocean. The bait house rents tackle and will advise you on a selection of

bait. Yellowtail have been caught off this pier. The good cafe here serves complete meals.

☐ Shelter Island Fishing Pier, Shelter Island.
This pier is smaller than some of the others, but catches are often made here. It is also the prettiest pier. A bait house rents tackle, and there is a snack bar.

Old Town State Park

Located just southeast of Interstates 5 and 8. (From I-5, take the Old Town off ramp.) (619) 237-6770. Daily, 10 A.M.–5 P.M. Shops open until 9 P.M. Free.

Old Town is the heart of old San Diego. The city began near here on Presidio Hill in 1769; from the 1820s to the 1870s, Old Town was the commercial, political, and social center of the city. Today it is a hodgepodge of homes, businesses, restored historical buildings, grassy areas, restaurants, and tourist shops. If the shops are avoided and historic sites are selected with care, children can spend an enjoyable afternoon here.

Washington Square is a big grassy plaza in the center of Old Town. It's a great place for kids to stretch their legs while their folks rest on a bench. There is even an old cannon to climb on. Various horse-drawn wagons and stagecoaches offer rides around Old Town, starting from this area.

Casa De Altamirano

On San Diego Avenue across from the Squibob Square. (619) 297-2219. Tuesday–Sunday, 10 A.M.–5 P.M. Free.

In 1868 this frame building became the home of the *San Diego Union* newspaper. The *Union* has since restored the building to look the way that first office did. You can see the old press, an ancient typewriter, and the bins full of lead type.

Mason Street School

On Mason Street between San Diego Avenue and Congress Street. Daily, 10 A.M.–4 P.M. Free.

Built in 1886, this was the first public school in San Diego. It has a potbellied stove, old-fashioned desks, and books. The blackboard has assignments on it, too.

The Seeley Stables
Calhoun Street between Mason and Twiggs streets. Daily, 10 A.M.–5 P.M. Adults, $1; children, 50¢; under 6, free. (The same ticket admits you to the Casa de Estudillo.)

The Seeley Stables houses an extensive collection of wagons and stagecoaches, including a Wells Fargo mail coach and the old Julian-to-San Diego stagecoach. There is no rope around any of the coaches, so you can get right next to them. Upstairs are displays of saddles, branding irons, and cowboy photos. Of interest to kids is a display of nineteenth-century children's toys and an old-fashioned telephone that can be touched.

Casa De Estudillo
Mason Street between Calhoun Street and San Diego Avenue. Daily, 10 A.M.–5 P.M. Adults, $1; children, 50¢; under 6, free. (The same ticket admits you to the Seeley Stables.)

This beautifully restored and refurnished adobe home was built by a wealthy rancher in 1827. The lovely gardens have a goldfish pond complete with fish. You look over half-doors into the rooms of the house, so small children will have to be lifted. Of special interest is the floor-warmer in the living room where hot rocks were placed to warm the room; at that time, there were no trees for firewood. Also note the children's room with its old dolls and the outdoor oven where all the baking was done.

Hamburguesa Restaurant
4016 Wallace Street, Old Town, San Diego. (619) 295-0584. Monday–Thursday, 11 A.M.–10 P.M.; Friday and Saturday, 10 A.M.–10 P.M.; Sunday, 9 A.M.–10 P.M.

Hamburguesa Restaurant offers sixteen varieties of hamburgers, including the concoction Hamburguesadilla, a hamburger on a crisp tortilla with shredded lettuce, cheese, and avocado. A kid's-size hamburger is $2.75 and child-size milk and soft drinks are available. Steaks, salads, desserts, and cocktails are also served. The atmosphere is very pleasing. Everything is brightly colored, and plants and paper flowers are everywhere. One nice place to eat is on the patio.

Whaley House

2482 San Diego Avenue (corner of Harney). (619) 298-2482. Wednesday–Sunday, 10 A.M.–4:30 P.M. (The last tour is at 4 P.M.) Adults, $2.50; seniors, $2; ages 12–16, $1; under 12, 50¢.

Built in 1856, the Whaley House is the oldest brick structure in Southern California. Once the center of social life for old San Diego, the house also served variously as a theater, granary, school, city hall, and courthouse, as well as a home for the Whaley family. Today the house has been restored to its original state, including the courtroom, and is open to visitors.

Kids will enjoy seeing the old courtroom, with its furnishings authentic down to a spittoon. The downstairs rooms include the furnished parlor and the kitchen with its metal bathtub. You can also see the rooms upstairs, which include a child's bedroom that is full of dolls. The house is one of the most interesting and least musty historic homes I have seen. If your children are old enough for ghost stories, ask one of the docents to tell you about the ghosts who are alleged to haunt this house. It's delightfully spooky.

Heritage Park

Corner of Juan and Harney streets (just above Old Town; signs point the way). (619) 565-5928. Most shops open daily, 10:30 A.M.–5:30 P.M. Free.

Heritage Park was created as a preserve for some of San Diego's endangered Victorian buildings. Once threatened with demolition, the buildings have been moved to this park from other sites and restored. The park looks like a picture-book page with a half-dozen brightly painted Victorian structures sitting on a grassy hill. The interiors of the homes have been leased to commercial interests and turned into shops. Children of junior high age and above will enjoy browsing in the shops, which fit comfortably into the restored rooms of the Victorian mansions. Younger children will enjoy seeing the outside of the buildings and playing in the park, which has a grassy hill to roll down.

Serra Museum/Presidio Park
2727 Presidio Drive (off Taylor Street). (619) 297-3258. Museum open Tuesday–Saturday, 10 A.M.–4:30 P.M.; Sunday, noon–4:30 P.M. Adults, $2; ages 12 and under, free.

On July 16, 1769, Father Junipero Serra, a Franciscan priest from Majorca, Spain, founded the first of California's twenty-one missions—and, in the process, the city of San Diego—on this hill. A walled city, the Presidio, was built around the mission and protected by garrisoned soldiers. The city's early settlers made their homes inside the Presidio, which was all there was to San Diego until the 1820s when people began moving off the hill into what is now Old Town. The mission remained on the hill for five more years, however, and then relocated at its present site in Mission Valley.

The Serra Museum, an impressive mission-style structure that can be seen for miles around, commemorates Father Serra and the history of San Diego. The museum's historical photos of San Diego, artifacts from Presidio excavations, and other Mission and Indian artifacts are rather dry for children. The outside areas, however, should interest them. The museum portico contains displays of early mission agricultural equipment such as wine and olive oil presses.

Below the museum, in an area surrounded by low walls, children can see the ridges and hollows in the ground that are the remains of the original Presidio. The park itself is beautiful and offers picnicking and lovely views of the surrounding city.

Mission Basilica San Diego de Alcala
10818 San Diego Mission Road. (Take I-8 east from San Diego. Exit at Mission Gorge Road and turn left. Turn left again on Twain Street and follow the signs to the mission.) (619) 281-8449. Daily, 9 A.M.–5 P.M. Over 12, $1; under 12, free.

The first of California's twenty-one missions, Mission San Diego moved to this site from Presidio Hill in 1774 to be nearer to the Indians, to have a better source of water, and to have better land for farming. The mission was destroyed by an Indian attack a year later and then rebuilt of adobe. The restored "Mother of the Missions" contains a reconstruction of the original monastery and living quarters of Father Serra, a magnificent belltower, an excavation site with models of early Indians and a Spanish soldier, and a small museum that includes models of Spanish galleons and arms and artifacts from the 1846 to 1862 U.S. Cavalry occupation of the mission.

Mission Bay Aquatic Park
Information Center: 2688 East Mission Bay Drive (just north of I-8 and west of I-5, reached via I-5). (619) 276-8200. Monday–Saturday, 9 A.M.–dusk; Sunday, 9:30 A.M.–dusk. Free.

A maze of islands, beaches, lagoons, and grass-covered coves, Mission Bay Park is a beautiful 4,600-acre aquatic playground. Almost every type of water sport activity is offered here, including swimming, motorboating, sailing, fishing, and water skiing. Traffic on the bay is organized so that one water activity is separated from another. Boat rentals are available. You can fish from the beach, a small boat, or a sportfishing boat. The swimming beaches have lifeguards during the summer. There are a number of children's playgrounds and miles of landscaped areas for picnicking. In addition to a number of hotels, campsites are available at the park. The visitors' center has information on all the park's activities, as well as activities throughout the city, and will make hotel reservations.

Sea World
1720 South Shores Road in Mission Bay. (Take the Sea World Drive exit west from I-5). (619) 226-3901. Daily, 9 A.M.–dusk. Ticket office closes 1½ hours earlier. (Hours extended during summer and holiday periods.) Admission and all shows: Adults, $19.95; ages 3–11, $14.95; under 3, free. Free parking.

Sea World is well worth a whole day's outing. It is one of the largest marine-life parks in the world: More than 100 marine mammals, 10,000 fish, and 1,600 birds inhabit its 135 acres. In addition to some very exciting shows—the most impressive being the killer whales—there are many exhibits where children can be active participants. They can pet and feed dolphins and whales, and they can toss fish to sea lions, seals, and walruses. Children can roll up their sleeves and explore a tide pool that duplicates California tidal life.

A fascinating exhibit for adults and children alike is Sea World's Penguin Encounter, one of the only places outside of Antarctica where you can see these charming creatures. The penguins live in a special enclosed compound that as nearly as possible duplicates their native habitat. First from a moving sidewalk in front of the 100-foot-long observation windows and then from an upper-observation deck, you'll watch the some four hundred penguins as they toddle on the ice, dine on fresh fish, and swim gracefully

A clear panel lets a young visitor get close to Shamu, one of Sea World's killer whales.

through clear water. Less charming, but certainly fascinating, are the large sharks, displayed in a 400,000-gallon aquarium.

Cap'N Kids World is a marvelous two-acre playground for children (thirty-seven to sixty-one inches in height) inside the park. Children can tangle with seven-foot-high foam-filled punching bags, jump on a giant air mattress, or wade through a lagoon filled with thousands of plastic balls. There are two dozen distinct activities in the playground, as well as comfortable observation stations for parents.

There are a number of places to eat at Sea World. Strollers and wheelchairs are available for rent.

Up the Coast

La Jolla Museum of Contemporary Art
700 Prospect Street, La Jolla. (619) 454-0267. Tuesday–Sunday, 10 A.M.–5 P.M.; Wednesday until 9 P.M. Adults, $3; seniors and students, $1; ages 5–12, 50¢. Free on Wednesday after 5 P.M.

The La Jolla Museum of Contemporary Art focuses on post-1945 painting, sculpture, photography, drawing, and graphic art. Kids will probably enjoy looking at some of the large colorful pop-art works and the conceptual art. The museum also offers stunning views of the Pacific Ocean.

The White Rabbit Children's Books
7755 Girard Avenue, La Jolla. (From northbound I-5, take the Ardath Road exit west to Torrey Pines Road. Continue on Torrey Pines until it ends, then turn right on Girard. From southbound I-5, exit at La Jolla Village Drive, go west to Torrey Pines, turn left, and continue as above.) (619) 454-3518. Monday–Saturday, 9 A.M.–5:30 P.M.

If you can't find the book you want at this extremely well-stocked children's bookstore, they will special order it for you. If a book is out of print, they will help you find it. The store has a lovely, bright atmosphere with a large window running across it, and all-natural wood fixtures. In addition to more than six thousand titles for children from infancy through junior high, the store stocks children's records, puzzles, puppets, educational games, stationery, and stuffed animals. A half-hour story hour for young children is held on Wednesday at 10:30 A.M. The staff is well trained and very helpful. They are right there if you need them, and they leave you alone if you want to be left alone. The White Rabbit also publishes a newsletter three times a year that keeps readers up to date on new children's books and provides reviews.

The Children's Museum of San Diego
8657 Villa La Jolla Drive, La Jolla. (Take I-5 to La Jolla Village Drive; go west. Turn left on Villa La Jolla Drive. Go ½ mile to La Jolla Village Square. Turn left on Noble, then turn right toward the May Co. Use the entrance to the mall that is closest to Bullocks Wilshire. The museum is on the

lower level of the mall, near the escalator.) (619) 450-0767. Wednesday–Friday, noon–5 P.M.; Saturday, 10 A.M.–5 P.M.; Sunday, noon–5 P.M. Open on Tuesday, noon–5 P.M., for groups only. $2.75 per person; $1.25 for seniors; children under 2, free.

Among the outstanding museums of San Diego County is one just for children. The exhibits in the Children's Museum of San Diego are all designed for children's participation. In a miniature television newsroom children can report news while other kids watch on a television set placed at their eye level. Children can get an understanding of what it is like to be visually impaired by walking through the museum's sensory tunnel. There is a well-equipped art studio, a theater area where children can dress up and play act on stage, a health center with examining equipment, and an exciting variety of changing exhibits. Workshops and special events are scheduled throughout the year. You can also arrange to have your child's birthday party at the museum. The cost of $6 per person includes cake and balloons. You should make reservations at least a month in advance.

Scripps Aquarium/Museum
8202 La Jolla Shores Drive (at the University of California, San Diego, Scripps Institute of Oceanography), just north of La Jolla. (Take either the Ardath Road or La Jolla Village Drive exit from I-5.) (619) 534-6933. Daily, 9 A.M.–5 P.M. Free.

Scripps Institute of Oceanography, a part of the University of California at San Diego, maintains an aquarium and oceanographic museum for the public. Sharks, eels, lobsters, and sea anemones are a few of the 150 or so species of marine life on display. If possible, schedule your visit for Sunday or Wednesday at 1:30 P.M., when the fish are fed. Museum exhibits include a wave channel display on how waves are formed and break, an underwater telecast, and an outside tide pool that simulates tide conditions and displays intertidal life.

Mingei International Museum of World Folk Art
Building I-7 in University Towne Shopping Centre, 4405 La Jolla Village Drive, La Jolla. (Take the La Jolla Village Drive exit east from I-5 or west from I-805. Turn south on Genesee Avenue into University Towne Shopping Centre. The museum is opposite Nordstrom's at the north end of the mall.)

(619) 453-5300. *Tuesday–Thursday, 11 A.M.–5 P.M.; Friday, 11 A.M.–9 P.M.; Saturday, 11 A.M.–5 P.M.; Sunday, 2–5 P.M. Adults, $2; children, free.*

Mingei combines the Japanese word for people (*min*) and art (*gei*) to mean "arts of the people." This bright museum, tucked away in the corner of a shopping center, offers changing exhibits of international folk art. Children's interest in the museum will vary with the exhibits. Past exhibits that have appealed to children include dolls and folk toys of the world, carousel pieces, Mexican folk art, dance costumes from Ecuador, and the horse in folk art.

Torrey Pines State Reserve
Off North Torrey Pines Road, south of Del Mar. (From I-5, take the Genesee Avenue exit and go west. Turn north on North Torrey Pines Road, follow it to the ocean, and turn left into the reserve.) (619) 755-2063. Daily, 9 A.M.–sunset. Visitors Center open 11 A.M.–4 P.M. $4 per car.

Torrey Pines State Reserve protects one of the world's rarest trees, the beautiful torrey pine. The five-needled pine, a survivor of the Ice Age, remains in only two places in the world—here and on isolated Santa Rosa Island off Santa Barbara. The reserve is easily one of the most beautiful spots in all of Southern California. The trees, surrounded by a vivid and undisturbed sage-scrub community, grow atop wind-eroded sandstone cliffs above the Pacific. Well-marked trails lead through the preserve and down to the ocean. The trails are easy enough to be negotiated by just about anyone, including parents carrying babies, although small children need to be watched carefully on the cliffs.

Strollers and wheelchairs are permitted on the trails, but not bicycles. No dogs are allowed on the reserve, and picnicking is not permitted. The flowers, pine cones, and all of the natural elements are protected.

The Visitors Center, located in an old Spanish-style building, offers slide shows on the reserve, and nature exhibits such as a stuffed coyote and bobcat. Nature walks leave the Visitors Center at 11:30 A.M. and 1:30 P.M. on weekends.

Quail Botanic Gardens
230 Quail Gardens Drive, Encinitas. (Take Encinitas Boulevard [S-9] east from I-5 to Quail Gardens Drive and go north about half a mile.)

(619) 436-3036. Daily, 8 A.M.–5 P.M. (until 6 P.M. in summer). Free. Parking, $1.

These thirty-one-acre gardens offer self-guided trails through chaparral, cacti, eucalyptus and jacaranda trees, star pines, and many varieties of plants and flowers. The area is also a bird refuge and feeding station. The sanctuary is formed by an area of chaparral in which you should be able to see a wide variety of birds, quail included.

Mission San Luis Rey de Francia
4050 Mission Avenue, San Luis Rey. (Four miles east of Oceanside via Highway 76. Take I-5 south from Los Angeles or north from San Diego to Highway 76.) (619) 757-3651. Monday–Saturday, 10 A.M.–4 P.M.; Sunday, noon–4 P.M. Adults, $1; ages 12 and under, 50¢.

One of the largest of California's missions, Mission San Luis Rey de Francia is a striking combination of Spanish, Moorish, and Mexican architecture. A self-guided tour will show you the padres' bedrooms and library, the sewing rooms, and kitchen. You'll also see the first pepper tree in California, the cloister garden, and the Indian cemetery. At the height of the mission's power, almost three thousand Indian converts lived there. Original decorations done by the Indians adorn the mission. Excavations are under way to unearth more of the mission's past, and you may be able to watch some work. A picnic area is in front of the mission.

Inland

San Diego Railway Museum
Campo Train Operations and Museum: 916 Sheridan Road, Campo. (Campo is located 45 miles east of San Diego. Take the Buckman Springs exit from I-8 and go south to Highway 94, then west 1 mile to Campo; follow signs to the museum.) (619) 697-7762. Weekends, 9 A.M.–5 P.M. Trains depart at 12:01 and 2:30 P.M. Adults, $7; ages 6–12, $3.50; under 6, free.
La Mesa Depot: La Mesa and Spring streets, La Mesa. (619) 478-9937. Weekends, 12:30–4:30 P.M., or by appointment. Free.

The San Diego Railroad Museum is a volunteer organization dedicated to preserving the nation's railroad heritage. The organization maintains an extensive collection of historic locomotives, freight cars, and passenger cars at its Campo Museum and Train Operation Center. (Among them are a pair of plush private cars used by Franklin D. Roosevelt when he was campaigning for his second term.) You can tour the cars and watch the members at work restoring the trains. But best of all, you can take a train ride. Trains leave Campo at 12:01 and 2:30 P.M. on weekends (you should be there at least an hour before) for a 1½-hour round-trip scenic ride through the hills of the San Diego back country. (The trains run over the old San Diego and Arizona Railway, originally built through Campo in 1915.) The excursions are geared for families. There are also picnic grounds at the Campo site.

The museum also maintains the 1894 La Mesa Depot, which their members restored, in downtown La Mesa. The depot, open weekends, is furnished with authentic turn-of-the-century equipment and artifacts. Outside you'll see a freight train with a steam locomotive.

Antique Gas and Steam Engine Museum
2040 North Santa Fe Drive, Vista. (Exit I-5 on Highway 76 in Oceanside. Take Highway 76 east 7 miles to North Santa Fe Street. Turn south and go 2 miles to the entrance.) (619) 941-1791. Daily, 10 A.M.–4 P.M. Free; however, admission is charged for the semiannual shows.

Located on forty acres of rolling farm land that is leased from the county, the Antique Gas and Steam Engine Museum preserves and restores farm equipment and machinery powered by steam and gas engines. The big events of the year here are the semiannual shows held the third and fourth weekends in June and October. There are farming demonstrations, a threshing bee, tractor and antique equipment parades, train rides, hayrides, fiddlers and square dancing, and an old-fashioned barbecue. You'll also see a blacksmith shop in operation, farmhouse exhibits, a steam-operated sawmill, horse-drawn equipment, and more.

If you come at other than a show event, the museum is very quiet, but still enjoyable. You can roam around the grounds and see the old equipment. Most days, you'll be able to see someone working on the machinery. There is a small park with a couple of swings and a museum with a jumble of antique equipment.

San Diego Wild Animal Park
Located 30 miles north of downtown San Diego via I-15/Highway 163. (From Los Angeles, take I-5 south to Highway 78 at Oceanside; take Highway 78 east to I-15 at Escondido; take I-15 south to Via Rancho Parkway and follow signs to the park.) (619) 234-6541 (tape) or 747-8702. Open daily. June 19–Labor Day: 9 A.M.–6 P.M. Rest of year: 9 A.M.–4 P.M. Ticket package includes admission, monorail, and all shows: Adults, $12.95; ages 3–15, $6.20; under 3, free. Parking, $1.

Within the city limits of San Diego is an eighteen-hundred-acre wildlife preserve where exotic animals roam freely in settings similar to their native homelands. You won't get as close a look at the animals as at the San Diego Zoo, the Wild Animal Park's parent institution. However, you will get to see how animals such as lions, Bengal tigers, elephants, rhinos, and giraffes behave in the wild, in African and Asian settings.

You enter the park through Nairobi Village, a recreated African village. Children will enjoy the large outdoor aviary, where more than one hundred exotic birds are perched, and the petting *kraal* where they can pet deer, sheep, and other gentle animals. They will also enjoy the Animal Care center where they can look through the windows to see the baby animals being cared for and fed. There are also a number of animal shows and exhibits—including the Gorilla Grotto—in this area, as well as a real elephant to ride.

To see the rhinoceroses, zebras, cheetahs, and other wild animals, you take a five-mile, fifty- to sixty-minute ride on a monorail from Nairobi Village. The train makes ample stops for observation, and the driver-guides identify the animals. The monorail ride is best taken in the early morning or late afternoon, because the animals often sleep in the midday heat. (The monorail ride can be very difficult with small children, however. You can't get off once the monorail starts, and sixty minutes can be a very long time on a crowded tram with a restless two-year-old.)

You can also see some of the animals from a safe distance on the 1¾-mile Kilimanjaro Hiking Trail that leads out of the Nairobi Village. There is a picnic place along the trail. The park also includes other picnic areas and a variety of restaurants and snack bars.

San Pasqual Battlefield State Historic Park
State Highway 78, just east of the San Diego Wild Animal Park. (619) 238-3380. Thursday–Monday, 10 A.M.–5 P.M. Closed Tuesday and Wednesday. Adults, $1; ages 6–17, 50¢.

One of the bloodier battles of the Mexican-American War was fought between American and native Californian troops in this quiet valley. The battle is commemorated by this state historic park. A visitors' center has displays (with text in both English and Spanish) on the battle and on the native Indians of the valley. A ten-minute video on the Mexican-American War is also shown. The park has a nature trail, and picnicking is permitted.

Bernardo Winery
13330 Paseo del Verano Norte, San Diego. (Located 6 miles south of Escondido. From San Diego: Go north on Highway 163 and I-15, take the Rancho Bernardo Road turnoff east to Pomerado Road, then go north 1½ miles on Pomerado Road to Paseo del Verano Norte. From Escondido: Go south on I-15 to Highland Valley-Pomerado Road exit. Take Pomerado Road 1¾ miles to Paseo del Verano Norte. Look for Bernardo Winery signs.) (619) 487-1866. Daily 9 A.M.–5 P.M.. Free.

One of the oldest continuously operating wineries in Southern California, the Bernardo Winery still grows its own grapes. There are no formal tours, but families are welcome to wander through the winery and vineyards at their own pace. Of interest are the old-style winepresses, which are still being used, and the large redwood storage vats, many of which are over seventy-five years old. There is wine-tasting for adults and a shady park with tables for picnicking.

Lake Wohlford
Northeast of Escondido. (From Escondido, take S-6 [Valley Parkway, then Valley Center Road] to Lake Wohlford road. Turn right and go about 2 miles to the lake.) (619) 749-2661.

There is a fine picnic area on the shores of this pleasant lake set in rugged hills. The lake offers boating and excellent fishing (a license is required), but no swimming. Lake Wohlford Resort (phone 619-749-2755) has boat rentals, bait, and tackle. The cafe also serves a really good catfish and hush puppy dinner.

Bates Brothers Nut Farm
15954 Woods Valley Road, Valley Center. (Take S-6 north from Escondido to Valley Center.) (619) 749-3333. Daily, 8 A.M.–5 P.M. Free.

This farm is a pleasure, offering visitors spacious green picnic grounds in a pretty country setting. Ducks, goats, sheep, and other farm animals reside behind fences and can be petted. A country store sells the farm's products and bags of feed for the animals. Although you can tour the nut-processing facilities by request on weekdays, the main attractions of this place for children are the animals and the green open spaces in which to run and play.

Palomar Observatory
From Oceanside, take Highway 76 past Pala and 5 miles beyond Rincon Springs; turn left on S-6 and continue up the mountain. (619) 742-2119. Daily, 9 A.M.–4 P.M. Free.

High on Palomar Mountain is the giant Hale telescope, whose 200-inch-diameter mirror gathers light beams from distant galaxies and focuses them on photographic plates to produce pictures of those galaxies. The massive telescope can be viewed from a glassed-in balcony viewing room. (Wear sweaters; it's cool inside.) Nearby is a small museum containing a model of Hale's mirror and illuminated color photographs of the planets, some of the galaxies, and some star clusters.

There are a number of nice spots for picnics and outdoor activities in the area. One picnic ground is close to the observatory near the Palomar Mountain Forest Station. Heading down the road from Palomar Mountain, you can go west at Summit Junction for about three miles on S-7 to Palomar Mountain State Park, nearly two thousand acres of parkland in a lush, densely wooded mountain region with magnificent views. The park has complete facilities for camping, good picnic areas, and plenty of hiking trails.

A short distance east of Summit Junction is Palomar Mountain County Park, a small but beautiful forested mountain park with eight picnic tables, five fireplaces, and restrooms.

You could also return to Highway 76 and travel east to the San Luis Rey Picnic Area, a lovely spot with a rushing stream, shade trees, and picnic facilities. If you go a little farther east on Highway 76, you can picnic at Lake Henshaw (which can also be reached by going east on S-7 from Summit Junction).

Julian
Sixty miles northeast of San Diego at the junction of Highways 78 and 79. (From Los Angeles, take I-5 south, then go east on 78. From San Diego, take I-8 east, then go north on 79.)

In the late 1860s, prospectors struck gold in the mountains near the settlement of Julian. False-front stores, gaudy hotels, saloons, and dance halls sprang up to serve the prosperous miners. When the boom ended, the town settled into being a sleepy little agricultural community.

Today the town still has its original false-front stores, wooden sidewalks, old homes, and elegant old hotel. You can sip a soda at an old-fashioned marble counter in the drugstore. Less than a block away is an old one-room school, now used as a library but still retaining its old-fashioned school desks.

A small museum is housed in an old masonry building that was once a brewery and a blacksmith shop. The Julian Museum, located at 2811 Washington Street, is open 10 A.M.–4 P.M. on weekends. Among the exhibits are turn-of-the-century clothing, household equipment, dolls, a foot-treadle printing press, and a mail pouch with a parachute that was dropped in 1938 on Julian's first airmail delivery.

Kids will enjoy most a tour of the Eagle Mine at the end of C Stret (open 10 A.M. to 2 P.M. daily; phone 619-765-9921). At the end of the tour, kids can pan for gold. There are also a number of home-style restaurants in the town. Julian can get very crowded on holiday and summer weekends; you might wish to schedule your trip to avoid these times.

Cuyamaca Rancho State Park
Highway 79 between Julian to the north and Descanso Junction to the south. (Take I-8 east from San Diego and go north on Highway 79.) (619) 765-0755. Open daily. Day use: $3 per vehicle. Campsites $10 (reservations should be made at least ten days in advance by phoning MISTIX, 1-800-444-7275).

Located about forty miles east of San Diego on the western slopes of the Laguna Range, this popular state park stretches over some twenty-one thousand acres. The terrain includes high mountain peaks; dense forests; many open meadows; and a wide range of flowering plants, streams, and springs. The varied bird and animal population includes deer, raccoons, squirrels, badgers, skunks, and bobcats. There are more than one hundred miles of hiking and riding trails, and the park generally has snow in the winter. Cuyamaca Lake is stocked with trout each year. Overnight camping is available in two campgrounds. This is a fine all-around, all-year park, although it gets heavy use on weekends.

Laguna Recreation Area
About 12½ miles north of the junction of I-8 and S-1. (Take I-8 east from San Diego past the towns of Alpine and Pine Valley. Go north on S-1 about 12½ miles to the recreation area.) (619) 473-8205. Open daily. Free. Information center: Monday–Friday, 9 A.M.–4 P.M.; Saturday and Sunday, 11 A.M.–6 P.M.

In the heart of the Cleveland National Forest, the Laguna Recreation Area is in a lovely setting of pine and oak trees. Most of the area is about six thousand feet in elevation, sunny and warm in the summer with cool nights, and cold with some snow during the winter. The area is beautiful, with high peaks, two small lakes, views of the desert below, vast stands of oak, sycamore, pine, big-cone spruce, fir, and incense cedar, wildflowers in the spring, and a variety of bird and animal life. Desert View offers the best picnic facilities in the area.

Stop in at the Mount Laguna visitors' center for detailed information on hiking trails, self-guided nature trails, and, in the summer, naturalist-led nature walks and evening campfire programs.

Anza-Borrego Desert State Park
Park headquarters is in Borrego Palm Canyon, 3 miles northwest of Borrego Springs. (619) 767-5311. For a list of lodgings, write to the Chamber of Commerce, Borrego Springs, CA 92004.

Extending almost the entire length of San Diego County's eastern border region, from Riverside County to the Mexican border, is Anza-Borrego Desert State Park. The nation's largest state park, it comprises more than a half-million acres. Although much of the land is a raw desert wilderness that should be explored only by experienced desert hands, the park still has a great deal to offer casual visitors. Along accessible trails are oases of fan palms, wild plum trees, elephant trees, tamarisks, oaks, cottonwoods, creek beds with lush vegetation, and surrealistic sandstone canyons sculpted by millions of years of wind and rain.

Borrego Palm Canyon, the site of the park headquarters, is probably the best spot for families. The main campground includes sun shelters, gas stoves, showers, and RV hookups. In this area are date groves, a view point overlooking the spectacularly eroded Borrego Badlands, and a self-guided nature trail leading up to a canyon of palms. Nature programs, tours, and campfire programs are given by park rangers on the weekends from November through May. The park headquarters will provide you with maps and all sorts of other information on the park.

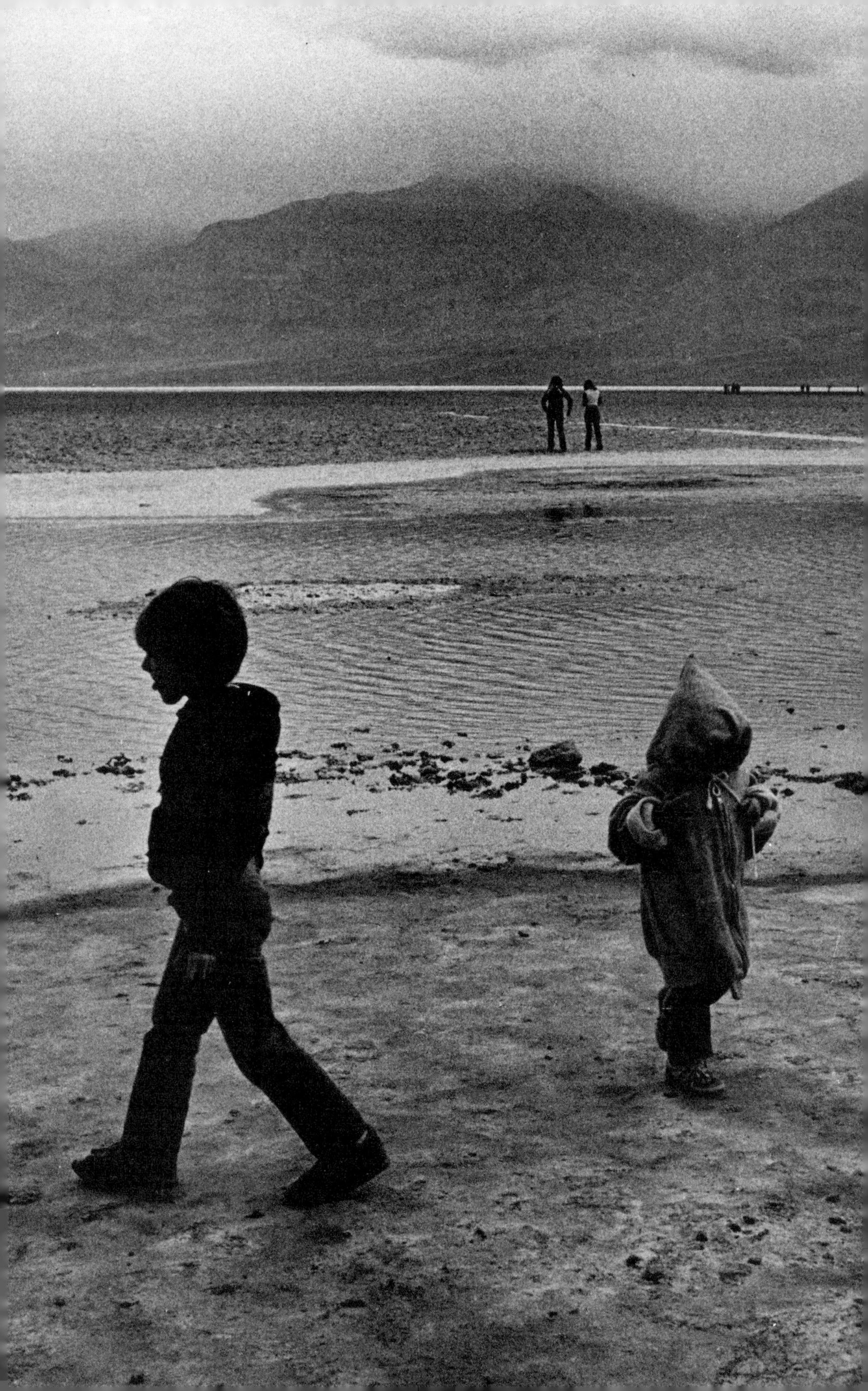

Inyo, Kern, and Tulare Counties

The heart of California's agricultural production, scenic forests, and a vast and fascinating desert are all part of the landscape of these counties. Many of the things to do with children in this region are nature activities, from an exploration of Death Valley, to a visit to see one of the last remaining herds of dwarf elk, or a trip to look at the world's oldest trees.

In addition to natural wonders, these counties also offer children some of the state's most exciting historical attractions. At Pioneer Village in Bakersfield, kids can explore the re-creation of an entire frontier town. At the town of Laws, near Bishop, they can play in an eleven-acre restoration of a nineteenth-century railroad community complete with trains. And on seven Sundays during the year, families can see a mock Civil War battle in a historic fort that once housed the country's only camel cavalry.

Although these counties cover a huge area, the places suggested in this chapter can be reached easily from either Bakersfield, Bishop, or Death Valley.

Badwater, Death Valley, is a desolate, yet fascinating place to explore.

In and Around Bakersfield

Pioneer Village/Kern County Museum
3801 Chester Avenue, Bakersfield. (805) 861-2132. Pioneer Village: Monday–Friday, 8 A.M.–5 P.M. Saturday, Sunday, and holidays, 10 A.M.–5 P.M. (Tickets sold until 3:30 P.M., daily.) Adults, $3; senior citizens, $2.50; children, $1.50; under 3, free. Kern County Museum: Monday–Friday, 8 A.M.–5 P.M.; Saturday, Sunday, and holidays, 10 A.M.–5 P.M. Free.

Pioneer Village is a fifteen-acre reconstruction of a nineteenth-century Kern County frontier town, and you'll find an exciting authenticity about it. The village's forty-odd buildings range from a completely furnished Victorian mansion to a log cabin, all either originals or painstakingly reproduced copies. There is an 1899 general store stocked the way it would have been; a one-room schoolhouse complete with McGuffy readers; authentically furnished doctor's, dentist's, lawyer's, and newspaper offices; and a jail. Other buildings include an old ranch house, a bank, a firehouse, a blacksmith shop, a railroad station, and so on—a complete town.

Though the insides of many buildings are glassed off, the richly detailed interiors, including period-costumed mannequins, provide a sense of visiting another time that holds children's interest. There is also much that can be touched and handled, such as the many farm and oil-drilling tools. The village is laid out with lots of space between the buildings, and there are many spots to stop and rest. A self-guided tour of this marvelous outdoor museum is relatively easy with the brochure supplied at the gate.

The Kern County Museum, housed in a large Spanish-style building, is adjacent to the village. Among the exhibits are displays of antique dolls, historic clothing, old rifles, local Yokuts Indian displays, and a dog-powered butter churn.

Lori Brock Children's Museum
3803 Chester Avenue, Bakersfield. (805) 395-1201. Monday–Friday, 11 A.M.–5 P.M.; Saturday, Sunday, and holidays, 10 A.M.–4 P.M. Adults, $1.50; ages 3–14 and seniors, $1.

Located next door to Pioneer Village, the Lori Brock Children's Museum offers kids a variety of hands-on exhibits. One room of the museum is devoted to a major thematic exhibit that changes yearly. The "Ocean in

Motion" exhibit, for example, offered kids the chance to crawl through a submarine equipped with sonar, radar, and a working periscope. The Discovery Room, across the hall, offers a variety of exhibits and activities. Children might try on costumes from around the world or put on a uniform and climb aboard a police motorcycle. There are art and science activities to participate in, computers to work, a climbing structure, and more. Outside the museum are picnic tables under shade trees and a play area with a wood play structure.

California Living Museum

Northeast of Bakersfield about 13 miles via Alfred Harrell Highway 178. Located on Frontage Road near Lake Ming. (805) 872-2256. Tuesday–Sunday, 10 A.M.–sunset. Closed Mondays, except for holiday Mondays. Closed Christmas. Adults, $2.50; seniors, $2; ages 6–17, $1.50; under 6, free.

The California Living Museum is a combination zoo, botanical garden, and natural history museum devoted to California wildlife. You'll get a close-up look at coyotes, bobcats, kit foxes, a pair of mountain lions, a porcupine, and other animals native to California. The museum's birds of prey collection, including a golden eagle, is composed entirely of handicapped birds who would not survive in the wild. Other exhibits include an earth-covered reptile house, a walk-in bird aviary, a tortoise enclosure, and a pleasant waterfowl lagoon. A nature trail follows a simulated Kern River, and a children's park allows kids to get up close to a variety of tame animals. All exhibits can be reached by wheelchair, and strollers are available. There are shaded picnic areas on the museum grounds and camping is possible next to the museum in Kern River Park. The museum is still young and expanding. The grounds are dusty, so dress accordingly. Also, it can get very hot in the desert sun, so you probably will want to avoid a midday visit in the summer.

Hart Memorial Park

East of Bakersfield 13 miles on Alfred Harrell Highway 178. (805) 872-5149. Daily, 5 A.M.–10 P.M. Free.

This eighty-acre park along the Kern River includes a safe place to play in the water, a casting pond, picnic grounds, and amusement rides.

Rankin Guest Ranch
P.O. Box 36, Caliente. (From Bakersfield, take Highway 58 east; turn onto the Caliente cutoff road and proceed 13 miles.) (805) 867-2511. Reservations required. Guest season: About April 1–October 30.

This thirty-one-thousand-acre working cattle and guest ranch has been in the same family since 1863. Guests can enjoy horseback riding, hayrides, swimming, family dances, fishing, tennis, archery, hiking, and other activities in a family environment. During the summer and school vacations, the ranch has a children's counselor on staff who supervises special programs for children from four to twelve, including picnics, crafts, horseback riding instruction, and horseback rides.

All activities—including the children's programs, fishing, and horseback riding—and all meals are included in the price. The daily rate for two adults sharing a cabin is $97.50 each. For each child under twelve in the same room the rate is $64.50. The rate for two children in a separate room adjoining the parents' room is $84.50 each. Children under a year old are free. Cribs and high chairs are available. Weekly rates and off-season rates are less. The top guest capacity is about thirty-five people at a time.

Tehachapi Mountain Park/Tehachapi Train Loop
Seven miles southwest of Tehachapi; 40 miles east of Bakersfield on Highway 58. (805) 822-4632. Free.

At an altitude ranging from five thousand to seven thousand feet, this pleasant mountain park offers hiking during the summer months and sledding and tobogganing during the winter. The pine-shaded 570-acre park is full of birds, squirrels, and occasionally deer.

About ten miles north of the park is the famous Tehachapi (Walong) Loop, built in 1876 to get trains through the rugged mountain pass. The rails here appear to be making two circles, winding around themselves in a knot. From a view point on a dirt road beside the tracks (off Highway 58 near Keene, just west of the historical marker), you can watch trains of more than eighty-five cars loop over themselves, with the engine passing just eleven feet above the cars still entering the tunnel below. The trains pass through fairly frequently, and it is worth a wait to see such an unusual sight.

Lake Isabella
South of Kernville. (From Bakersfield, take Highway 178 east.) (619) 379-2742. Open daily, year round. Free.

Lake Isabella is the largest freshwater lake in Southern California. Nine miles across at its widest point, the lake has thirty-eight miles of shoreline. It is ranked as the top lake for catching bass in California. Rainbow trout, bluegill, and catfish also make their home here. Boat rentals are available. There are numerous camping and picnicking areas around the lake.

Buena Vista Aquatic Recreation Area
Near Taft via Highway 119. (Located about 35 miles west of Bakersfield. From Bakersfield, take Highway 99 south to Highway 119; go west on 119 to Enos Lane and turn left.) (805) 763-1526. Open daily, 5 A.M.–10 P.M. Day use: $2 per vehicle (up to six people). Dogs, $2; boats, $3.50.

This Kern County-operated 980-acre recreation area includes an 86-acre fishing lake and an 873-acre boating lake. A comfortably large picnic area with complete facilities is adjacent to the larger lake. Overnight camping is permitted in designated areas.

Tule Elk State Reserve
Located 25 miles west of Bakersfield near Tupman. (From Bakersfield, take Highway 119 west to Tupman Road and go north.) (805) 765-5004. Open daily until sunset. Free.

One of the last herds of the rare California tule elk resides in a park created especially for their preservation. The animals are about two-thirds the size of other species of elk and are much lighter in color. The herd of about forty bulls, cows, and calves can best be seen at 2 P.M., when they come to the park headquarters area to be fed. (However, in the winter season when there is sufficient grass, the elk may not visit the feeding area for several days at a time.) Park personnel are around at feeding time and are glad to answer questions about the animals.

There are shady picnic tables, barbecue pits, water, and restrooms in the grassy viewing area. It is a good idea to plan coming here for a picnic or in combination with a visit to the nearby Buena Vista Aquatic Center, in case the elk don't show. Bring along binoculars.

Fort Tejon State Historic Park
Fort Tejon exit off I-5, 3½ miles north of Lebec (thirty-six miles south of Bakersfield.) (805) 248-6692. Park open daily, 8 A.M.–5 P.M. (until 6 P.M. in summer). Buildings open 10 A.M.–4:30 P.M. Adults, $1; ages 6–17, 50¢; under 6, free. Battle weekend admission: Adults, $2; ages 6–17, 50¢.

Fort Tejon was established by the U.S. Army in 1854 to protect the Indians in the southern San Joaquin Valley and the government property at the reservation. In addition to protecting the Indians, the troopers guarded miners, chased bandits, and generally offered protection to the southern part of the state. The fort also had the only camel cavalry in the United States. On the orders of the then-secretary-of-war, Jefferson Davis, who was later to be president of the Confederacy, camels were imported to the post for carrying supplies to isolated desert posts. The camels worked out splendidly, but the experiment was abandoned at the outbreak of Civil War. The fort itself was abandoned in 1864.

Fort Tejon is now restored as a state historic park. A map is available at the headquarters museum and leads you to the barracks building and the officers' and orderlies' quarters. A stream and a grassy picnic area are under big shade trees. On the third Sunday of the month from April through October, a mock Civil War battle takes place in the park, complete with blue- and gray-uniformed soldiers, old guns, and cannons. (Bring your own folding chairs or blankets, as no seating is provided.) On the first Sunday of the month year round, people at the park are costumed in historic dress.

Colonel Allensworth State Historic Park
Twenty miles north of Wasco on Highway 43. (Take Highway 46 east from I-5 or west from Highway 99, then go north on Highway 43.) (805) 849-3433. Open daily. Free.

The town of Allensworth was founded in 1908 by Col. Allen Allensworth as a self-governing and completely self-sufficient community for Black Americans—a place where Blacks could live and work in peace. An escaped slave who served with the Union forces during the Civil War, Allensworth was also a successful restaurateur, a minister, an army chaplain, and the highest-ranking Black military officer of his time. The town he founded prospered—there was a school, church, library, post office, a hotel, and shops—until its water supply eventually failed. Allensworth was slowly abandoned, its building left to decay.

In 1974 the town became a state historic park, and the town's appearance is slowly being restored. The Visitors Center, open daily from 10 A.M. to 5 P.M., has displays and shows a thirty-minute film on Colonel Allensworth and the town. Nearby is the restored school and the reconstructed home of Colonel Allensworth. Both buildings are open on request. This area includes green lawns and shaded picnic grounds. Five other buildings have been restored—you look through their windows. The rest of the town awaits restoration and is rather desolate.

The park has a semi-improved campground (no hookups).

The Bishop Area

Bishop City Park and Visitors Center
690 North Main Street (corner of Main [Highway 395] and Park Avenue), Bishop. Free. Visitors Center: (619) 873-8405. Hours: Monday–Friday, 8 A.M.–5 P.M.; Saturday and Sunday, 10 A.M.–4 P.M.

Children will enjoy feeding the ducks who make their home on the lake in this scenic city park. In addition to a beautiful setting, the large park includes a stream where you can fish for trout, a swimming pool with showers, well-equipped children's playgrounds, a gazebo, picnic facilities—including a pavilion for sheltered eating—ball fields, tennis courts, and a friendly, relaxed atmosphere.

The Visitors Center adjacent to the park offers tourist information for the region and a most helpful staff.

Laws Railroad Museum and Historical Site
Laws. (From Bishop, take U.S. 6 northeast 5 miles, then go east half a mile on Silver Canyon Road.) (619) 873-5950. March–mid-November: Daily, 10 A.M.–4 P.M. Rest of year: Weekends only, weather permitting. Closed New Year's, Thanksgiving, and Christmas Day. Free.

The Laws Railroad Museum and Historical Site is an eleven-acre restoration of the once-active railroad community of Laws. You'll see the 1883 depot—with its displays of railroad artifacts, western items, and a working model railroad—and the old stationmaster's house, restored and furnished with turn-of-the-century items. Other buildings include the Laws post office with old-fashioned equipment and the Wells Fargo Building with gold-weighing scales and displays of Indian artifacts. There are loading bunkers, a water tower, an oil tank, a hand-operated turntable, a boxcar town, a farm wagon display, mining equipment left over from the Nevada gold rush, and more. Best of all is the *Slim Princess*, a narrow-gauge locomotive that is just waiting for kids to crawl on it and ring the old cattle-warning bell in its cab.

Ancient Bristlecone Pine Forest
East of Big Pine. (From Big Pine, south of Bishop, go east on Highway 168 to Westgard Pass; turn north on White Mountain Road.) Daily, June–October, weather and road conditions permitting. Free. For more information contact White Mountain District Visitors Center, 798 North Main Street, Bishop. (619) 873-4207.

The oldest known living things on earth can be examined in the Bristlecone Pine Forest, a part of the Inyo National Forest. The bristlecone pines here in the White Mountains have survived more than four thousand years, exceeding the age of the oldest giant sequoia by fifteen hundred years. A paved road takes you to Schulman Grove, where the gnarled trees have been sculpted into astonishingly beautiful shapes and forms by the elements of centuries. An information center displays some of the things scientists have learned from studying the trees. There are two self-guided nature trails. One leads you to Pine Alpha, the first tree dated at over four thousand years. The other trail leads you by the oldest of the trees, including the forty-seven-hundred-year-old Methuselah tree. There is a picnic area and toilets at Schulman Grove, but no water is available.

Patriarch Grove is eleven miles farther up the mountain by way of a dirt road; the drive is spectacular, with views of great open spaces and colorful ranges. The Patriarch Grove is set within a large open bowl, exposed to wind and weather. The trees here have been molded into unusual abstract sculptures by the elements. A self-guided trail leads past the Patriarch tree, the largest bristlecone pine in the world. There are picnic tables, an outdoor display case, and toilets at the grove.

Dress warmly when you visit the forest, bring an adequate supply of water, and make sure you have a full tank of gas.

Eastern California Museum
Corner of Grant and Center streets, Independence. (Independence is south of Bishop and Big Pine on Highway 395. From Highway 395, exit at Center Street.) (619) 878-2411 weekdays. (619) 878-2010 weekends. Thursday–Monday, 12–4 P.M. Free.

Perhaps this fine museum's most interesting feature for children is its Little Pine Village, a group of old buildings furnished with original items. The buildings include a general store, a blacksmith's shop, a livery stable, a millinery shop, and a barber-beauty shop. The five-acre museum grounds also have displays of Indian dwellings and antique wagons. The museum building houses Indian and pioneer artifacts, historical photographs, and natural history displays relating to this eastern Sierra region.

The Eastern California Museum also administers the Commander's House, a restored and furnished eleven-room Victorian that is the only structure remaining of Camp Independence, established in 1862 to protect early Owens Valley residents from Indian attacks. You can take a free guided tour of the house, which is located one block north of Center Street on Highway 395, on Sundays, March through October, from 1 to 4:45 P.M. (It's a good idea to call ahead to make sure a docent will be available the Sunday you are going to be in Independence.)

Mount Whitney Fish Hatchery
Located a mile west of Highway 395, 2 miles north of Independence. (Follow the signs from Highway 395.) (619) 878-2272. Daily, 8 A.M.–5 P.M. Free.

The Mount Whitney Fish Hatchery is one of the sources for the fish that are planted in Southern California streams. The fish hatchery building is currently closed, and no fingerlings are being hatched due to the infestation of Whirling disease in their waters. (Whirling disease is not contagious to humans.) When the disease is eradicated, the hatchery will resume operation. You can still see rainbow and brook trout, however, swimming in the concrete raceways just north of the building. The hatchery, built of native stone in 1917, is a very attractive place, and its tree-shaded grounds include an inviting area for picnicking.

Death Valley

Death Valley Monument
Park headquarters is located at Furnace Creek. (Take Highway 190 east from Highway 395 at Olancha, or take Highway 127 north from I-15 at Baker.) (619) 786-2331. Open year round, although it is uncomfortably hot in the summer. Free.

This enormous desert valley is a place of great extremes. During the summer months, temperatures frequently reach 120 degrees, and they've been known to go as high as 134 degrees. The area contains the lowest point in the United States, Badwater, which is 282 feet below sea level. Nearby is Telescope Peak at 11,049 feet above sea level. In spite of the desolate environment, plant and animal life are found everywhere. Some plants—such as Death Valley sage, rattleweed, and the panamint daisy—can be found only in this area.

It is recommended that you begin your visit at the Monument Headquarters and Visitors Center in Furnace Creek. Guidebooks and maps are available here, as well as a leaflet giving hints on safe driving in the desert. There is also a small museum to acquaint you with the area's geology and plant and animal life. Near the monument headquarters, the Borax Museum displays original mining tools and equipment, a railroad handcar, stagecoach, buckboard, and wagon and mining artifacts. Two miles north, the famous twenty-mule-team wagons mark the site of the Harmony Borax Works, a restored processing plant.

The tourist season begins in October and lasts until May. There are nine campgrounds in the monument; hotels and motels are in Furnace Creek. The Death Valley roads and campgrounds get extremely crowded during winter three-day weekends, Thanksgiving weekend, Christmas–New Year's week, Easter week, and the annual Death Valley Forty-Niner's encampment the first or second week in November. Also, make sure you have plenty of gas and oil when traveling in this area. Carry water both for your family and your car. Do not venture off the paved roads, and never leave your car in case of trouble.

Devil's Postpile National Monument
The monument is reached via Highway 203, which leads west from Highway 395 and the Mammoth Visitors Center. (619) 934-2289. Open daily, mid-

June to early October. Free. Except for vehicles with camping permits, private vehicles are not allowed beyond Minaret Summit between 7:30 A.M. and 5:30 P.M., July 1–September 7. A shuttle bus service stops a half-mile from the Postpile. Tickets and schedule information are available at the Mammoth Mountain Ski Area. Fee: $3.50 per person.

When nature appears to be an imitation of manmade things, it causes us to stop and wonder. The Devil's Postpile is just such a place. At this remote national monument up in the Sierra Nevada near the Mammoth ski area, thousands of symmetrical gray granite columns rise to a height of more than sixty feet. Caused by volcanic upheaval in the distant past, the formation presents a striking example of the wonders of nature. Pieces of granite have broken off and created a large pile at the base of the formation, which you can walk up and touch. An easy trail leads to the top of the columns, where glaciers have polished the surface to resemble tile inlays.

Scotty's Castle
North end of Death Valley. Monument headquarters phone: (619) 786-2331. Open daily, 9 A.M.–5 P.M. Adults, $4; ages 6–11, $2; under 6, free.

In the middle of this lonely desert area is a Spanish-Moorish mansion that was built by two thousand workmen at a cost of $2.5 million. It was built many years ago at the whim of an eccentric millionaire who loved the valley, Walter Scott, known as Death Valley Scotty. The Death Valley Park Service offers tours through the castle, which is furnished with luxurious rugs, tapestries, rare art treasures, and elaborate furniture. The castle is quite a contrast to the starkness of many of the local desert towns.

Amargosa Opera House
Death Valley Junction. (Death Valley Junction is located near the junction of Highways 190 and 127 on the east side of Death Valley Monument, 28 miles from Furnace Creek.) (619) 852-4316. Open October–May. November–April: Performances Monday, Friday, and Saturday at 8:15 P.M. October and May: Saturdays only. Adults, $5; children $3.

Marta Becket is known for the one-woman family-oriented dance pantomime shows she presents at her Amargosa Opera House in the little town of Amargosa near the eastern entrance of Death Valley. The audience

The Spanish-Moorish Scotty's Castle is quite a contrast from the starkness of Death Valley.

watches the performance seated on metal chairs gathered around an old potbellied stove that is lit on chilly nights. Becket has decorated the walls of this converted old movie theater with painted murals jammed with sixteenth-century kings, queens, gypsies, and other characters shown sitting in balcony seats. The ceiling is a field of cupids and clouds. Reservations are a good idea.

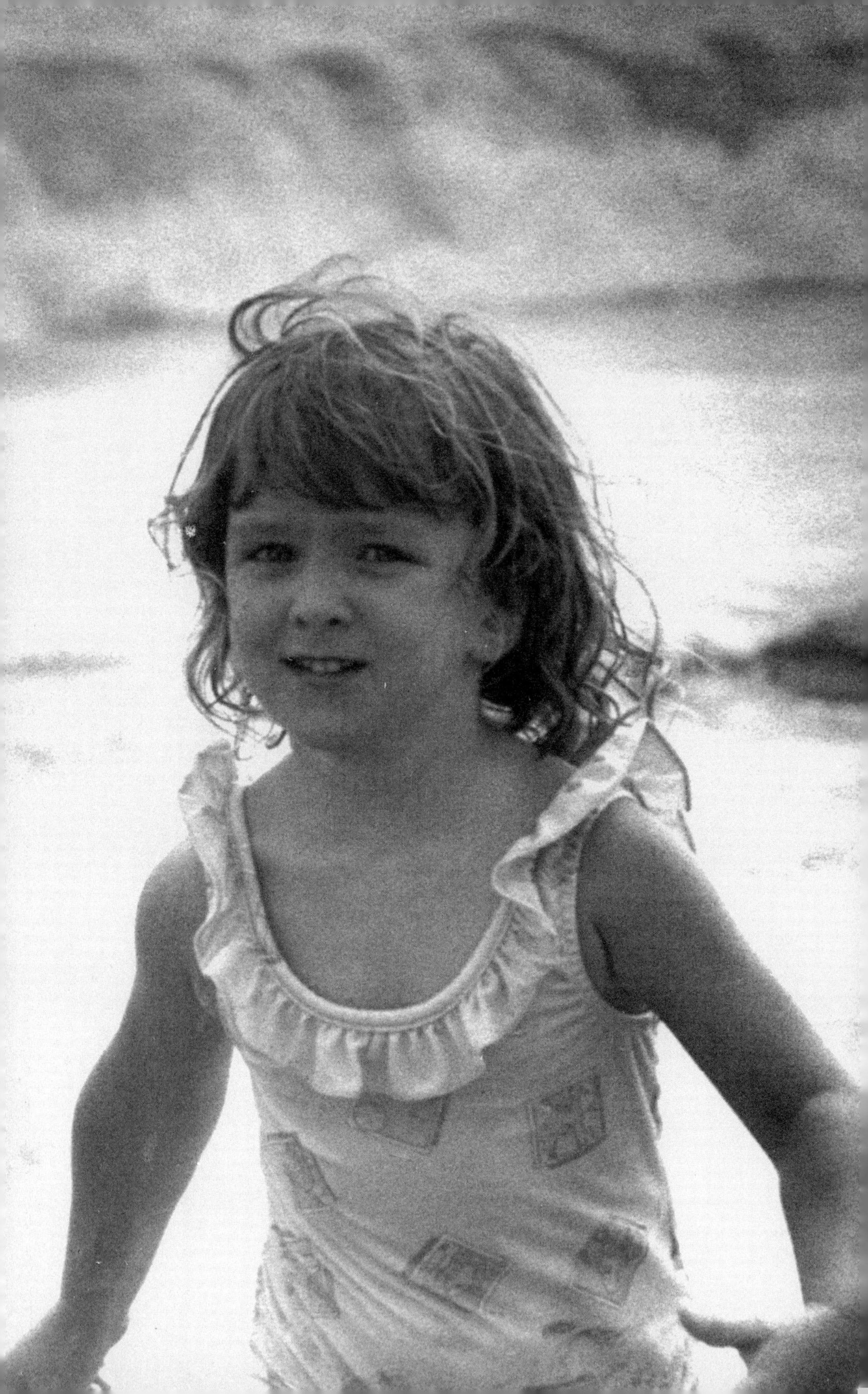

Santa Barbara, Ventura, and San Luis Obispo Counties

There may be an ugly spot between Morro Bay and Ventura, but I haven't seen it. Santa Barbara, with its Mediterranean setting and architecture, is one of California's most beautiful cities. The year-round good weather and slower-paced lifestyle here make outdoor activities—from boating to horseback riding to walking—a pleasure for families. The city has worked to preserve its history, and the lovely Mission Santa Barbara is among the many places where kids can get a sense of Santa Barbara's colorful past. The Santa Barbara Visitors Information Office at 1 Santa Barbara Street (phone: 805-965-3021) provides visitors with accommodation information, maps, a calendar of current events, and other helpful information.

North of Santa Barbara, the Santa Ynez Valley offers some wonderful small towns to explore. South and east of Santa Barbara in Ventura, Ojai, and the Santa Clara Valley, the variety of places to go with children includes uninhabited islands in the Pacific.

Up the coast, San Luis Obispo is a city that has preserved its history as well as its small-town charm. The San Luis Obispo Chamber of Commerce at 1039 Chorro Street (phone: 805-543-1323) offers a variety of literature for visitors, including a guide to the city just for kids. A few miles away, the once-quiet fishing village of Morro Bay offers families a wide choice of waterfront activities, including a trip by water taxi to an island of sand dunes.

Santa Barbara has wonderful beaches to enjoy.

In and Around Santa Barbara

Santa Barbara County Courthouse
1120 Anacapa Street (one block east of State Street and one block north of Carrillo Street), downtown Santa Barbara. (805) 962-6464. Monday–Friday, 8 A.M.–5 P.M.; Saturday, Sunday, and holidays, 10 A.M.–5 P.M. Guided tour Wednesday and Friday at 10:30 A.M. and Thursday at 2 P.M. Free.

The beautiful Santa Barbara County Courthouse is a good place to begin a tour of the city. Resembling a Spanish-Moorish castle, the courthouse has wrought-iron balconies, hand-carved doors, a great archway, towers, and a red tile roof. Inside the building you are greeted with an amazing variety of colorful tiles set in the floor, stairways, and walls. There are handpainted ceilings, wrought-iron chandeliers, and bright red curtains at the windows. A clocktower above the fourth floor provides a panoramic view of the city, coastline, and mountains; you will also be able to see some of the places, such as the mission, that you may be visiting later.

In the Assembly Room, the two-story-high walls are painted with murals depicting such events in Santa Barbara's history as the arrival of Juan Rodriguez Cabrillo in 1542 and the founding of Mission Santa Barbara in 1786. After walking down a winding staircase to the lowest level, children will be interested to find a well-preserved old stagecoach that is quite different from the kind usually seen on television westerns. Other relics include an old wine cart. The courthouse is surrounded by tropical gardens and lush lawns. You can either tour the courthouse on your own or take a forty-five-minute guided tour offered on Wednesday and Friday mornings and Thursday afternoons.

Santa Barbara Museum of Art
1130 State Street (at Anapamu Street), downtown Santa Barbara. (805) 963-4364. Tuesday, Wednesday, Friday, and Saturday, 11 A.M.–5 P.M.; Thursday, 11 A.M.–9 P.M.; Sunday, noon–5 P.M. Free.

It should come as no surprise that the art-minded town of Santa Barbara has a fine local museum. In fact, most of the objects on permanent display were donated by Santa Barbara residents. Housed in a bright, airy building, the collection includes ancient Greek, Roman, and Egyptian sculpture, Oriental art, West African art and artifacts, and American and European paintings. Children should enjoy seeing the interesting Alice F. Schott Doll Collection—which ranges from B.C. Egyptian to eighteenth-century French dolls—and the museum's collection of four hundred rare historical Oriental musical instruments. The museum mounts an annual Christmas exhibit designed for children.

El Cuartel/El Presidio de Santa Barbara
122 East Canon Perdido Street (one block south of Carrillo Street, two blocks east of State Street), downtown Santa Barbara. (805) 966-9719. Monday–Friday, 10:30 A.M.–4:30 P.M.; Saturday–Sunday, noon–4 P.M. Free.

The center of Spanish Santa Barbara was the Presidio Real, the fourth military post established in California by Imperial Spain. El Cuartel, the oldest building in Santa Barbara open to the public, was a soldiers' barracks built shortly after the Presidio was founded in 1782. Inside are scale models of what the Presidio looked like in its day and an exhibit of artifacts recovered from an archaeological dig that is exploring the remains of the rest of the fort. The padres' quarters on the Presidio grounds has recently been rebuilt using the original style of handmade adobe bricks. The Presidio chapel is also being rebuilt.

Historical Society Museum
136 East de la Guerra Street (two blocks south of Carrillo Street and two blocks east of State Street), downtown Santa Barbara. (805) 966-1601. Tuesday–Friday, noon–5 P.M.; Saturday–Sunday, 1–5 P.M. Guided tours Wednesday, Saturday, and Sunday at 1:30 P.M. Free.

Embracing four distinct eras—Indian, Spanish, Mexican, and American—Santa Barbara's colorful past is presented to the public in this museum. Mementos from each era are displayed. Of interest to children are lots of period costumes, including a seventeenth-century Spanish cape and a Mexican ranchero's outfit; relics of Richard Henry Dana's visits to the city, including a model of his ship, *Pilgrim;* saddle and horsemanship displays; and antique dolls, teddy bears, and a bright red carriage.

Art Show on the Boulevard
Cabrillo Boulevard east of State Street, Santa Barbara. (From Highway 101, take either Cabrillo Boulevard or State Street exit.) Sunday, 10 A.M.–sunset. Free.

On Sundays, local printers, sculptors, leather workers, potters, toymakers, and other craftspeople display their wares on the grass between the beach and the boulevard. It's a colorful display that can stretch as far as a mile. The variety is pleasing and the atmosphere can be fun for older children.

Moreton Bay Fig Tree
Chapala and Montecito streets, Santa Barbara. (Chapala is one block west of State Street; the tree is one block south of Highway 101.) Daily, sunrise to sunset. Free.

Admittedly, a tree is an odd sightseeing destination, but this one is really something. Native to Moreton Bay in eastern Australia, this tree was planted in Santa Barbara in 1877 by a pioneer family. The tree is enormous; it's among the largest of its kind in the world. The *Guinness Book of Records* reports that ten thousand people could stand in its shade at noon. The tree would fill half a football field. The last measurement of its spread branches indicated that this giant was 160 feet wide.

Yacht Harbor and Breakwater
West Cabrillo Boulevard, Santa Barbara. (From Highway 101, take either the State Street or Castillo Street exit, go south to Cabrillo, and then west to the harbor and breakwater.) Open daily. The walkway is lighted at night.

A paved walkway on top of the breakwater protecting the Santa Barbara Yacht Harbor provides a captivating half-mile walking tour of the harbor. In addition to seeing hundreds of pleasure craft, kids will get a closeup view of the local fishing boats. If you want to get out on the water yourself, you can rent one of a variety of various-sized motorboats, sailboats, and rowboats from Santa Barbara Boat Rentals (phone: 805-962-2862) at the breakwater.

Sealanding Sportfishing (phone: 805-963-3564) sells bait, rents tackle, and runs daily sportfishing boats. Half-day boats usually leave at 7 A.M. and 12:30 P.M. and cost $18 for adults and $14 for children fourteen and under.

Longer trips are also available. Rates include bait, and all boats have a galley. They also offer whale-watching cruises in the winter.

Carriage Museum
129 Castillo Street, Santa Barbara. (From Highway 101, take the Castillo Street exit south.) (805) 962-2353. Sunday, 2–4 P.M. Free, but donation requested.

The horse-drawn carts and carriages in this museum were used by pioneer Santa Barbara residents and donated by their descendants. During Santa Barbara's annual Old Spanish Days parade in August, the carriages leave the museum to ride down the streets of Santa Barbara once again. On their trip to the museum, children may see some of the work being done to restore the carriages. Adjacent to the Carriage Museum is Pershing Park, a large grassy park that is a nice spot for picnics.

Santa Barbara Zoological Gardens
500 Niños Drive, Santa Barbara. (From Highway 101, take Milpas Street south to Niños Drive). (805) 962-6310. Daily, 10 A.M.–5 P.M. (Open 9 A.M.– 6 P.M. during summer.) Adults, $4; ages 2–12 and seniors, $2; under 2, free.

This small zoo is a delight. Situated on a beautiful eighty-one-acre hilltop overlooking the Pacific, the zoo houses some five hundred animals, including lions, tigers, red pandas, gibbons, lemurs, sea lions, elephants, giraffes, and llamas. Most of the animals reside in habitats that resemble their natural homes. The zoo's small size makes it easy for children to see everything, and the exhibits are designed so that small children can see without having to be lifted.

There is a farmyard where children can pet and feed sheep, goats, donkeys, chickens, and other domestic animals. The zoo also includes a pleasant playground and a tiny children's carousel. Above the playground is a large grassy picnic area with a spectacular view of Santa Barbara Harbor. (The zoo is so manageable in size that one adult can walk back to the car to get the picnic lunch when you're ready to eat.) The zoo also has a miniature train that circles the park about every fifteen minutes, charging $1 a ride. There is a snack bar. Strollers and red wagons are available to rent. A zoo birthday party package is also available. During the summer, a Zoo Camp is offered for children aged three to eleven.

All sorts of animals reside in the beautiful Santa Barbara Zoo.

Andree Clark Bird Refuge
1400 East Cabrillo Boulevard (just west of the Cabrillo Boulevard exit from Highway 101, south of downtown Santa Barbara). Open daily during daylight hours. Parking on north side of lagoon. Free.

Adjoining the Zoological Gardens is a lovely lagoon in a garden setting that serves as a refuge for freshwater birds. Children will enjoy bringing bread crumbs to feed the birds. (The best location to feed them from is the clear area on the eastern shore.) A footpath and bikeway skirt the lagoon.

Mission Santa Barbara
Upper end of Laguna Street, Santa Barbara. (From Highway 101, take the Mission Street exit and turn left at Laguna Street.) (805) 682-4713. Daily, 9 A.M.–5 P.M. Adults, $1; under 16, free.

On a hill overlooking the city is the beautiful Mission Santa Barbara. Established in 1786, the mission is still used as a parish church. It is the only one of the California missions that has remained continuously in the hands of the Franciscans; the altar light has burned constantly since the mission was built.

On a self-guided tour through the mission, you'll see a typical padre's bedroom, the kitchen, eighteenth- and nineteenth-century furniture and kitchen utensils, examples of mission crafts and tools, and a Chumash Indian room. Displays include a history of the mission site, an exhibit on the mission's construction, and a collection of early photographs. The tour also passes through the flower-filled courtyard, the sanctuary, and the cemetery, whose crypts reflect the various degrees of wealth of the parishioner. In front of the church, a Moorish fountain flows into an ancient laundry trough. The mission faces a spacious and lovely grassy park where you can relax in the sun.

Museum of Natural History
2559 Puesta de Sol Road (two blocks north of the mission; follow the signs), Santa Barbara. (805) 682-4711. Monday–Saturday, 9 A.M.–5 P.M.; Sunday, 10 A.M.–5 P.M. Adults, $3; seniors and ages 13–17, $2; under 13, $1. Free admission the first Sunday of every month.

Surrounded by two acres of wooded ground, this museum focuses on the natural history and anthropology of the Pacific Coast. Each of the fourteen halls houses a different permanent collection, such as butterflies or Indian artifacts. The Bird Hall includes two giant California condors, one hanging from the ceiling with its great wings outstretched. An exhibit in the Insect Hall shows how a spider spins its web. Dioramas depict the lives of the local Chumash Indians before the Europeans arrived, and there is a full-size replica of a Chumash canoe. There are no steps or stairs between any of the exhibit halls, so strollers are easily used throughout the museum.

Other highlights of the museum include the seismograph just outside Fleischmann Auditorium on which you can watch the constant motion of Southern California, and the complete skeleton of a gray whale. The museum planetarium presents shows on Saturday and Sunday afternoons. (Telephone 805-682-3224 for information on planetarium shows.)

The museum buildings are attractive Spanish-style adobe with red tile roofs. A central courtyard provides a resting place between exhibits.

Santa Barbara Botanic Garden
1212 Mission Canyon Road (1½ miles north of the mission), Santa Barbara. (805) 682-4726. Daily, 8 A.M.–sunset. Free.

Up the canyon from Mission Santa Barbara, the city has transformed sixty acres of land into a garden that includes a 170-year-old dam and three miles of easy-to-walk nature trails. Native California trees, shrubs, wildflowers, and cacti all grow in their natural settings. The redwood grove is a particularly impressive-looking and pleasant-smelling area. Trails lead up, down, and along the sides of the canyon, which contains a small stream.

Benches are placed all along the trails, providing ample resting spots. Near the end of the gardens is a historic dam built by Indians at the beginning of the nineteenth century under direction of the mission fathers. It originally supplied water for the mission and surrounding Indian village.

Santa Barbara by Bike
Directions to the bike paths are available from the Santa Barbara Visitors Information Service, 1 Santa Barbara Street, Santa Barbara. (805) 965-3021.

Santa Barbara is a marvelous place for bicycling. The area is both scenic and relatively flat, and the weather is nearly always comfortable. A four-mile bikeway runs along the beachfront from the bird refuge to the mesa on the west. Branches of the bikeway also extend through the city, and a path runs from Goleta through the University of California campus. There are also plenty of bicycle racks throughout downtown and along the traveled routes. If you wish to rent bikes, Beach Rentals at State and Cabrillo streets, across from the pier, has a good selection (phone: 805-963-2524). Rates start at about $4 an hour. They are open daily.

Santa Barbara Polo Grounds
Highway 101 at Nidever Road (just south of the city of Santa Barbara). (805) 684-5819.

For a change of pace in the world of spectator sports, you might want to take your children to see a polo game. One of the country's better-known fields is here in Santa Barbara. There are practice matches (which are free) and trophy matches practically every weekend. Check with the polo grounds to see who's playing when.

Stow House
304 Los Carneros Road, Goleta. (From Highway 101 just north of Santa Barbara, take the Los Carneros Road exit north.) (805) 964-4407. Saturday and Sunday, 2–4 P.M. $1 per person.

The oldest frame house in Goleta Valley (dating from 1872) has been completely restored and furnished with Victorian trappings. More interesting to children than the tour of the house, though, are its grounds; these feature a bunkhouse, a museum, and a blacksmith's barn complete with tools from the past century.

Goleta Depot Railroad Museum
300 North Los Carneros Road, Goleta. (805) 964-3540. Wednesday–Sunday, 1–4 P.M. Free.

Also located on the grounds of Stow House is Goleta's relocated 1901 Southern Pacific Depot. The depot has been authentically restored to look the way it did in the early part of this century.

Stow Grove County Park
La Patera Lane, Goleta. (From Highway 101, take the Los Carneros Road exit north, turn right on Cathedral Oaks Road, and proceed to the park.) Open daily. Free.

Near Stow House is Stow Grove Park, where you can picnic in a grove of redwood trees. The thirteen-acre park was formerly a part of Stow Ranch. There are picnic tables and barbecues.

The Big Yellow House Restaurant
108 Pierpont Avenue, Summerland (5 miles south of Santa Barbara). (805) 969-4140. Daily, 7:30 A.M.–9 P.M.

The Big Yellow House Restaurant is easy to spot from Highway 101. The name is apt—it's a big yellow house overlooking the highway. If you are traveling with children to Santa Barbara from a southern location, you might want to use the restaurant as a landmark—something for the kids to spot on the way there and a place to eat on the way back.

There are six dining rooms in the refurbished nineteenth-century house.

Breakfast, lunch, and family-style dinner are served daily (except on Sunday when brunch and dinner are served). You have a choice of dinner entrees, and the side dishes are served family-style. Dinner starts at $6.95 for adults, and children are weighed on an old-fashioned scale to determine the price of their dinner. It's a good idea to phone ahead for reservations.

Santa Claus Lane
Eight miles south of Santa Barbara on Highway 101. Open daily.

This short side street between Summerland and Carpenteria is a year-round village with a Christmas theme. The Toyland shop features a wide range of toys and games. Another shop features Christmas cookies; as you walk in, all the traditional smells of Christmas hit you. Several restaurants serve a variety of food that is not tied to December 25. There is also a post office where letters can be postmarked Santa Claus Lane, CA. Santa Claus Lane does not merit a special visit on its own, but it can be a pleasant stop if you are traveling past.

Ventura, Thousand Oaks Area, and the Santa Clara Valley

Ventura County Historical Museum
100 East Main Street, Ventura. (Take California Street exit from Highway 101 and turn left on Main Street.) (805) 653-0323. Tuesday–Sunday, 10 A.M.–5 P.M. Free.

When I walked into this museum, I encountered a little boy loudly complaining to his parents that he didn't want to leave. Who could blame him? Housed in a bright new building, the museum presents a series of colorful displays on the history of Ventura County from the Chumash Indian days through the early part of this century. Among the exhibits are authentic reproductions of Chumash Indian rock paintings; a Spanish breastplate, excavated on the Ventura beach in the 1870s; rancho and Victorian costumes; a firearms collection, including the gun of the notorious bandit Vasquez; and a stuffed California condor. Other exhibits that should interest kids are the doll-size historical figures dressed in detailed costumes and the exact-scale replica of the San Buenaventura Mission and early Ventura business section as it stood in 1880. Outside are an extensive and fascinating collection of early farm equipment, displays of the early oil-drilling process, and an old oil pump. Surrounding the museum is a grassy park with picnic tables.

Mission San Buenaventura
211 East Main Street, Ventura. (From Highway 101, take the California Street exit and turn left on Main Street.) (805) 643-4318. Daily, 8:30 A.M.–5:30 P.M. Free.

Founded in 1782, this was the ninth California mission. The mission building has been beautifully restored. Children will be interested in the garden, which contains an olive press and an old water pump.

Albinger Archaeological Museum
113 East Main Street, Ventura. (805) 648-5823. Tuesday–Sunday. 10 A.M.–3:30 P.M. Free.

In the ground next to the mission, archaeologists are digging for bits and pieces of history. The artifacts that have been excavated on the site, including even some old bottles tossed from a long-ago saloon, are on display in this museum. Exhibits explain what archaeology is and what archaeologists do. If you ask her, the curator will gladly show you a ten-minute slide show on the area's history. Outside, you can take a close-up look at the digs.

Adventures for Kids
3457 Telegraph Road (at Mills Road), Ventura. (805) 650-9688. Monday–Saturday, 10 A.M.–5 P.M. Open Sundays, mid-November to Christmas.

Kids can climb into a wooden boat to look over books in this charming children's bookstore. There is also plenty of room to sprawl in the recently relocated and expanded store. The owner, Jody Fickes, is a former librarian, and she has arranged her store like a library: The books are organized by subject matter. The selection ranges in age appeal from a baby's first books to a substantial collection of young adult books. There's a large section of young-children's books; and there are books on prenatal care, child-rearing, and other subjects of interest to parents.

The store will special order books for you if they do not have them in stock. There is a story time every Tuesday at 10:30 from October through July; these are open to all kids, although groups are requested to call ahead. The store's extremely knowledgeable staff includes former teachers and a grandmother. The bookstore has wooden blocks in open stock. (You can purchase as few or as many as you want.) They also sell children's records, cassettes, rhythm instruments, puzzles, puppets, rubber stamps, and stickers. Adventures for Kids publishes an excellent newsletter three times a year that reviews children's books and lists upcoming special events.

Channel Islands National Park/Island Packer Cruises
1867 Spinnaker Drive, Ventura. (805) 642-1393. Reservations required.

Eight islands extending over a range of 150 miles make up this chain off the Southern California coast. Five of these islands have been set aside by the government as Channel Islands National Park. You can reach the five islands on boat trips offered by Island Packers.

Anacapa, the closest island, some fourteen miles off the shore of Ventura, is reached by a three-hour round-trip boat ride. (Daily excursions are offered year round. The boat leaves Ventura dock at 9 A.M. and returns at 5 P.M.) It's quite an adventure for kids. Seals and sea lions are pointed out along the way, and during the trip you may sight migrating whales. An eighteen-foot skiff takes five people at a time from the boat to the island. Anacapa, actually a chain of three small adjacent islets, is undeveloped and has wild areas, trails, and tide pools. Adults should be in good physical condition and children should have the stamina for a rugged outdoor day. (You must climb 153 steps to get from the landing cove to the island top, for a start.) There are no facilities on the island (except latrines), so bring your own food and water. Special weekend trips are also made to Frenchy's Cove on West Anacapa. There is a beautiful beach here with clear water where you can swim, picnic, and explore the tide pools. The cost for Anacapa is $28 for adults and $14 for children twelve and under. Half-day, nonlanding excursions to Anacapa that include a narrated cruise along the island's rugged north shore are available from April through November (adults, $16; children, $9.50).

Santa Barbara Island, forty-six miles offshore from Ventura, is home to the huge northern elephant seal. Reached by a three-hour trip each way, this island offers the opportunity to observe the elephant seals and other wildlife. The fare is $40 for adults and $27 for children. Trips are made only in the summer.

Other excursions are available to San Miguel Island and to Santa Rosa Island, home of the rare torrey pine. The crossings to both islands, however, can be long and rough. Trips are also available to Scorpion Ranch, a late-1800s ranch on Santa Cruz Island, and to the Pelican Bay preserve on Santa Cruz (no children under ten are permitted on the Pelican Bay trip). Camping trips and whale-watching trips are also available. Reservations should be made at least a month in advance for any weekend trip.

Channel Islands National Park Visitors Center
1901 Spinnaker Drive, Ventura. (805) 644-8262. Daily, 8 A.M.–5:30 P.M. Free.

A good place to prepare you for your visit to the Channel Islands—or as a stop in itself—is the Channel Islands National Park Visitors Center in Ventura. Exhibits include photo displays, Chumash Indian artifacts, a simulated caliche ghost forest, a native plant display, and an indoor tide pool. A twenty-five-minute film on the Channel Islands is also shown.

Olivas Adobe
4200 Olivas Park Drive, Ventura. (Take the Victoria Avenue exit from Highway 101 and follow the signs.) (805) 644-0346. Grounds open daily, 9 A.M.–4 P.M. House open weekends, 10 A.M.–4 P.M. Free.

In 1841 Raimundo Olivas and Felipe Lorenzana were awarded a grant of land near the mouth of the Santa Clara River as payment for their service in the Mexican army. Calling their land Rancho San Miguel, they planted grain, fruit trees, and grapevines and raised cattle. When the gold rush of 1848 brought hordes of gold-seekers to California, rancho owners like Olivas became rich by driving their cattle north to meet the miners' demands for food.

The large two-story adobe you see today was begun in 1847 to accommodate Olivas's growing family. It was the first two-story adobe in the area. (The family's original one-room adobe is still standing in the southwest corner of the courtyard.) The house was inhabited by a succession of owners almost continually until it was donated to the city.

On a tour of the nicely restored adobe, you can see the upstairs bedrooms with rancho-style hats hanging on the bed posts. Downstairs are the furnished living room, dining room, kitchen, and chapel. Kids will be impressed by the short doorways and the old newspaper—once used as insulating material—exposed in a wall section. Some old farm equipment is in the yard, and a Chumash Indian thatched hut is among the displays at the visitors' center. The adobe is surrounded by a lovely 6½ acre park.

CEA/Seabee Museum
U.S. Naval Construction Battalion Center, Gate A (Channel Islands and Ventura Road, southwest of Highway 101), Port Hueneme. (805) 982-5163. Monday–Friday, 8 A.M.–5 P.M.; Saturday, 9 A.M.–4:30 P.M.; Sunday, 12:30–4:30 P.M. Free.

Seebees fought in the Navy with bulldozers and shovels rather than with ships and guns. Their equipment is on display here along with some of their history. Exhibits include uniforms, an underwater diving display, outrigger canoes, World War II dioramas, weapons, flags, and tools. The museum is located on an operating navy base.

Stagecoach Inn Museum
51 South Ventu Park Road, Newberry Park. (From Los Angeles, take the Ventura Freeway past Thousand Oaks; exit at Ventu Park Road.) (805) 498-9441. Wednesday–Friday and Sunday, 1–4 P.M. Closed Monday, Tuesday, and Saturday. Free.

The Stagecoach Inn opened in 1876 as a stopover for weary travelers journeying between Los Angeles and Santa Barbara by stagecoach. The inn, which was originally located where the freeway meets Ventu Park Road, has been recreated with detailed authenticity. The docent-led tour begins in the hotel's parlor and dining room, which is furnished exactly as it might have been when the stage travelers relaxed there. The kitchen has a coal-burning stove, wooden sink, water pump, and old-time utensils. There is an authentic 1850s Wells Fargo safe in the hotel office. Among the rooms you'll see upstairs is a furnished guestroom said to be inhabited by a ghost.

Outside you can see a real stagecoach. Also on the museum grounds is a tri-village complex, including a Spanish-Mexican adobe of early 1800s, a wooden pioneer cabin, and two Chumash thatched huts. (The tri-village is open only on Sunday). There's a park with picnicking and a children's playground adjacent to the museum.

Moorpark College Exotic Animal Compound
7975 Campus Drive, Moorpark. (Located at the west end of Highway 118 between the cities of Simi Valley and Moorpark.) (805) 378-1441. Shows on Sunday at 3 P.M. Adults, $2; children 12 and under, $1.

Moorpark College offers a unique program in the training and management of exotic animals for students interested in becoming zookeepers or animal trainers. Every Sunday at 3 P.M. the students demonstrate what they are learning in a forty-five-minute show for the public. Sea lions, a baboon, parrots, and ponies are among the animals performing in the intimate outdoor theater. Students explain about the animals and take questions from the audience. Children get a chance to touch some of the animals, including a large snake. There is also a petting zoo open from 10 A.M. to 2:30 P.M. on Sundays before the show. The petting zoo, which includes rabbits, ducks, and goats, costs 50¢. You can see the animals in their compound on a visit to the campus any day.

Ojai Valley Museum and Historical Society
109 South Montgomery, Ojai. (A sign in the center of town on Ojai Avenue points the way.) (805) 646-2290. Wednesday–Monday, 1–4:30 P.M. Free.

Located in the former Ventura County Fire Station, the Ojai Museum displays Chumash Indian artifacts, early pioneer items, and stuffed animals and birds native to the Ojai Valley. The Civic Center Park on Ojai Avenue in the heart of town is a nice shady spot for a picnic.

Union Oil Co. Museum
1003 East Main Street, Santa Paula. (Santa Paula is located 53 miles east of Santa Barbara via Highway 150.) (805) 525-6672. Wednesday–Sunday, 10 A.M.–4:30 P.M. Free.

The Union Oil Co. Museum traces the history of the search for crude oil in California and the subsequent development of the industry. On display are oil-drilling machinery and old tools, including an early wooden drilling rig. Other exhibits explain how oil pools are located and how the drillers reach them. There are many historical photographs, as well.

Fillmore Museum and Historical Society
447 Main Street, Fillmore. (Fillmore is located on Highway 126 east of Santa Paula.) (805) 524-0948. Tuesday–Sunday, 1–4:30 P.M. Free.

Fillmore's 1887 Southern Pacific railroad depot was moved away from the tracks to house this museum. A large mural inside the museum depicts Fillmore around 1910, and many exhibits relate to the history of the area. There are pioneer household items, old business machines and typewriters, antique tools, railroad and oil industry memorabilia, and Indian artifacts. A special exhibit is a model of a condor cave.

The Santa Ynez Valley

Lake Cachuma
On Highway 154, 24 miles north of Santa Barbara. (805) 688-4658. Open daily. Day use: $3 per vehicle.

Set in a valley of the Santa Ynez Mountains, this large manmade lake offers picnic and playground facilities, boating, and fishing in lovely surroundings. The freshwater lake is stocked with thousands of fish. Bait, tackle, and boat rentals are available. Horseback riding is permitted, and there are camping facilities.

Solvang
Three miles east of Buellton and about 40 miles northwest of Santa Barbara. (You can either travel north on Highway 101 from Santa Barbara and east on Highway 246 at Buellton, or take the scenic route: Highway 154 from outside Santa Barbara, then west on Highway 246). Most shops and restaurants open daily, 9:30 A.M.–5 P.M. Closed Christmas.

Solvang is a blend of commercialism and cultural expression (leaning toward commercialism). It was founded in 1911 by Danes who copied the architecture of their homeland. The businesses have an old-world appearance with thatched-style roofs, inlaid timbers on the outside walls, and stained-glass windows. Many of the roofs have the traditional stork perched on top; and, of course, there are windmills. The renowned bakeries are probably the highlight of the town. The shops generally feature imports from Europe. There are some toy, doll, and hobby shops that might interest children. A horse-drawn replica of a Danish streetcar gives tours of the town, starting at Solvang Park.

Mission Santa Ines
1760 Mission Drive (a short distance east of the main business district), Solvang. (805) 688-4815. Winter: Monday–Saturday, 9:30 A.M.–4:30 P.M.; Sunday, noon–4:30 P.M.. Summer: Monday–Friday, 9 A.M.–5 P.M.; Saturday, 9 A.M.–4:30 P.M.; Sunday, noon–5 P.M. Adults, $1; under 16, free.

Founded in 1804, Santa Ines is a well-restored mission with a red tile roof and an arched colonnade in front. Highlights include artifacts from the time the Santa Ynez Valley was first settled by the padres; these items were used in the daily life of both priests and their Indian parishioners. There is also a pretty garden.

Pea Soup Andersen's Restaurant
Avenue of the Flags, Buellton. (805) 688-5581. Daily, 7 A.M.–11 P.M.

A few years ago you could eat all the pea soup you wanted here for 95¢. Now the price is $4.25, but the restaurant is as popular as ever. For those who don't like pea soup, other soups and a full menu are offered. The restaurant, at a central location in the Santa Ynez Valley, is large and colorful and has a number of different dining rooms. There are some coin-operated children's rides outside and a toy shop upstairs.

The Little Red Schoolhouse in Ballard
Located about 4 miles north of Solvang. (From Santa Barbara, take Highway 101 north, go east on Highway 246 through Solvang, and north on Alamo Pintado Road. Go east on Baseline Avenue to Ballard. Turn north on Cottonwood Avenue to the school). Free.

In a setting that is absolutely genuine, children can experience the era of their great-grandparents when they visit the little red schoolhouse in the sleepy town of Ballard. The steepled one-room schoolhouse was built in 1882 and has been in continuous use by schoolchildren since 1883. A sign at the schoolyard gate reads: "No dogs or livestock." The school is painted bright red with white trim. A rope swing hangs from a tree in front, a nice playground is in back, and there is also a big green lawn. Kindergartners are still being taught in the schoolhouse, but the yard is open to visitors on weekends and in the summer.

Mattei's Tavern

On Highway 154, Los Olivos. (Los Olivos is about 6 miles north of Solvang and about 2 miles north of Ballard. From Santa Barbara, take Highway 101 north past Buellton and turn right on Highway 154; or take Highway 154 directly from Highway 101 just north of Santa Barbara.) (805) 688-4820. Monday–Friday, 5:30–9 P.M.; Saturday, noon–3 P.M. and 4:30–10 P.M.; Sunday, noon–3 P.M. and 4–9 P.M.

Los Olivos was a stagecoach stop for the famous Butterfield Stage Lines. Mattei's Tavern, built in 1886, provided food and lodging for the tired and hungry passengers. The inn, now a state historic landmark, is still serving dinner to travelers. Of course, now the travelers arrive by car and the restaurant is operated by the Chart House—but never mind, the tavern still retains some of its old atmosphere. It's in a lovely rural setting, and kids will enjoy looking around the old inn. Dinners are served in a number of attractive dining rooms furnished in the style of the late 1800s; the fare is predominantly steak and chicken with bread and a salad bar. Adult dinners range from $8.95 to $23.95. Children's dinners are available for $6.95.

Union Hotel/Los Alamos

Los Alamos. (Fourteen miles north of Solvang and 17 miles south of Santa Maria. Take the Los Alamos turnoff from Highway 101. Follow the signs to town. The hotel is on the main street; you can't miss it.) (805) 344-2744. Hotel dining room open Friday and Saturday, 5–8 P.M.; Sunday, noon–7 P.M. (Hotel rooms are available for adults only.)

Kids step on a big butcher's scale and are charged by their weight for dinner at the historic Union Hotel in Los Alamos. Built of wood in 1880, the original Union Hotel provided lodging for Wells Fargo stagecoach passengers. The hotel later burned down and was rebuilt of adobe bricks. When the present owner bought the old hotel in 1972, he restored it to look as it did originally, using wood from 50- to 100-year-old barns. The hotel is completely furnished in antiques, down to an old-fashioned telephone on the lobby desk. Parked outside the hotel is a 1918 fifteen-passenger White touring car.

Dinners are served family-style in a dining room, which is furnished with pieces from a Mississippi plantation. The homestyle dinners include homemade soup, salad, corn bread, country-baked chicken, a platter of roast beef, potatoes, and fresh vegetables. The friendly waitresses wear old-fashioned dresses. The price of dinner for grown-ups is $12. The price for children is less and depends on their weight.

Los Alamos is a quiet little country town of seven hundred people, and city kids may enjoy just strolling through it. Los Alamos also has a very nice county park (follow the signs) open daily from 8 A.M. to sunset. The park features an old covered wagon, a children's playground, lots of lovely grassy areas, wooden bridges, hiking trails, and picnic tables.

La Purisima Mission State Historic Park
Northeast of Lompoc on Highway 246. (Take Highway 1 from its junction with Highway 101, or take Highway 246 west from Buellton. The mission is about 12 miles from Buellton and about 4 miles from Lompoc.) (805) 733-3713. Daily, 9 A.M.–5 P.M. Adults, $1; ages 6–17, 50¢; under 6, free.

La Purisima is the most interesting of all the missions for children. Beautifully restored, it gives you the feeling you are actually visiting a mission in the early 1800s. The major restoration work was done in the 1930s by Civilian Conservation Corps workers. After careful research, they performed the restoration using the original tools and methods of the early 1800s. While only the church remains at most California missions, La Purisima has been restored almost in its entirety, enabling you to grasp more fully what mission life was like. The mission system was established as a way for the Spanish government to set up territorial outposts without great expense, and, as such, the missions had to be self-supporting. Each mission was a self-sufficient economic unit which, in addition to its religious functions, quartered soldiers, provided for visitors, raised livestock, grew crops, and produced tradeable commodities such as hides.

At La Purisima, you can see real cattle hides on the drying racks, reconstructions of the original tallow vats used for making soap and candles, the *cuartel*—used for housing soldiers—with its dirt floor and narrow cots, the candle maker's shop, the weaving room with its looms, the olive mill and press, the kitchens, the apartments of married soldiers, the carpenter's and potter's shops, as well as the church and chapel. Sheep, burros, horses, and goats are kept together in an old-style pen; and pigs are kept in another pen. You can even see the ruts of a segment of the old Camino Real—the original highway that connected the California missions. A museum near the visitors' entrance has displays on the mission and the Chumash Indians.

In addition to the fine restoration of the mission grounds, the sense of the mission's past is heightened by its location off the beaten track in a rural area surrounded by agriculture and grazing land. Plan to spend a couple of hours at this highly recommended family destination.

San Luis Obispo and Morro Bay

San Luis Obispo Path of History
San Luis Obispo Chamber of Commerce, 1039 Chorro Street (between Monterey and Higuera streets), downtown San Luis Obispo. (805) 543-1323. Monday–Friday, 8 A.M.–5 P.M.; Saturday and Sunday, 9 A.M.–5 P.M. (Closed during lunch on weekends.) Free.

Nestled in a beautiful rural valley, San Luis Obispo has preserved not only its small-town atmosphere, but also its history. Many of the city's original buildings remain, restored and adapted for modern use. The city has marked out a Path of History linking nineteen historic sites in the downtown area. The path includes the mission, a history museum, and such intriguing spots as the Ah Louis Store, founded in 1874 by a Cantonese entrepreneur to serve the Chinese community and run today by his son. A guide to the Path of History is available from the Chamber of Commerce. If your children are old enough and you have the energy, you can cover the two-mile tour in a leisurely two hours on foot. Otherwise, you and your children can use the guide to select the spots you want to see.

A Kid's Guide to San Luis Obispo
San Luis Obispo Chamber of Commerce. (See above.) The guide costs $1.25.

San Luis Obispo may be historic but it's not stuffy. In fact, the San Luis Obispo Chamber of Commerce provides a guide to the city just for kids. In the form of a big treasure map that can be colored, it includes a pet shop, a toy store, a hobby center, a park, the mission, places to eat, and much more. Our favorite was Bubble Gum Alley, an alley (off Higuera Street between Garden and Broad streets) that has been brightly decorated with bubble gum.

Mission San Luis Obispo de Tolosa/Mission Plaza
Chorro and Monterey streets, San Luis Obispo. (805) 543-6850. Daily, 9 A.M.–4 P.M. Open until 5 P.M. during summer. 50¢ per person or $1 per family.

The fifth of the California missions was constructed in 1772 with adobe bricks made by the local Chumash Indians. The mission was restored in the 1930s and today serves as a parish church and a museum. In the museum, children can see an acorn mortar used by the Chumash—along with other Indian artifacts, some antique dolls, and Early California saddles, guns, and tools.

The Mission Plaza between the mission and San Luis Creek was designed by Cal Poly students as an attractive recreation of the historic center of the city. With its lush landscaping, benches, bridges, and creekside walkways, the plaza makes a lovely spot for resting or playing. It is also the center of many community activities throughout the year.

Best of all for kids is San Luis Creek. They can walk down to the water's edge and, when the water is not high, hop across the rocks in the stream.

San Luis Obispo County Historical Museum
696 Monterey Street, San Luis Obispo. (805) 543-0638. Wednesday–Sunday, 10 A.M.–4 P.M. Free.

An old-time U.S. mail carriage, a "Wanted" poster for Jesse James, and a giant model of the RCA Victor dog listening to an early phonograph are some of the exhibits in this thoroughly enjoyable historical museum. Housed in a 1905 red brick Carnegie library (point out the face on the frieze above the door to your kids), the museum also contains a room furnished in the style of an 1880s parlor, complete with models of women and children dressed in the fashion of an era. Kids will enjoy trying out the stereopticon viewer lying out in the open with a number of pictures to examine. Other exhibits that will interest children include a lighthouse lantern that magnifies fifty thousand times, nineteenth-century children's books and shoes, Civil War hats, old sheriff's badges, a model of Hearst

Castle, and a working model of a trolley made by a fifteen-year-old boy in 1911.

Cal Poly's Animal Farm
School of Agriculture, California Polytechnic University, San Luis Obispo. (From Highway 101, take the Grand Avenue off ramp north and follow the signs to campus.) (805) 756-0111. The farm is open daily. Free.

Most of Cal Poly's beautiful 5,169-acre campus is devoted to agricultural studies. The campus includes some thirty-four hundred acres of model farms, gardens, and livestock ranches where students get practical experience in their chosen fields. Visitors are welcome to tour most of the agricultural units. Kids will want to see the swine unit, which includes a nursery for baby pigs; the horses; the sheep unit; the dairy, where cows are milked every day at noon; and the cattle. The agriculture facilities are spread out, but you can get a map and pamphlet for a self-guided tour weekdays from the School of Agriculture. (Agricultural Sciences Building, Room 211; the building is near the campus store). On weekends you can get directions from students on the campus, or you can request that a map be sent to you ahead of time.

The horse and beef units and feed mill are to the right of Via Carta. The swine units are to the left of Via Carta. The sheep unit can be reached from Highland Avenue, and the dairy from Mount Bishop Road. On the weekend, Saturday is the best day to visit because everything is in operation (although you can still see animals on Sunday).

Atascadero Lake County Park
In Atascadero, about 15 miles north of San Luis Obispo. (Take Highway 101 north from San Luis Obispo and exit at Highway 41/Morro Bay. The park is located 2 miles west of Highway 101 on Highway 41.) Open daily. Free.

A visit to this large rural park is like returning to a slower, easier time. There is fishing, swimming, and pedalboating on the large lake. The park has a children's playground, picnic facilities, concession stands, and acres of tree-shaded lawn. Best of all is the uncrowded, soothing atmosphere.

Paddock Zoo
Located in Atascadero Lake County Park (see above). (805) 466-9037. Daily, 10 A.M.–4 P.M. Adults, $1; ages 6–17, 50¢; under 6, free.

This small zoo was put together by ranger Chuck Paddock. It has more than one hundred different species of animals, including lions, bears, and coyotes. There is a pleasant walk-through aviary and a lion-shaped drinking fountain for kids.

Morro Bay State Park
Located a mile south of the town of Morro Bay on State Park Road. (Take Bay Boulevard west from Highway 1 to the park; or from town, take Main Street south to the park.) (805) 772-2560 or 772-7434. Open daily. Day use, $3; campsite, $10; RV hookup, $16.

The nearly fifteen hundred seaside acres of Morro Bay State Park offer outstanding opportunities for picnicking, camping, hiking, bicycling, fishing, boating, and studying the wildlife of the central California coast. The park boasts one of the largest natural areas of marshland remaining along the coast, which is a haven for countless birds. In the spring, wildflowers are spread over the grass and the brush-covered hills. There are 135 family campsites, each with table, stove, and food locker; and the restrooms have hot showers. If you plan to stay overnight, you should reserve a campsite at least ten days in advance.

Morro Bay Museum of Natural History
State Park Road, Morro Bay State Park. (805) 772-2694. Daily, 10 A.M.–5 P.M. Adults, $1; ages 6–17, 50¢; under 6, free.

Located on a rocky cliff overlooking Morro Bay, this nature museum focuses on the birds and sea creatures of the area. There are exhibits on tide pools, low-tide animals, local birds, abalone, and various fish, as well as on the Chumash Indians. Perhaps the nicest feature of this museum is that it overlooks Morro Bay. Kids can use the telescope in the lobby or go out on the observation deck to match the specimens with the real thing.

Marina Rentals Clam Taxi
699 Embarcadero (at Pacific), Morro Bay. (805) 772-8085. Summer: Daily, except Wednesday, 9 A.M.–4 P.M.; launches leave every hour on the hour. Runs only on weekends during the winter. Adults, $3 round trip; children, $1.50 round trip; dogs, free.

The sandy strand with a strip of high dunes that separates the bay from the ocean here is part of Morro Bay State Park. For kids, a trip out to the strand is an adventure out of Robinson Crusoe. The adventure begins with a trip on a clam taxi, an open launch that takes you from the Morro Bay Marina across the bay to the uninhabited (by people, at least) strand. There are no facilities on the strand, just miles of sand to play in, as well as sand dunes to slide down. Bring sand toys, lunch, and drinking water.

Morro Bay Aquarium
595 Embarcadero, Morro Bay. (805) 772-7647. Winter: Monday–Friday, 10 A.M.–5 P.M. Saturday, Sunday, and holidays, 9 A.M.–6 P.M.; closed Thanksgiving and Christmas. Summer: Daily, 9 A.M.–7 P.M. Adults, $1; ages 5–11, 50¢; under 5, free.

You walk through a door in the Morro Bay Gift Shop and find yourself face to face with a group of barking seals and sea otters. Naturally, the seals are adept at begging for handouts from the visitors. The lady who sells tickets to the aquarium also sells seal food. One sea otter has even developed his own smoothly unique style: While the others bark and clap, he looks at the visitors and gives them a jaunty little wave.

An inside area contains about twenty tanks with some three hundred live marine occupants, including eels, octopi, abalone, crabs, lobsters, and all sorts of fish. A display of preserved marine specimens includes a great white shark. The inside is old, dark, and damp and consequently might scare small children. However, in this era of sleek amusement parks, there is something charming about this aquarium's aging unpretentiousness.

Tigers Folly II
1205 Embarcadero (behind the Harbor Hut Restaurant opposite the power plant), Morro Bay. (805) 772-2255. Daily during summer. Rest of year on weekends. Phone for the schedule.

You can take a one-hour narrated cruise of Morro Bay on the old-fashioned-style paddlewheeler *Tigers Folly II* past Morro Rock, the Embarcadero, and the harbor entrance.

Montana de Oro State Park
Located on the coast south of Morro Bay. (From Highway 101 south of San Luis Obispo, exit at the Los Osos off ramp. Follow Los Osos Valley Road through the town of Los Osos to Pecho Road. Follow Pecho Road to the park.) (805) 528-0513. Open daily. Free.

Dramatic and unspoiled, Montana de Oro State Park is a vivid reminder of the natural beauty of this state. The park's seven thousand acres of rolling hills, rugged cliffs and capes, beaches, and small coves are breathtakingly lovely. In the spring, the area is covered with brilliant wildflowers whose predominantly gold color gave the park its name: mountain of gold. There are miles of hiking trails through hills that overlook the ocean. Camping is available in an undeveloped campsite. For kids, the park offers a quiet beach covered with smooth, colored stones; it has natural jetties to climb on, and kids can wade in a stream that empties into the ocean.

Hearst Castle–San Simeon State Historical Monument
Off Highway 1 at San Simeon, 43 miles north of San Luis Obispo. (805) 927-2000. Daily, except Thanksgiving and Christmas Day. Minimum tour hours are from 8:20 A.M. to 3 P.M., with tours leaving every half hour. (Hours increase during summer and holiday periods.) You can buy your tickets at the ticket office, but reservations are strongly recommended. Reservations can be made by phoning MISTIX or in person at any MISTIX outlet. Phone 1-800-444-7275 to charge tickets by phone or for the address of the nearest MISTIX outlet. Adults, $10; ages 6–12, $5; under 6, free (provided the child sits on your lap on the bus.) No strollers are allowed.

On a par with any castle that a powerful seventeenth-century monarch might have built is the residence that William Randolph Hearst created for himself. The vastly wealthy publisher began building his home—apparently he never referred to it as a castle—in 1919. The work was never completed, but by the time of his death in 1951 there were more than a hundred rooms, including thirty-eight bedrooms, thirty-one bathrooms, fourteen sitting rooms, two libraries, a movie theater, and an indoor and an outdoor swimming pool. Hearst reputedly spent fifty million dollars collecting art treasures, many of them for showcasing in or as part of his estate.

Hearst's mansion and 123 surrounding acres of terraces, gardens, and palatial guest houses were donated to the state in 1958 by Hearst's descendants. Four separate two-hour tours of the estate are available to the public. Tour I is suggested as an overall first look. It includes the main floor of the castle, the gardens, the pools, and a guest house. Tour II visits about twenty-six rooms on the upper floors, including bedrooms, bath and sitting rooms, the libraries, and the kitchen. Tour III includes the guest wing of the mansion, a guest house, the grounds, and the pools. Tour IV focuses on the formal area and the lower level of the largest guest house. Each of the four tours requires climbing about three hundred steps.

Special Annual Events

January

Tournament of Roses Parade

This New Year's parade has been a tradition for years. No matter how good your color TV may be, you can't imagine how spectacular this event is until you see it in person. Hardy souls camp out the night before along the parade route to get a good vantage point. Grandstand seats usually go on sale in February and can be sold out by August. Check with the Tournament of Roses Association, Pasadena, CA 91184 (phone: 818-449-4100) early in the year to find out where to buy tickets. You can also see the floats the afternoon of the parade and the next day at Victory Park, 2575 Paloma Street, Pasadena.

Chinese New Year

Los Angeles's Chinatown celebrates Chinese New Year in January or early February. Highlights include the dragon parade and children's lantern procession. Phone or write the Chinese Chamber of Commerce, 978 Broadway, Room 206, Los Angeles, CA 90012. Phone: (213) 617-0396.

Greater Los Angeles Auto Show

More than five hundred domestic and imported cars are showcased along with antique and specialty cars. Phone the Los Angeles Convention Center for details: (213) 748-8531.

February

Children's Camellia Float Parade

Kids design and propel their own floats in this annual parade in Los Angeles County, usually held on the last Saturday in February. Write or phone early to enter a float. Temple City Camellia Festival, c/o Temple City Chamber of Commerce, 5827 North Temple City Boulevard, Temple City, CA 91780. Phone: (818) 287-9150.

Whale Festival

The annual twelve-thousand-mile migration of the California gray whales is celebrated in this festival sponsored by the Dana Point Harbor Association. Events include a film festival, whale-watching cruises, and opportunities to meet famous scientists and adventurers. Dana Point is located between San Juan Capistrano and San Clemente. For more information phone the Dana Point Harbor Association at (714) 498-2591.

Laguna Beach Winter Carnival

This Orange County festival has folk dancing, an arts and crafts fair, surfing and sand castle contests, a pancake breakfast, a parade, and often art exhibits. Contact the Laguna Beach Chamber of Commerce, P.O. Box 396, Laguna Beach, CA 92652. Phone: (714) 494-1018.

National Date Festival and Camel Races

Comical camel races, an amusement fair, and stands serving all sorts of date concoctions are some of the highlights of this ten-day festival in Riverside County. Write the National Date Festival, P.O. Drawer NNNN, Indio, CA 92202 (phone: 619-342-8247); or call the Indio Chamber of Commerce at (619) 347-9676 for details.

March

Blessing of the Animals

One of the loveliest events in Los Angeles occurs in front of the Plaza Church on Olvera Street on the Holy Saturday before Easter, when children bring their beribboned pets to be blessed by the priests. Even some of the animals from the zoo join the procession. Phone: (213) 625-5045.

Ocean Beach Kite Festival

Both adults and children can participate in this San Diego County kite festival. The festival, which includes kite decorating and flying contests, is sponsored by the Ocean Beach Recreational Council and Kiwanis. Phone: (619) 223-1175.

Girl's Day in Little Tokyo

The Japanese honor girls in the month of March, and March 3 is set aside as Girls' Day, or Doll Festival Day. Special food is served, and beautiful Japanese dolls are displayed along First Street in Little Tokyo. For details, check with the Japanese Chamber of Commerce of Southern California, 244 South San Pedro Street, Los Angeles, CA 90012. Phone: (213) 626-3067.

Fiesta de las Golondrinas

The return of the swallows to Mission San Juan Capistrano is celebrated in this festival in Orange County. There's a fiesta, a parade, a dance pageant, art exhibitions, and a pancake breakfast. For more information, contact the San Juan Capistrano Chamber of Commerce, 31882 Camino Capistrano, Suite 218, San Juan Capistrano, CA 92675. Phone (714) 493-4700.

April

Poly Royal

The students of the California Polytechnic State University at San Luis Obispo hold a big fair on the last Friday and Saturday of April. The highlight is an intercollegiate rodeo. For details, contact the California Polytechnic State University, San Luis Obispo, CA 93407. Phone: (805) 756-0111.

Renaissance Pleasure Faire

A whole Elizabethan village is set up on the Paramount Ranch in Agoura every spring from late April through May. There are arts and crafts booths, food, parades, dances, children's games, and strolling musicians, jugglers, and other entertainers. Visitors come dressed in their own period costumes. Agoura is located at the west end of Los Angeles County on Highway 101. Phone the Agoura Chamber of Commerce at (818) 889-3150 for details.

Ramona Pageant

Helen Hunt Jackson's Early California love story, *Ramona,* is dramatized three weekends every year in an outdoor amphitheater set in a canyon on the slopes of Mount San Jacinto in Riverside County. The natural acoustics are excellent. It's a colorful production with a cast of more than 350; music, dancing, authentic Indian rituals, and even horses are presented on the stage. Early reservations for the play are a good idea. Mail orders are accepted beginning January 1; send them to the Ramona Pageant Association, P.O. Box 755, Hemet, CA 92343. Phone: (714) 658-3111.

Kern County Museum Heritage Days

A parade, a Model A Ford car show, contests, quilting and candlemaking demonstrations, singing, and dancing are all a part of the Heritage Days celebration at the Kern County Museum and Pioneer Village, 3801 Chester Avenue, Bakersfield, CA 93302. Phone: (805) 861-2132.

Long Beach Grand Prix

This international auto race is held on the streets of Long Beach. Phone (213) 437-0341 for details.

National Orange Show

Animated citrus exhibits, a Polynesian music and dance competition, a hobbies and crafts show, an Armed Forces parade, a championship rodeo, 4-H exhibits, a midway and carnival area, a youth band competition, model railroad displays, and a free marionette show are just *some* of the activities at the annual National Orange Show in San Bernardino. For more information, contact the San Bernardino Chamber of Commerce, P.O. Box 658, San Bernardino, CA 92402. Phone: (714) 885-7515.

May

Bishop's Mule Days

A mule-shoeing contest, a mule show, and a mule sale are some of the events of Bishop's Mule Days. There's a barbecue and a pancake breakfast, too. For details on this Inyo County event, write to the Bishop Chamber of

Commerce, 690 North Main Street, Bishop, CA 93514; or phone (619) 873-8405.

Fiesta de la Primavera

This Early California-style celebration is held in San Diego's Old Town. There are mariachis, fiddle and banjo contests, Spanish and Mexican dancers, an arts and crafts show, and a buffalo barbecue. Phone Old Town State Park (619-237-6770) for details.

Cinco de Mayo

One of Mexico's great holidays is celebrated in El Pueblo de Los Angeles Historic Monument with puppet shows, mariachi music, Spanish dancing, and food. Phone El Pueblo Park (213-625-5045) for information.

Strawberry Festival

Pie-eating contests, a parade, amusement rides, games, and the world's largest strawberry shortcake are all a part of this celebration, which is held in Garden Grove (Orange County) over the Memorial Day weekend. Telephone the Garden Grove Chamber of Commerce for more information. Phone: (714) 638-7590.

Boys' Day in Little Tokyo

Carp flags will be flying and special food served on May 5, the day the Japanese honor boys. For details, contact the Japanese Chamber of Commerce of Southern California, 244 South San Pedro Street, Los Angeles, CA 90012. Phone: (213) 626-3067.

Children's Celebration of the Arts

Puppet-making, etching, weaving, and face painting are just a few of the hands-on activities featured in this children's arts festival held along Main

Street in Ventura. For more information, phone Ventura Parks and Recreation: (805) 654-7837.

Creative Rancho Days

Rancho life as it was one hundred years ago is reenacted this month at Rancho Los Alamitos in Long Beach. You'll see horseshoeing, butter churning, and many other tasks of nineteenth-century ranch life demonstrated. For details, phone Rancho Los Alamitos: (213) 431-3541.

June

Huck Finn Jubilee

Mojave Narrows Regional Park outside of Victorville is the site of this annual celebration of a bygone time. Events include river raft-building contests, nickel-in-the-haystack games, fence painting, clog dancing, bluegrass music, and more. For details, phone Mojave Narrows Regional Park: (619) 245-2226.

Cherry Festival

The festival in Beaumont (Riverside County) features a parade, fireworks, and amusement rides. Kids can pick cherries. Contact the Beaumont Chamber of Commerce, P.O. Box 291, Beaumont, CA 92223. Phone: (714) 845-9541.

Southern California Exposition/San Diego County Fair

Held at the fairgrounds in Del Mar, this fair features an impressive performing horse show. Phone the San Diego Visitors Bureau, (619) 236-1212, for more information.

Whale Fiesta

Sand sculpture contests, arts, crafts, games, films, lectures, and much more are part of this annual celebration of the whale sponsored by the Cabrillo Marine Museum and the American Cetacean Society. For details, phone the Cabrillo Marine Museum at (213) 548-7546.

Summer Solstice Celebration

The longest day of the year is celebrated in Santa Barbara with a colorful parade down State Street and other activities. Phone the Santa Barbara Visitors Information Office at (805) 965-3021 for more information.

Lompoc Flower Festival

A parade of flower floats, tours of the flower fields, a carnival, and other festivities highlight this Lompoc celebration. Contact Lompoc Valley Chamber of Commerce, 119 East Cypress, Lompoc, CA 93436. Phone: (805) 736-4567.

July

Laguna Beach Living Art Pageant

Laguna Beach citizens are costumed and posed inside frames to recreate famous art works during the nightly Pageant of the Masters in Orange County. During the day there is an outdoor display of arts and crafts. Write early for tickets: Festival of the Arts, 650 Laguna Canyon Road, Laguna Beach, CA 92651. Phone: (714) 494-1145.

Surf, Sand and Sandcastle Days

Held in conjunction with the U.S. Open Sandcastle Competition, this celebration features a parade, fireworks, and, of course, sand castle building. The three-day event takes place in the City of Imperial Beach. For more information, phone the City of Imperial Beach at (619) 423-8300.

Santa Barbara National Horse and Flower Show

Held at the Earl Warren Showgrounds, this is one of the best horse shows in the nation. Phone: (805) 687-0766.

Santa Barbara Kennel Club Dog Show

Held on the campus of the University of California at Santa Barbara, this is one of the largest shows of its kind in the country. Contact the Santa Barbara Convention and Visitors Bureau, P.O. Box 299, Santa Barbara, CA 93102. Phone: (805) 965-3021.

Orange County Fair

A rodeo, a horse fair, 4-H project displays, motorcycle races, an arts and crafts show, a laser show, a carnival, and professional entertainers are a few of the main events in this ten-day fair held in Costa Mesa. Phone: (714) 751-3247.

July Fourth Street Fair in Ventura

The highlight of this street fair for kids is the "Push 'em-pull 'em" procession, where kids parade down the street in or on decorated strollers, wagons, bikes, skateboards, and all sorts of other nonmotorized conveyances. The event also features food, music, dancing, and entertainment. Contact the Ventura Visitors and Convention Bureau Information Center: (805) 648-2075.

August

Santa Barbara's Old Spanish Days Fiesta

This five-day festival celebrates the heritage of Santa Barbara. The highlight is the historical parade including brightly decorated antique horse-drawn carriages. For details, call the Santa Barbara Visitors Information Office: (805) 965-3021.

International Children's Film and Television Festival

Children's films from around the world are screened at this annual festival sponsored by the Children's Film and Television Center of America. Performances by clowns, mimes, and musicians, and other children's entertainment, takes place before each matinee. The festival is held on the USC campus at the Norris Cinema Theatre. For more information contact the Children's Film and Television Center of America, USC School of Cinema-TV, University Park, Los Angeles, CA 90089-2211. Phone: (213) 743-8632.

Little Tokyo Nisei Festival

Karate, judo, and sword tournaments; a carnival; and a street parade are among the attractions at this celebration in Los Angeles's Little Tokyo. Contact the Japanese Chamber of Commerce of Southern California, 244 South San Pedro Street, Los Angeles, CA 90012. Phone: (213) 626-3067.

Old Miner's Days in Big Bear

Long before the skiers started coming here, these San Bernardino County mountains were inhabited by gold miners. This Old West-style celebration commemorates that time with parades, dances, contests, and a burro derby. Contact the Big Bear Lake Chamber of Commerce, P.O. Box 2860, Big Bear Lake, CA 92315. Phone: (714) 866-4607.

Antelope Valley Fair

Tractor races highlight this six-day fair held at Lancaster in Los Angeles County. For more information phone the Lancaster Chamber of Commerce: (805) 948-4518.

Long Beach Sea Festival

Boat races, a swim meet, and a sand-sculpture contest are some of the events of this Los Angeles County summer festival. Contact the Long Beach Convention and Tourism Bureau, 180 East Ocean Boulevard, Long Beach, CA 90802. Phone: (213) 436-3645.

Newport Beach Harbor Character Boat Parade

More than a hundred one-of-a-kind boats parade through this Orange County harbor on the third Saturday in August each year. The boats are decorated with flags, balloons, animated characters, and streamers; and the crews wear costumes. Contact the Newport Beach Chamber of Commerce, 1470 Jamboree Avenue, Newport Beach, CA 92660. Phone: (714) 644-8211.

Ventura County Fair

A parade, a rodeo, and a carnival are some of the highlights of this county fair held on the Ventura Fairground. Contact the Ventura Visitors and Convention Bureau Information Center, 785 South Seaward Avenue, Ventura, CA 93001. Phone: (805) 648-2075.

Thundertub Regatta

Contestants design their own imaginative bathtubs and race them on the water in this slapstick regatta held on Enchanted Cove, Fiesta Island on Mission Bay, San Diego. For more information, phone (619) 236-1212.

America's Finest City Week

San Diego celebrates itself in this annual event. Activities include a half-marathon run, fireworks, concerts, a Bay Day for children, and more. Phone the San Diego Visitors and Convention Bureau at (619) 236-1212.

September

Los Angeles County Fair

One of the largest fairs in the nation, the Los Angeles County Fair in Pomona lasts most of the month of September. Featured are rides, food, livestock, arts and crafts, horse shows, and you name it. Phone: (714) 623-3111.

Bishop Wild West Rodeo Weekend

Every year on Labor Day weekend, Bishop plays host to four days of Old West family entertainment including rodeos, parades, bed races, picnics, children's games, pancake breakfasts, and barbecues. For more information, contact the Bishop Chamber of Commerce, 690 North Main Street, Bishop, CA 93514. Phone: (619) 873-8405.

Mexican Independence Day

Mexico's Independence Day is celebrated in a two-day fiesta in El Pueblo de Los Angeles Historic Monument. Phone El Pueblo Park: (213) 625-5045.

Kern County Fair

A junior livestock auction, games, and rides are featured at the fair. Telephone the Bakersfield Chamber of Commerce for details: (805) 327-4421.

Cabrillo Festival

This festival celebrates the discovery of the West Coast with a reenactment of Juan Cabrillo's landing at Point Loma. For details, call the San Diego Convention and Visitors Bureau at (619) 236-1212.

Solvang Danish Days Festival

Denmark's Independence Day is celebrated with Danish music, costumed singing and dancing, and special pancakes cooked outdoors and served along the main street. For more information, contact the Solvang Chamber of Commerce, 1623 Mission Drive, Solvang, CA 93463. Phone: (805) 688-3317.

October

Calico Days

A greased-pig contest and mock gunfight are two of the events held during Calico Days at Calico Ghost Town (San Bernardino County), P.O. Box 638, Yermo, CA 92398. Phone: (619) 254-2122.

Anaheim Halloween Festival

Children have their own costume parade with bands and floats during this celebration in Orange County. Other events include outdoor costume breakfasts and another elaborate Halloween parade with animated floats. For more information, contact the Anaheim Chamber of Commerce, 100 South Anaheim Boulevard, No. 300, Anaheim, CA 92805. Phone: (714) 758-0222.

Silverado Days

A youth parade, a carnival, food booths, an arts and crafts fair, plays, and a big parade are all part of this four-day celebration in Buena Park (Orange County). For details, contact the Buena Park Visitors and Convention Bureau, P.O. Box 5308, Buena Park, CA 90622. Phone: (714) 994-1511.

Pismo Beach Clam Festival

All sorts of activities are held during this weekend-long event in San Luis Obispo County, including clam-digging contests, sand castle contests, and arts and crafts exhibitions. Telephone or write the Pismo Beach Chamber of Commerce, 581 Dolliver Street, Pismo Beach, CA 93449. Phone: (805) 773-4382.

November

Hollywood's Santa Claus Lane Parade of the Stars

Santa Claus is joined by television and movie stars in this parade along Hollywood Boulevard on the Sunday after Thanksgiving. Call the Hollywood Chamber of Commerce: (213) 469-8311.

Mother Goose Parade

Mother Goose characters are portrayed on colorful floats during this parade in El Cajon designed entirely for children. For details, contact the San Diego Visitors and Convention Bureau: (619) 232-1212.

December

Long Beach Christmas Water Parade

Boats decorated with Christmas lights make their way through the Naples Canals in Long Beach while a choir sings from barges during this Los Angeles County Christmas pageant. Contact the Long Beach Convention and Tourism Bureau, 180 East Ocean Boulevard, Long Beach, CA 90802, for details. Phone: (213) 436-3645.

Lights on the Water

Boats strung with Christmas lights parade through San Diego's Mission Bay. The parade ends with the lighting of Sea World's Sky Tower Christmas tree. In a separate water parade, lighted boats tour San Diego Bay from the Embarcadero to Shelter Island. Contact the San Diego Convention and Visitors Bureau, First Avenue and F Street, 11 Horton Plaza, San Diego, CA 92101. Phone: (619) 232-1212.

San Diego Community Christmas Center

On the first three Sundays in December, Spreckels Outdoor Organ Pavilion in Balboa Park is the location for a fifty-foot lighted Christmas tree, Nativity scenes, and special programs. Phone: (619) 236-1212.

Los Posadas

A traditional Mexican Christmas festival is held for nine days on Olvera Street in Los Angeles. Each night at 8 P.M. there is a candlelight procession through the street, reenacting the journey of Mary and Joseph into Bethlehem. After the procession each night, children break an enormous candy-filled piñata. Phone: (213) 625-5045.

Index

Adobe De Palomares, 82
Adventures for Kids (bookstore), 185–186
Adventure Playground, 97
Aerospace Building, 17
Aerospace Museum, 136
Agua Caliente Indian Reservation, 118
Air and Space Garden, 17
Albinger Archaeological Museum, 185
Amargosa Opera House, 171–172
America's Finest City Week, 212
Anaheim Halloween Festival, 213
Anaheim Stadium Tours, 91
Ancient Bristlecone Pine Forest, 168
Andree Clark Bird Refuge, 180
Andres Pico Adobe, 66
Angeles National Forest, 75–76
Angel's Attic, 42
Angel's Gate Park, 51
Annual Events, 201–215
Antelope Valley Fair, 211
Antique Gas & Steam Engine Museum, 152
Anza-Borrego Desert State Park, 157–158
Atascadero Lake County Park, 196
Atlantis Play Center, 92
Avila Adobe, 3–5

Babes at the Beach, 39
Babes in the Woods, 39
Balboa Island Ferryboat Ride & Fun Zone, 98–99
Balboa Park, 130–131
Banning Residence Museum and Park, 53
Barnsdall Park, 31–33
Barstow Station, 124
Barstow Way Station, 123–124
Bates Brothers Nut Farm, 155
Berkeley (ferryboat), 139
Bernardo Winery, 154

Beverly Hills
  Public Library Story Hours, 37–38
  Recreation & Parks Department, 38
The Big Yellow House Restaurant, 183–184
Birthday party programs, 8, 14, 28, 34, 40, 41, 42, 57, 73, 92, 96, 104, 113, 149
Bishop
  City Park and Visitors Center, 167
  Mule Days, 205
  Wild West Rodeo Weekend, 212
Blessing of the Animals, 203
Boatrides, 45, 50, 52–53, 56, 98–99, 140, 186, 198
Bob Baker Marionette Theater, 34
Botanical Building (Balboa Park), 133
Boys' Day in Little Tokyo, 206
Brand Park, 70
Brand Park Library and Art Center, 70
Buena Vista Aquatic Recreation Area, 165
Burton Chase Park, 44

Cabot's Old Indian Pueblo and Museum, 120
Cabrillo Festival, 213
Cabrillo Marine Museum 49–50
Cabrillo National Monument, 140
Calico Days, 213
Calico Ghost Town, 124–125
California Living Museum, 163
California Museum of Afro-American History & Culture, 18
California Museum of Science and Industry, 16–18
Cal Poly's Animal Farm, 196
Camp Snoopy, 86, 87
Carriage Museum, 179
Casa de Adobe, 25

Casa de Altamirano, 142
Casa De Estudillo, 143
Catalina Island, 52–53
CEA/Seabee Museum, 188
Century City Playhouse, 40
Channel Islands National Park, 186
  Island Packer Cruises, 186
  Visitors Center, 187
Charles W. Bowers Museum, 92–93
Chatsworth Park South, 65
Cherry Festival, 207
Chilao Visitors Center (Angeles National Forest), 76
Children's
  Book and Music Center, 40
  Book Shop, 97–98
  Camellia Float Parade, 202
  Celebration of the Arts, 206
  Film and Television Center of America, 16
  Museum of San Diego, 148–149
  Zoo (San Diego Zoo), 131–132
Chinatown, 6
Chinese New Year, 201
Clifton's Cafeterias, 14
Colonel Allensworth State Historic Park, 166–167
Cottonwood Springs, 123
Craft and Folk Art Museum, 36
Creative Rancho Days, 207
Crystal Pier, 141
Cuyamaca Rancho State Park, 156

Danish Days Festival, 214
Death Valley Monument, 170
DeMille, Cecil B., 33
Descanso Gardens, 71
Devil's Postpile National Monument, 170–171
Discovery Center, 18, 19
Discovery Museum of Orange County, 92
Disneyland, 90
Disneyland Hotel, 90–91

217

218 INDEX

Dominguez Adobe, 21
Douglas Park, 41
"The Dream is Alive" (film), 17
Dwight D. Eisenhower
  Park, 93–94

Eastern California
  Museum, 169
Eaton Canyon County Park &
  Nature Center, 74
El Dorado Park & Nature
  Center, 58–59
El Mercado (Los Angeles), 15
El Presidio de Santa
  Barbara, 177
  El Cuartel, 177
El Pueblo de Los Angeles
  Historical Monument, 2
Elysian Park, 22
The Enchanted Forest, 63
Exposition Park Rose
  Garden, 20

Fairmount Park, 109
The Farm, 64
Farmer's Market, 37
Fiesta de la Primavera, 206
Fiesta de las Golondrinas, 204
Fillmore Museum & Historical
  Society, 190
Fort Tejon State Historic
  Park, 166
Fortynine Palms Oasis, 123
Fullerton Museum Center, 95
Fullerton Youth Science
  Center, 95

Garden Grove Park, 91–92
  Atlantis Play Center, 92
Gardens, 17, 71, 74, 99, 119
Gene Autry Western Heritage
  Museum, 30–31
Geology Road Tour, 123
George C. Page Museum, 35
George Izay Park Maze, 70
Girl's Day in Little Tokyo, 203
Glendale Young People's
  Library, 70–71
  Family Film Festival, 70–71
Goleta Depot Railroad
  Museum, 183

Grand Central Market, 11
Greater Los Angeles Auto
  Show, 202
Grier-Musser Museum, 35
Griffith Observatory and
  Planetarium, 27–28
  Hall of Science, 27
Griffith Park, 25–31
Griswold's Smorasbord, 82–83

Hacienda Heights Youth
  Science Center, 80–81
Hall of Health, 18
Hamburguesa Restaurant, 143
Happily-Ever-After
  (bookstore), 31
Harbor Regional Park, 53
Hart Memorial Park, 163
Hearst Castle-San Simeon State
  Historical Monument,
  199–200
Heritage Hill Historical Park, 101
Heritage House, 108–109
Heritage Park (El Monte),
  78–79
Heritage Park (San Diego), 144
Heritage Square, 23
Hidden Valley, 123
Hi-Desert Nature Museum,
  122
Historical Society Museum,
  177
Hobby City Doll & Toy
  Museum, 89–90
Hollyhock House, 31, 32, 33
Hollywood Bowl Museum, 34
Hollywood's Santa Clause Lane
  Parade of Stars, 214
The Hollywood Studio
  Museum, 33
Holographic Visions, 12–13
Huck Finn Jubilee, 207
Huntington Central Park, 97
  Adventure Playground, 97
Huntington Library/Art
  Gallery/Botanical Gardens,
  74–75

IMAX Theater, 16
Independent Press-Telegram
  tours, 57

International Children's Film
  and Television Festival, 210
Inyo/Kern/Tulare counties, 161
Irvine Regional Park, 94

Jensen's Date and Citrus
  Gardens, 119
Joshua Tree National
  Monument, 122–123
  Geology Road Tour, 123
J. Paul Getty Museum, 46
Julian, town of, 156
July Fourth Street Fair in
  Ventura, 209
Junior Arts Center, 32–33
Junior Programs of California,
  39

Kellogg's Arabian Horse Center,
  82
Kern County Fair, 212
Kern County Museum, 162
  Heritage Days, 205
Kidspace, 72–73
A Kid's Guide to San Luis
  Obispo, 194
A Kid's Place Annex
  (bookstore), 100
Kingdom of the Dolls,
  120–121
Knott's Berry Farm
  (amusement park), 86–87
Knott, Walter, 124
Korean Friendship Bell, 51

LaBrea Tar Pits, 35
  George C. Page Museum of,
  discoveries, 35
Lacy Park, 75
Laguna Beach
  Laguna Art Museum, 103
  Living Art Pageant, 208
  Winter Carnival, 202
Laguna Recreation Area, 157
LaHabra Children's Museum,
  96
La Jolla Museum of
  Contemporary Art, 148
Lake Cachuma, 190
Lake Isabella, 165
Lake Perris, 110

Lake Wohlford, 154
La Purisima Mission State
  Historic Park, 193–194
Lawry's California Center, 22
Laws Railroad Museum &
  Historical Site, 167
Leonis Adobe, 65–66
Lights on the Water, 215
Lincoln Park, 15
The Little Red Schoolhouse in
  Ballard, 191
Little Tokyo, 1, 8–10
  Nisei Festival, 210
Living Desert Reserve, 118
Lomita Railroad Museum, 48
Lompoc Flower Festival, 208
Long Beach
  Children's Museum, 56–57
  Christmas Water Parade,
    215
  Firefighters Museum, 57
  Grand Prix, 205
  Harbor Cruises, 56
  Sea Festival, 211
Lori Brock Children's Museum,
  162–163
Los Angeles
  Bonaventure Hotel, 13–14
  Children's Museum, 7–8
  County, 1
  County Fair, 212
  County Museum of Art, 36
  County Natural History
    Museum, 18
  Maritime Museum, 51
  Municipal Art Gallery, 32
  Philharmonic Symphonies
    for Youth, 11
  State and County
    Arboretum, 77
  Visitors Information
    Centers, 1
  Zoo, 29
Los Angeles Times tours, 10
Los Coyotes Regional Park, 89
Los Encinos State Historic
  Park, 62
Los Posadas, 215
Lummis Home, 24–25

McCallum Adobe, 115
McGroarty's Arts Center, 61

Magical Mystery Tour, 32
Magic Mountain (amusement
  park), 68–69
March Field Museum,
  109–110
Marina del Rey
  Beach, 44
  Burton Chase Park, 44
  Fisherman's Village, 44–45
Marina Rentals Clam Taxi, 198
Maritime Museum, 139
Mark Taper Hall of Economics
  and Finance, 18
Mason Street School, 142–143
Mattei's Tavern, 192
McCallum Adobe, 115
McGroarty's Arts Center,
  60–61
Medea (old English yacht), 139
Medieval Times, 87–89
Merry-go-rounds, 29, 35, 42,
  48, 56, 69, 99, 130, 138
Mexican Independence Day,
  212
Mile Square Park, 97
Mingei International Museum
  of World Folk Art, 149–150
Miniature train rides, 28–29,
  130. *See Also* Train rides
Miss Cornelia White's House,
  115
Mission(s)
  Basilica San Diego de Alcala,
    145
  San Buenaventura, 185
  San Fernando Rey de
    Espana, 66
  San Juan Capistrano, 103
  San Luis Obispo de Tolosa,
    195
  San Luis Rey de Francia, 151
  Santa Barbara, 180–181
  Santa Ines, 191
Mission Bay Aquatic Books,
  146
Mission Plaza, 195
Mitchell Caverns, 127
Mojave Narrows Regional Park,
  126–127
Mojave River Valley Museum,
  124

Montana de Oro State Park,
  199
Moorpark College Exotic
  Animal Compound, 189
Moorten's Botanical Gardens,
  116
Morongo Wildlife Reserve,
  121–122
Morro Bay
  Aquarium, 198
  Museum of Natural History,
    197
  State Park, 197
Mother Goose Parade, 214
Mount Whitney Fish Hatchery,
  169
Mount Wilson, 76
Movieland Wax Museum, 87
Mrs. Nelson's Toy and Book
  Shop, 80
Museum of Contemporary Art,
  12
The Museum of Natural
  History and Science,
  99–100
Museum of Natural History,
  181
Museum of Photographic Arts,
  134
Museum of San Diego History,
  134
Museum of World Wars, 89

National Date Festival and
  Camel Races, 203
National Orange Show, 205
Natural History Museum
  (Balboa Park), 135
Natural History Museum of
  Los Angeles County, 18–19
  Discovery Center, 18, 19
Navy Ships' Open House, 139
NBC Television Studio Tour, 69
Newport Beach Harbor
  Character Boat Parade, 211
Newport Dunes Aquatic Park,
  98
Nisei Festival, 210
Norton Simon Museum of Art,
  73
Nursery Nature Walks, 46

Oak Glen Apple Farms,
  112–113
Oak Tree Village, 112–113
Oasis Waterpark, 116
Ocean Beach Kite Festival, 203
Oceanside Pier, 141
Ojai Valley Museum &
  Historical Society, 189
Old Miner's Days in Big Bear,
  210
Old Plaza Firehouse, 5
The Old Spaghetti Factory,
  137
Old Spanish Days Fiesta, 210
Old Town Mall, 48
Old Town State Park, 142
Old Woman Meteorite,
  123–124
Olivas Adobe, 187
Olvera Street (Los Angeles),
  1, 3
One-Day Train Rides, 5
Open House at Hollywood
  Bowl, 12
Orange County, 85
Orange County Marine
  Institute, 103–104
Orange Empire Railway
  Museum, 110–111
Orcutt Ranch Horticulture
  Center, 65

Pacific Asia Museum, 72
Pacific Coast Stock Exchange,
  14
Paddock Zoo, 197
Pages Books for Children &
  Young Adults, 62–63
Palm Canyon, 118
Palm Springs
  Arial Tramway, 107, 114
  Bicycle Trails, 117
  Desert Museum, 114–115
  Public Library, 116
  Swim Center, 117
Palomar Observatory, 155
Pasadena Arts Workshops, 73
Pea Soup Andersen's
  Restaurant, 191
Pier fishing, 141–142
Pierce College Farm, 64

Pilgrim (sailing ship/
  laboratory), 104
Pioneer Village, 162
Pio Pico State Historic Park,
  79–80
Pismo Beach Clam Festival,
  214
Placerita Canyon State/County
  Park and Nature Center, 67
Planes of Fame Air Museum,
  111–112
Plaza de la Raza (Lincoln Park),
  15
Point Vincent Interpretive
  Center (whales), 49
Polo games, 45
Poly Royal (fair), 204
Pony rides, 28–29, 64, 113,
  117
Ports O'Call Village, 50
Presidio Park, 145
Puppets/marionettes, 11, 34,
  38, 48, 63, 73, 113
Prado Regional Park, 111
Princess Louise Restaurant, 51
Providence Mountains State
  Recreational Area, 127
Pyramid Lake Recreation Area,
  69

Quail Botanic Gardens, 150
Queen Mary (ocean liner),
  54–55

Raging Waters (aquatic
  playground), 81
Rainbow Basin, 126
Ramona Pageant, 204
Rancho(s)
  Los Alamitos, 58
  Los Cerritos, 57
  San Pedro, 21
  Santa Ana Botanic Garden,
    83
Rankin Guest Ranch, 164
Raymond M. Alf Museum, 83
Renaissance Pleasure Faire,
  204
Reseda Park, 63
Reuben H. Fleet Space Theater
  & Science Center, 135

Riverside Art Museum, 108
Riverside Municipal Museum,
  108
Riverside/San Bernardino
  Counties, 107
Roy Rogers-Dale Evans
  Museum, 126
Rustic Canyon Recreation
  Center, 45

Santa Barbara
  by Bike, 182
  Botanic Gardens, 182
  County Courthouse, 176
  Kennel Club Show, 209
  Museum of Art, 176
  National Horse & Flower
    Show, 209
  Old Spanish Days Festival,
    210
  Polo Grounds, 182
  Zoological Gardens, 179
San Bernardino County
  Museum, 112
Sand Dune Park, 47
San Diego
  Community Christmas
    Center, 215
  County, 129–130
  County Fair, 207
  Hall of Champions, 135
  Harbor Excursion, 140
  Model Railroad Museum,
    134
  Museum of Man, 132–133
  Museum of Art, 133
  Public Fishing Pier, 141
  Railway Museum, 151–152
  Wild Animal Park, 153
  Zoo/Children's Zoo,
    131–132
San Gabriel Mountains
  (Angeles National Forest),
  75
San Gabriel Municipal Park,
  76–77
San Luis Obispo County
  Historical Museum, 195
San Luis Obispo Path of
  History, 194

San Pasqual battlefield State Historic Park, 153–154
Santa Ana Zoo, 93
Santa Anita Workouts (race horses), 77–78
Santa Claus Lane, 184
Santa Monica
 Heritage Square Museum, 43–44
 Pier, 42–43
 Playhouse, 42
Santa Monica Mountains Recreation Area, 47
Santa's Village, 113
Santiago Oaks Regional Park, 94
Scotty's Castle, 171
Scripps Aquarium/Museum, 149
Seaport Village/Marina Park, 138
Sea World, 146
 Cap'N Kids World, 147
The Seeley Stables, 143
Serra Museum, 145
Shelter Island Fishing Pier, 142
Sherman Indian Museum, 109
Sherman Library and Gardens, 99
Shield Date Gardens, 119
Shoreline Village, 56
Silverado Days, 214
Smoketree Stables, 117
Solvang, 190–191
 Danish Days Festival, 213
South Coast Botanic Gardens, 49
Southern California Exposition, 207
Southern California Rapid Transit District, 1, 85
Southwest Museum, 23–24
Spruce Goose (Howard Hughes' aircraft), 54, 55
Stagecoach Inn Museum, 188
Stagecoach rides, 28–29
Star of India (sailing ship), 139
Story hours, 31, 37–38, 40, 63, 80, 98, 100
Stow Grove County Park, 183

Stow House, 183
Strawberry Festival, 206
Summer Solstice Celebration, 208
Sunrise Park, 117
Surf, Sand and Sandcastle Days, 208
Sycamore Grove Park, 25

Tehachapi Mountain Park, 164
Tehachapi Train Loop, 164
Temporary Contemporary, 10
Thundertub Regatta, 211
Tiger's Folly (cruise boat), 198
Timken Art Gallery, 133–134
Torrey Pines State Reserve, 150
Tournament of Roses Parade, 201
Train rides, 5, 111, 125, 152, 153. *See Also* Miniature train rides
Travel Town, 28
Treepeople Tours, 39
Tucker Wildlife Sanctuary, 101–102
Tule Elk State Reserve, 165
Turtle Rock Nature Center, 101
Twentynine Palms, 122, 123
Tykes on Hikes, 39
Union Hotel/Los Alamos, 192–193
Union Oil Co. Museum, 189
Universal Studios, 59–60

Van Nuys Airport Tour, 61–62
Vasquez Rocks County Park, 67–68
Ventura County Fair, 211
Ventura County Historical Museum, 184
Verdugo Park, 71
Village Green Heritage Center, 115
Villa Montezuma Museum, 137

Watts Towers, 21
Watts Towers Art Center, 21
Westside Arts Center, 40–41
Westside Children's Museum, 41

Whale Festival, 202
Whale Fiesta, 208
Whaler's Wharf, 50
Whale Watching, 141
Whaley House, 144
The White Rabbit Children's Books, 148
Whitewater Trout Farm, 121
Whittier Narrows Nature Center, 78
Wild Rivers (aquatic park), 102
William O. Douglas Outdoor Classroom, 38–39
William S. Hart Park, 66–67
Will Rogers State Historic Park, 45
Wonderworld Puppet Productions, 48

Zoos, 29, 93, 94, 131, 197

Photo Credits

Michael Coates: pages ix, 4, 17, 43
Courtesy of the Los Angeles Children's Museum: page 8
©Claire Henze 1988: pages 9, 24, 26
Courtesy of the Natural History Museum of Los Angeles County: pages 19, 20
Courtesy of the Los Angeles Zoo: page 30
Courtesy of the *Queen Mary/Spruce Goose:* page 55
Courtesy of the Universal Studios Tour: pages 60, 61
Courtesy of Magic Mountain: page 68
Stephanie Kegan: page 79
Courtesy of Knott's Berry Farm: pages 84, 86, 88
Courtesy of Palm Springs Aerial Tramway: page 106
Courtesy of Calico Ghost Town: page 125
Courtesy of Sea World: pages 128, 147
Courtesy of the San Diego Zoo: page 132
Courtesy of the National Park Service: page 172
Ruth Ann Laws: page 174
Courtesy of the Santa Barbara Zoo: page 180